Daily Strength for Daily Needs

Daily Strength for Daily Needs

AN INSPIRING COLLECTION OF
SPIRITUAL PASSAGES IN PROSE & VERSE
ONE FOR EVERY DAY OF THE YEAR

Selected by Mary W. Tileston

SMITHMARK

This edition published in 1995 by
SMITHMARK Publishers, Inc.
16 East 32nd Street, New York, NY 10016.

SMITHMARK books are available for bulk purchase
for sales promotion and premium use. For details
write or call the manager of special sales,
SMITHMARK Publishers Inc., 16 East 32nd Street,
New York, NY 10016; (212) 532-6600.

Cover photograph: Larry Ulrich/Tony Stone
Worldwide
Cover design: Mike Stromberg

ISBN 0-8317-2393-9

Printed in the United States of America

2 4 6 8 10 9 7 5 3 1

PREFACE

THIS little book of brief selections in prose and verse, with accompanying texts of Scripture, is intended for a daily companion and counsellor. These words of the goodly fellowship of wise and holy men of many times, it is hoped may help to strengthen the reader to perform the duties and to bear the burdens of each day with cheerfulness and courage.

M. W. T.

They go from strength to strength.—PS. lxxxiv. 7.

First the blade, then the ear, after that the full corn in the ear.—MARK iv. 28.

BUILD thee more stately mansions, O my soul,
    As the swift seasons roll !
    Leave thy low-vaulted past !
Let each new temple, nobler than the last,
Shut thee from heaven with a dome more vast,
    Till thou at length art free,
Leaving thine outgrown shell by life's unresting
    sea !

O. W. HOLMES

HIGH hearts are never long without hearing some new call, some distant clarion of God, even in their dreams ; and soon they are observed to break up the camp of ease, and start on some fresh march of faithful service. And, looking higher still, we find those who never wait till their moral work accumulates, and who reward resolution with no rest ; with whom, therefore, the alternation is instantaneous and constant ; who do the good only to see the better, and see the better only to achieve it ; who are too meek for transport, too faithful for remorse, too earnest for repose ; whose worship is action, and whose action ceaseless aspiration.

J. MARTINEAU

The Lord shall preserve thy going out and thy coming in from this time forth, and even for ever-more.—PS. cxxi. 8.

Lord, Thou hast been our dwelling-place in all generations.—PS. xc. 1.

WITH grateful hearts the past we own ;
The future, all to us unknown,
We to Thy guardian care commit,
And peaceful leave before Thy feet.

P. DODDRIDGE

WE are like to Him with whom there is no past or future, with whom a day is as a thousand years, and a thousand years as one day, when we do our work in the great present, leaving both past and future to Him to whom they are ever present, and fearing nothing, because He is in our future as much as He is in our past, as much as, and far more than, we can feel Him to be in our present. Partakers thus of the divine nature, resting in that perfect All-in-all in whom our nature is eternal too, we walk without fear, full of hope and courage and strength to do His will, waiting for the endless good which He is always giving as fast as He can get us able to take it in.

G. MACDONALD

As thy days, so shall thy strength be.—DEUT. xxxiii. 25.

Sufficient unto the day is the evil thereof.—MATT. vi. 34.

OH, ask not thou, How shall I bear
   The burden of to-morrow ?
Sufficient for to-day, its care,
   Its evil and its sorrow ;
God imparteth by the way
Strength sufficient for the day.

J. E. SAXBY

HE that hath so many causes of joy, and so great, is very much in love with sorrow and peevishness, who loses all these pleasures, and chooses to sit down upon his little handful of thorns. Enjoy the blessings of this day, if God sends them ; and the evils of it bear patiently and sweetly : for this day is only ours, we are dead to yesterday, and we are not yet born to the morrow. But if we look abroad, and bring into one day's thoughts the evil of many, certain and uncertain, what will be and what will never be, our load will be as intolerable as it is unreasonable.

JEREMY TAYLOR

*If we sin, we are Thine, knowing Thy power :
but we will not sin, knowing that we are counted
Thine. For to know Thee is perfect righteousness :
yea, to know Thy power is the root of immortality.*
—WISDOM OF SOLOMON XV. 2, 3.

OH, empty us of self, the world, and sin,
And then in all Thy fulness enter in ;
Take full possession, Lord, and let each thought
Into obedience unto Thee be brought ;
Thine is the power, and Thine the will, that we
Be wholly sanctified, O Lord, to Thee.

C. E. J.

TAKE steadily some one sin, which seems
to stand out before thee, to root it out, by
God's grace, and every fibre of it. Purpose
strongly, by the grace and strength of God,
wholly to sacrifice this sin or sinful inclination
to the love of God, to spare it not, until thou
leave of it none remaining, neither root nor
branch.

Fix, by God's help, not only to root out this
sin, but to set thyself to gain, by that same
help, the opposite grace. If thou art tempted
to be angry, try hard, by God's grace, to be
very meek ; if to be proud, seek to be *very*
humble.

E. B. PUSEY

That He might present it to Himself a glorious church, not having spot, or wrinkle, or any such thing, but that it should be holy and without blemish.—EPH. V. 27.

Ye also, as lively stones, are built up a spiritual house.—I PETER ii. 5.

ONE holy Church of God appears
  Through every age and race,
Unwasted by the lapse of years,
  Unchanged by changing place.

S. LONGFELLOW.

A TEMPLE there has been upon earth, a spiritual Temple, made up of living stones ; a Temple, as I may say, composed of souls ; a Temple with God for its light, and Christ for the high priest ; with wings of angels for its arches, with saints and teachers for its pillars, and with worshippers for its pavement. Wherever there is faith and love. this Temple is.

J. H. NEWMAN

TO whatever worlds He carries our souls when they shall pass out of these imprisoning bodies, in those worlds these souls of ours shall find themselves part of the same great Temple ; for it belongs not to this earth alone. There can be no end of the universe where God is, to which that growing Temple does not reach,— the Temple of a creation to be wrought at last into a perfect utterance of God by a perfect obedience to God.

PHILLIPS BROOKS

In all ages entering into holy souls, she [Wisdom] maketh them friends of God, and prophets.— WISDOM OF SOLOMON vii. 27.

MEANWHILE with every son and saint of Thine
    Along the glorious line,
Sitting by turns beneath Thy sacred feet
    We'll hold communion sweet,
Know them by look and voice, and thank them all
    For helping us in thrall,
For words of hope, and bright examples given
To shew through moonless skies that there is light in
    heaven.
                                J. KEBLE

IF we cannot live at once and alone with Him, we may at least live with those who have lived with Him ; and find, in our admiring love for their purity, their truth, their goodness, an intercession with His pity on our behalf. To study the lives, to meditate the sorrows, to commune with the thoughts, of the great and holy men and women of this rich world, is a sacred discipline, which deserves at least to rank as the forecourt of the temple of true worship, and may train the tastes, ere we pass the very gate, of heaven. . . . We forfeit the chief source of dignity and sweetness in life, next to the direct communion with God, if we do not seek converse with the greater minds that have left their vestiges on the world.

                              J. MARTINEAU

DO not think it wasted time to submit yourself to any influence which may bring upon you any noble feeling.
                              J. RUSKIN

The exceeding greatness of His power to usward who believe, according to the working of His mighty power.—EPH. i. 19.

THE lives which seem so poor, so low,
   The hearts which are so cramped and dull,
The baffled hopes, the impulse slow,
   Thou takest, touchest all, and lo !
They blossom to the beautiful.

                   SUSAN COOLIDGE

A ROOT set in the finest soil, in the best climate, and blessed with all that sun and air and rain can do for it, is not in so sure a way of its growth to perfection, as every man may be, whose spirit aspires after all that which God is ready and infinitely desirous to give him. For the sun meets not the springing bud that stretches towards him with half that certainty, as God, the source of all good, communicates Himself to the soul that longs to partake of Him.

                   WM. LAW

IF we stand in the openings of the present moment, with all the length and breadth of our faculties unselfishly adjusted to what it reveals, we are in the best condition to receive what God is always ready to communicate.

                   T. C. UPHAM

As we have therefore opportunity, let us do good unto all men.—GAL. vi. 10.

Let brotherly love continue.—HEB. xiii. 1.

I ASK Thee for a thoughtful love,
  Through constant watching wise,
To meet the glad with joyful smiles,
  And to wipe the weeping eyes,
And a heart at leisure from itself,
  To sooth and sympathize.

A. L. WARING

SURELY none are so full of cares, or so poor in gifts, that to them also, waiting patiently and trustfully on God for His daily commands, He will not give direct ministry for Him, increasing according to their strength and their desire. There is so much to be set right in the world, there are so many to be led and helped and comforted, that we must continually come in contact with such in our daily life. Let us only take care, that, by the glance being turned inward, or strained onward, or lost in vacant reverie, we do not miss our turn of service, and pass by those to whom we might have been sent on an errand straight from God.

ELIZABETH CHARLES

LOOK up and not down ; look forward and not back ; look out and not in ; and lend a hand.

EDWARD E. HALE

And in every work that he began in the service of the house of God, and in the law, and in the commandments, to seek his God, he did it with all his heart, and prospered.—2 CHRON. xxxi. 21.

What shall we do, that we might work the works of God?—JOHN vi. 28.

GIVE me within the work which calls to-day,
   To see Thy finger gently beckoning on ;
So struggle grows to freedom, work to play,
   And toils begun from Thee to Thee are done.
               J. F. CLARKE

GOD is a kind Father. He sets us all in the places where He wishes us to be employed ; and that employment is truly 'our Father's business'. He chooses work for every creature which will be delightful to them, if they do it simply and humbly. He gives us always strength enough, and sense enough, for what He wants us to do ; if we either tire ourselves or puzzle ourselves, it is our own fault. And we may always be sure, whatever we are doing, that we cannot be pleasing Him, if we are not happy ourselves.

               J. RUSKIN

*Because Thy loving-kindness is better than life,
my lips shall praise Thee.*—PS. lxiii. 3.

*Whosoever shall seek to save his life shall lose it ;
and whosoever shall lose his life shall preserve it.*—
LUKE xvii. 33.

> O LORD ! my best desires fulfil.
>   And help me to resign
> Life, health, and comfort, to Thy will,
>   And make Thy pleasure mine.
>
> WM. COWPER

WHAT do our heavy hearts prove but that
other things are sweeter to us than His
will, that we have not attained to the full
mastery of our true freedom, the full perception
of its power, that our sonship is yet but faintly
realized, and its blessedness not yet proved and
known ? Our consent would turn all our trials
into obedience. By consenting we make them
our own, and offer them with ourselves again
to Him.

H. E. MANNING

NOTHING is intolerable that is necessary. Now
God hath bound thy trouble upon thee, with a
design to try thee, and with purposes to reward
and crown thee. These cords thou canst not
break ; and therefore lie thou down gently, and
suffer the hand of God to do what He please.

JEREMY TAYLOR

I will be glad, and rejoice in Thy mercy ; for Thou has considered my trouble ; Thou hast known my soul in adversities.—PS. xxxi. 7.

NAY, all by Thee is ordered, chosen, planned—
Each drop that fills my daily cup ; Thy hand
Prescribes for ills none else can understand.
              All, all is known to Thee.
                         A. L. NEWTON

GOD knows us through and through. Not the most secret thought, which we most hide from ourselves, is hidden from Him. As then we come to know ourselves through and through, we come to see ourselves more as God sees us, and then we catch some little glimpse of His designs with us, how each ordering of His Providence, each check to our desires, each failure of our hopes, is just fitted for us, and for something in our own spiritual state, which others know not of, and which, till then, we knew not. Until we come to this knowledge, we must take all in faith, believing, though we know not, the goodness of God towards us. As we know ourselves, we, thus far, know God.
                         E. B. PUSEY

Let the words of my mouth, and the meditation of my heart, be acceptable in Thy sight, O Lord, my strength, and my redeemer.—PS. xix. 14.

THE thoughts that in our hearts keep place,
  Lord, make a holy, heavenly throng,
And steep in innocence and grace
  The issue of each guarded tongue.

T. H. GILL

THERE is another kind of silence to be cultivated, besides that of the tongue as regards others. I mean silence as regards one's self,—restraining the imagination, not permitting it to dwell overmuch on what we have heard or said, not indulging in the phantasmagoria of picture-thoughts, whether of the past or future. Be sure that you have made no small progress in the spiritual life, when you can control your imagination, so as to fix it on the duty and occupation actually existing, to the exclusion of the crowd of thoughts which are perpetually sweeping across the mind. No doubt, you cannot prevent those thoughts from arising, but you can prevent yourself from dwelling on them ; you can put them aside, you can check the self-complacency, or irritation, or earthly longings which feed them, and by the practice of such control of your thoughts you will attain that spirit of inward silence which draws the soul into a close intercourse with God.

JEAN N. GROU

Speak not evil one of another, brethren.—JAMES
iv. 11.

*Let all bitterness, and wrath, and anger, and
clamor, and evil speaking, be put away from you,
with all malice.*—EPH. iv. 31.

IF aught good thou canst not say
  Of thy brother, foe, or friend,
Take thou, then, the silent way,
  Lest in word thou shouldst offend.

ANON.

IF there is any person to whom you feel dis-
like, that is the person of whom you ought
never to speak.

R. CECIL

TO recognize with delight all high and gener-
ous and beautiful actions ; to find a joy even in
seeing the good qualities of your bitterest op-
ponents, and to admire those qualities even in
those with whom you have least sympathy,—
be it either the Romanist or the Unitarian,—
this is the only spirit which can heal the love
of slander and of calumny.

F. W. ROBERTSON

Thy servants are ready to do whatsoever my lord the king shall appoint.—2 SAM. XV. 15.

I LOVE to think that God appoints
  My portion day by day ;
Events of life are in His hand,
  And I would only say,
Appoint them in Thine own good time,
  And in Thine own best way.

A. L. WARING

IF we are really, and always, and equally ready to do whatsoever the King appoints, all the trials and vexations arising from any change in His appointments, great or small, simply do not exist. If He appoints me to work there, shall I lament that I am not to work here ? If He appoints me to wait indoors to-day, am I to be annoyed because I am not to work out-of-doors ? If I meant to *write* His messages this morning, shall I grumble because He sends interrupting visitors, rich or poor, to whom I am to *speak* them, or ' show kindness ' for His sake, or at least obey His command, ' Be courteous ' ? If all my members are really at His disposal, why should I be put out if to-day's appointment is some simple work for my hands or errands for my feet, instead of some seemingly more important doing of head or tongue ?

F. R. HAVERGAL

For this is the will of God, even your sanctification.—I THESS. iv. 3.

BETWEEN us and Thyself remove
Whatever hindrances may be,
That so our inmost heart may prove
A holy temple, meet for Thee.

LATIN MSS. OF 15TH CENTURY

BEAR, in the presence of God, to know thyself. Then seek to know for what God sent thee into the world ; how thou hast fulfilled it ; art thou yet what God willed thee to be ; what yet lacketh unto thee ; what is God's will for thee *now* ; what thing thou mayest *now* do, by His grace, to obtain His favour, and approve thyself unto Him. Say to Him, ' Teach me to do Thy will, for Thou art my God ', and He will say unto thy soul, ' Fear not ; I am thy salvation '. He will speak peace unto thy soul ; He will set thee in the way ; He will bear thee above things of sense, and praise of man, and things which perish in thy grasp, and give thee, if but afar off, some glimpse of His own, unfading, unsetting, unperishing brightness and bliss and love.

E. B. PUSEY

God, even our Father, which hath loved us, and hath given us everlasting consolation, and good hope through grace, comfort your hearts, and stablish you in every good word and work.— 2 THESS. ii. 16, 17.

WHEN sorrow all our heart would ask,
We need not shun our daily task,
   And hide ourselves for calm ;
The herbs we seek to heal our woe
Familiar by our path way grow,
   Our common air is balm.

J. KEBLE

OH, when we turn away from some duty or some fellow-creature, saying that our hearts are too sick and sore with some great yearning of our own, we may often sever the line on which a divine message was coming to us. We shut out the man, and we shut out the angel who had sent him on to open the door. . . . There is a plan working in our lives ; and if we keep our hearts quiet and our eyes open, it all works together ; and, if we don't, it all fights together, and goes on fighting till it comes right, somehow, somewhere.

ANNIE KEARY

Beloved, think it not strange concerning the fiery trial which is to try you, as though some strange thing happened unto you : but rejoice, inasmuch as ye are partakers of Christ's sufferings.—I PETER iv. 12, 13.

> WE take with solemn thankfulness
> Our burden up, nor ask it less,
> And count it joy that even we
> May suffer, serve, or wait for Thee,
>   Whose will be done !
>
> J. G. WHITTIER

RECEIVE every inward and outward trouble, every disappointment, pain, uneasiness, temptation, darkness, and desolation, with both thy hands, as a true opportunity and blessed occasion of dying to self, and entering into a fuller fellowship with thy self-denying, suffering Saviour. Look at no inward or outward trouble in any other view ; reject every other thought about it ; and then every kind of trial and distress will become the blessed day of thy prosperity. That state is best, which exerciseth the highest faith in, and fullest resignation to God.

WM. LAW

Thou shalt rejoice in every good thing which the Lord thy God hath given unto thee.—DEUT. XXVI. 11.

Rejoice evermore. In everything give thanks.—I THESS. V. 16, 18.

GRAVE on thy heart each past ' red-letter day ' !
Forget not all the sunshine of the way
By which the Lord hath led thee ; answered prayers,
And joys unasked, strange blessings, lifted cares,
Grand promise-echoes ! Thus thy life shall be
One record of His love and faithfulness to thee.

F. R. HAVERGAL

GRATITUDE consists in a watchful, minute attention to the particulars of our state, and to the multitude of God's gifts, taken one by one. It fills us with a consciousness that God loves and cares for us, even to the least event and smallest need of life. It is a blessed thought, that from our childhood God has been laying His fatherly hands upon us, and always in benediction ; that even the strokes of His Hands are blessings, and among the chiefest we have ever received. When this feeling is awakened, the heart beats with a pulse of thankfulness. Every gift has its return of praise. It awakens an unceasing daily converse with our Father,—He speaking to us by the descent of blessings, we to Him by the ascent of thanksgiving. And all our whole life is thereby drawn under the light of His countenance, and is filled with a gladness, serenity, and peace which only thankful hearts can know.

H. E. MANNING

Let the heart of them rejoice that seek the Lord.—
PS. CV. 3.

*The joy of the Lord is your strength.—*NEH. viii.
10.

BE Thou my Sun, my selfishness destroy,
Thy atmosphere of Love be all my joy;
Thy Presence be my sunshine ever bright,
My soul the little mote that lives but in Thy light.
GERHARD TERSTEEGEN

I DO not know when I have had happier
times in my soul, than when I have been
sitting at work, with nothing before me but a
candle and a white cloth, and hearing no sound
but that of my own breath, with God in my soul
and heaven in my eye. . . . I rejoice in being
exactly what I am,—a creature capable of loving
God, and who, as long as God lives, must be
happy. I get up and look for a while out of the
window, and gaze at the moon and stars, the
work of an Almighty hand. I think of the
grandeur of the universe, and then sit down,
and think myself one of the happiest beings
in it.

A POOR METHODIST WOMAN, 18TH CENTURY

The Lord taketh pleasure in His people : He will beautify the meek with salvation.—PS. cxlix. 4.

SEND down Thy likeness from above.
And let this my adorning be :
Clothe me with wisdom, patience, love,
With lowliness and purity.

JOACHIM LANGE

IT is not in words explicable, with what divine lines and lights the exercise of godliness and charity will mould and gild the hardest and coldest countenance, neither to what darkness their departure will consign the loveliest. For there is not any virtue the exercise of which, even momentarily, will not impress a new fairness upon the features ; neither on them only, but on the whole body the moral and intellectual faculties have operation, for all the movements and gestures, however slight, are different in their modes according to the mind that governs them—and on the gentleness and decision of right feeling follows grace of actions, and, through continuance of this, grace of form.

J. RUSKIN

THERE is no beautifier of complexion, or form, or behaviour, like the wish to scatter joy and not pain around us.

R. W. EMERSON

Even the youths shall faint and be weary, and the young men shall utterly fall ; but they that wait upon the Lord shall renew their strength ; they shall mount up with wings as eagles ; they shall run, and not be weary ; and they shall walk and not faint.—ISA. xl. 30, 31.

> LORD, with what courage and delight
> I do each thing,
> When Thy least breath sustains my wing !
> I shine and move
> Like those above,
> And, with much gladness
> Quitting sadness,
> Make me fair days of every night.
>
> H. VAUGHAN

MAN, by living wholly in submission to the Divine Influence, becomes surrounded with, and creates for himself, internal pleasures infinitely greater than any he can otherwise attain to—a state of heavenly Beatitude.

J. P. GREAVES

BY persisting in a habit of self-denial, we shall, beyond what I can express, increase the inward powers of the mind, and shall produce that cheerfulness and greatness of spirit as will fit us for all good purposes ; and shall not have lost pleasure, but *changed* it ; the soul being then filled with its own intrinsic pleasures.

HENRY MORE

Then shall we know, if we follow on to know the Lord.—HOSEA vi. 3.

AND, as the path of duty is made plain,
May grace be given that I may walk therein,
  Not like the hireling, for his selfish gain,
With backward glances and reluctant tread,
Making a merit of his coward dread,—
  But cheerful, in the light around me thrown,
  Walking as one to pleasant service led ;
  Doing God's will as if it were my own,
Yet trusting not in mine, but in His strength alone !

J. G. WHITTIER

IT is by doing our duty that we learn to do it. So long as men dispute whether or no a thing is their duty, they get never the nearer. Let them set ever so weakly about doing it, and the face of things alters. They find in themselves strength which they knew not of. Difficulties which it seemed to them they could not get over, disappear. For He accompanies it with the influences of His blessed Spirit, and each performance opens our minds for larger influxes of His grace, and places them in communion with Him.

E. B. PUSEY

THAT which is called considering what is our duty in a particular case, is very often nothing but endeavouring to explain it away.

BISHOP BUTLER

If thou draw out thy soul to the hungry, and satisfy the afflicted soul ; then shall thy light rise in obscurity, and thy darkness be as the noonday ; and the Lord shall guide thee continually.—ISA. lviii. 10, 11.

IF thou hast Yesterday thy duty done,
   And thereby cleared firm footing for To-day
Whatever clouds make dark To-morrow's sun,
   Thou shalt not miss thy solitary way.

               J. W. VON GOETHE

O LORD, who art our Guide even unto death, grant us, I pray Thee, grace to follow Thee whithersoever Thou goest. In little daily duties to which Thou callest us, bow down our wills to simple obedience, patience under pain or provocation, strict truthfulness of word and manner, humility, kindness ; in great acts of duty or perfection, if Thou shouldest call us to them, uplift us to self-sacrifice, heroic courage, laying down of life for Thy truth's sake, or for a brother. Amen.

               C. G. ROSSETTI

I will bless the Lord, who hath given me counsel.
—PS. xvi. 7.

Not slothful in business ; fervent in spirit ; serv-ing the Lord.—ROM. xii. 11.

> MINE be the reverent, listening love
> That waits all day on Thee,
> With the service of a watchful heart
> Which no one else can see.
>
> A. L. WARING

NOTHING is small or great in God's sight ;
whatever He wills becomes great to us,
however seemingly trifling, and if once the voice
of conscience tells us that He requires anything
of us, we have no right to measure its import-
ance. On the other hand, whatever He would
not have us do, however important we may
think it, is as nought to us. How do you know
what you may lose by neglecting this duty,
which you think so trifling, or the blessing
which its faithful performance may bring ?
Be sure that if you do your very best in that
which is laid upon you daily, you will not be left
without sufficient help when some weightier
occasion arises. Give yourself to Him, trust
Him, fix your eye upon Him, listen to His voice,
and then go on bravely and cheerfully.

JEAN NICOLAS GROU

If ye know these things, happy are ye if ye do them.—JOHN xiii. 17.

Therefore to him that knoweth to do good, and doeth it not, to him it is sin.—JAMES iv. 17.

> WE cannot kindle when we will
>   The fire that in the heart resides,
> The spirit bloweth and is still,
>   In mystery our soul abides :
> But tasks in hours of insight willed
> Can be through hours of gloom fulfilled.
>
> MATTHEW ARNOLD

HURT not your conscience with any known sin.

S. RUTHERFORD

DEEP-ROOTED customs, though wrong, are not easily altered ; but it is the duty of all to be firm in that which they certainly know is right for them.

JOHN WOOLMAN

HE often acts unjustly who does not do a certain thing ; not only he who does a certain thing.

MARCUS ANTONINUS

EVERY duty we omit obscures some truth we should have known.

JOHN RUSKIN

O the depth of the riches both of the wisdom and knowledge of God ! how unsearchable are His judgments, and His ways past finding out !—ROM. xi. 33.

It doth not yet appear what we shall be.—1 JOHN iii. 2.

NO star is ever lost we once have seen,
We always may be what we might have been.
Since Good, though only thought, has life and breath,
God's life—can always be redeemed from death ;
And evil, in its nature, is decay,
And any hour can blot it all away ;
The hopes that lost in some far distance seem,
May be the truer life, and this the dream.

A. A. PROCTER

ST. BERNARD has said : ' Man, if thou desirest a noble and holy life, and unceasingly prayest to God for it, if thou continue constant in this thy desire, it will be granted unto thee without fail, even if only in the day or hour of thy death ; and if God should not give it to thee then, thou shalt find it in Him in eternity : of this be assured.' Therefore do not relinquish your desire, though it be not fulfilled immediately, or though ye may swerve from your aspirations, or even forget them for a time. . . . The love and aspiration which once really existed live forever before God, and in Him ye shall find the fruit thereof ; that is, to all eternity it shall be better for you than if you had never felt them.

J. TAULER. 1290–1361

For thus saith the high and lofty One that inhabiteth eternity, whose name is Holy ; I dwell in the high and holy place, with him also that is of a contrite and humble spirit, to revive the spirit of the humble, and to revive the heart of the contrite ones.—ISA. lvii. 15.

WITHOUT an end or bound
  Thy life lies all outspread in light ;
    Our lives feel Thy life all around,
  Making our weakness strong, our darkness bright ;
Yet is it neither wilderness nor sea,
But the calm gladness of a full eternity.

                      F. W. FABER

O TRUTH who art Eternity ! And Love who art Truth ! And Eternity who art Love ! Thou art my God, to Thee do I sigh night and day. When I first knew Thee, Thou liftedst me up, that I might see there was somewhat for me to see, and that I was not yet such as to see. And Thou streaming forth Thy beams of light upon me most strongly, didst beat back the weakness of my sight, and I trembled with love and awe : and I perceived myself to be far off from Thee in the region of unlikeness.

                ST. AUGUSTINE

O fear the Lord, ye His saints ; for there is no want to them that fear Him.—PS. xxxiv. 9.

Thou openest Thine hand, and satisfiest the desire of every living thing.—PS. cxlv. 16.

WHAT Thou shalt to-day provide,
　Let me as a child receive ;
What to-morrow may betide,
　Calmly to Thy wisdom leave.
'Tis enough that Thou wilt care ;
Why should I the burden bear ?

J. NEWTON

HAVE we found that anxiety about possible consequences increased the clearness of our judgment, made us wiser and braver in meeting the present, and arming ourselves for the future ? . . . If we had prayed for this day's bread, and left the next to itself, if we had not huddled our days together, not allotting to each its appointed task, but ever deferring that to the future, and drawing upon the future for its own troubles, which must be met when they come whether we have anticipated them or not, we should have found a simplicity and honesty in our lives, a capacity for work, an enjoyment in it, to which we are now, for the most part, strangers.

F. D. MAURICE

I the Lord will hold thy right hand, saying unto thee, Fear not ; I will help thee.—ISA. xli. 13.

Show Thy marvellous loving-kindness, O Thou that savest by Thy right hand them which put their trust in Thee.—PS. xvii. 7.

I TAKE Thy hand, and fears grow still ;
  Behold Thy face, and doubts remove ;
Who would not yield his wavering will
  To perfect Truth and boundless Love ?

S. JOHNSON

DO not look forward to the changes and chances of this life in fear ; rather look to them with full hope that, as they arise, God, whose you are, will deliver you out of them. He has kept you hitherto,—do you but hold fast to His dear hand, and He will lead you safely through all things ; and, when you cannot stand, He will bear you in His arms. Do not look forward to what may happen to-morrow ; the same everlasting Father who cares for you to-day, will take care of you to-morrow, and every day. Either He will shield you from suffering, or He will give you unfailing strength to bear it. Be at peace then, and put aside all anxious thoughts and imaginations.

FRANCIS DE SALES

If I take the wings of the morning, and dwell in the uttermost parts of the sea ; even there shall Thy hand lead me, and Thy right hand shall hold me.— PS. CXXXIX. 9, 10.

I CANNOT lose Thee ! Still in Thee abiding,
  The end is clear, how wide soe'er I roam ;
The Hand that holds the worlds my steps is guiding,
  And I must rest at last in Thee, my home.

E. SCUDDER

HOW can we come to perceive this direct leading of God ? By a careful looking at home, and abiding within the gates of thy own soul. Therefore, let a man be at home in his own heart, and cease from his restless chase of and search after outward things. If he is thus at home while on earth, he will surely come to see what there is to do at home,—what God commands him inwardly without means, and also outwardly by the help of means ; and then let him surrender himself, and follow God along whatever path his loving Lord thinks fit to lead him : whether it be to contemplation or action, to usefulness or enjoyment ; whether in sorrow or in joy, let him follow on. And if God do not give him thus to feel His hand in all things, let him still simply yield himself up, and go without, for God's sake, out of love, and still press forward.

J. TAULER

In all thy ways acknowledge Him, and He shall direct thy paths.—PROV. iii. 6.

He leadeth me.—PS. xxiii. 2.

IN ' pastures green ' ? Not always ; sometimes He
Who knoweth best, in kindness leadeth me
In weary ways, where heavy shadows be.

So, whether on the hill-tops high and fair
I dwell, or in the sunless valleys, where
The shadows lie, what matter ? He is there.

HENRY H. BARRY

THE Shepherd knows what pastures are best for his sheep, and they must not question nor doubt, but trustingly follow Him. Perhaps He sees that the best pastures for some of us are to be found in the midst of opposition or of earthly trials. If He leads you there, you may be sure they are green for you, and you will grow and be made strong by feeding there. Perhaps He sees that the best waters for you to walk beside will be raging waves of trouble and sorrow. If this should be the case, He will make them still waters for you, and you must go and lie down beside them, and let them have all their blessed influences upon you.

H. W. S.

Now the God of patience and consolation grant you to be like-minded one toward another, according to Christ Jesus.—ROM. xv. 5.

Let patience have her perfect work.—JAMES i. 4.

MAKE me patient, kind, and gentle,
　　　Day by day ;
Teach me how to live more nearly
　　　As I pray.

SHARPE'S MAGAZINE

THE exercise of patience involves a continual practice of the presence of God ; for we may be come upon at any moment for an almost heroic display of good temper, and it is a short road to unselfishness, for nothing is left to self ; all that seems to belong most intimately to self, to be self's private property, such as time, home, and rest, are invaded by these continual trials of patience. The family is full of such opportunities.

F. W. FABER

Now we exhort you, brethren, warn them that are unruly, comfort the feeble-minded, support the weak, be patient toward all men.—I THESS. V. 14.

THE little worries which we meet each day
May lie as stumbling-blocks across our way,
Or we may make them stepping-stones to be
    Of grace, O Lord, to Thee.

A. E. HAMILTON

WE must be continually sacrificing our own wills, as opportunity serves, to the will of others ; bearing, without notice, sights and sounds that annoy us ; setting about this or that task, when we had far rather be doing something very different ; persevering in it, often, when we are thoroughly tired of it ; keeping company for duty's sake, when it would be a great joy to us to be by ourselves ; besides all the trifling untoward accidents of life ; bodily pain and weakness long continued, and perplexing us often when it does not amount to illness ; losing what we value, missing what we desire ; disappointment in other persons, wilfulness, unkindness, ingratitude, folly, in cases where we least expect it.

J. KEBLE

Search me, O God, and know my heart ; try me, and know my thoughts ; and see if there be any wicked way in me, and lead me in the way ever-lasting.—PS. CXXXIX. 23, 24.

> SAVE us from the evil tongue,
> From the heart that thinketh wrong,
> From the sins, whate'er they be,
> That divide the soul from Thee.
>
> ANON.

SUCH as are thy habitual thoughts, such also will be the character of thy mind ; for the soul is dyed by the thoughts. Dye it then with a continuous series of such thoughts as these : for instance, that where a man can live, there he can also live well. But he must live in a palace : well, then, he can also live well in a palace.

MARCUS ANTONINUS

WHO is there that sets himself to the task of steadily watching his thoughts for the space of one hour, with the view of preserving his mind in a simple, humble, healthful condition, but will speedily discern in the multiform, self-reflecting, self-admiring emotions, which, like locusts, are ready to ' eat up every green thing in his land ', a state as much opposed to simplicity and humility as night is to day ?

M. A. KELTY

If any man offend not in word, the same is a perfect man, and able also to bridle the whole body. —JAMES iii. 2.

Set a watch, O Lord, before my mouth ; keep the door of my lips.—PS. cxli. 3.

> WHAT ! never speak one evil word,
>   Or rash, or idle, or unkind !
> Oh, how shall I, most gracious Lord,
>   This mark of true perfection find ?
>
> C. WESLEY

WHEN we remember our temptations to give quick indulgence to disappointment or irritation or unsympathizing weariness, . . . and how hard a thing it is from day to day to meet our fellow-men, our neighbours, or even our own households, in all moods, in all discordances between the world without us and the frames within, in all states of health, of solicitude, of preoccupation, and show no signs of impatience, ungentleness, or unobservant self-absorption,—with only kindly feeling finding expression and ungenial feeling at least inwardly imprisoned ;—we shall be ready to acknowledge that the man who has thus attained is master of himself, and in the graciousness of his power is fashioned upon the style of a Perfect Man.

J. H. THOM

Blessed are they that keep judgment, and he that doeth righteousness at all times.—PS. cvi. 3.

Thou shalt be stedfast, and shalt not fear : because thou shalt forget thy misery, and remember it as waters that pass away.—JOB xi. 15, 16.

IN the bitter waves of woe,
  Beaten and tossed about
By the sullen winds that blow
  From the desolate shores of doubt,
Where the anchors that faith has cast
  Are dragging in the gale,
I am quietly holding fast
  To the things that cannot fail.

WASHINGTON GLADDEN

IN the darkest hour through which a human soul can pass, whatever else is doubtful, this at least is certain. If there be no God and no future state, yet, even then, it is better to be generous than selfish, better to be chaste than licentious, better to be true than false, better to be brave than to be a coward. Blessed beyond all earthly blessedness is the man who, in the tempestuous darkness of the soul, has dared to hold fast to these venerable landmarks. Thrice blessed is he, who, when all is drear and cheerless within and without, when his teachers terrify him, and his friends shrink from him, has obstinately clung to moral good. Thrice blessed, because *his* night shall pass into clear, bright day.

F. W. ROBERTSON

Whoso putteth his trust in the Lord shall be safe.—PROV. xxix. 25.

I will cry unto God most high ; unto God, that performeth all things for me.—PS. lvii. 2.

ONLY thy restless heart keep still,
   And wait in cheerful hope ; content
To take whate'er His gracious will,
   His all-discerning love hath sent ;
Nor doubt our inmost wants are known
   To Him who chose us for His own.

G. NEUMARCK

GOD has brought us into this time ; He, and not ourselves or some dark demon. If we are not fit to cope with that which He has prepared for us, we should have been utterly unfit for any condition that we imagine for ourselves. In this time we are to live and wrestle, and in no other. Let us humbly, tremblingly, manfully look at it, and we shall not wish that the sun could go back its ten degrees, or that we could go back with it. If easy times are departed, it is that the difficult times may make us more in earnest ; that they may teach us not to depend upon ourselves. If easy belief is impossible, it is that we may learn what belief is, and in whom it is to be placed.

F. D. MAURICE

Obey my voice, and I will be your God, and ye shall be my people : and walk ye in all the ways that I have commanded you, that it may be well unto you.—JER. vii. 23.

AND oft, when in my heart was heard
Thy timely mandate, I deferred
The task, in smoother walks to stray ;
But thee I now would serve more strictly, if I may.
                              W. WORDSWORTH

PRAY Him to give you what Scripture calls ' an honest and good heart ', or ' a perfect heart ' ; and, without waiting, begin at once to obey Him with the best heart you have. Any obedience is better than none. You have to seek His face ; obedience is the only way of seeing Him. All your duties are obediences. To do what He bids is to obey Him, and to obey Him is to approach Him. Every act of obedience is an approach—an approach to Him who is not far off, though He seems so, but close behind this visible screen of things which hides Him from us.

                              J. H. NEWMAN

AS soon as we lay ourselves entirely at His feet, we have enough light given us to guide our own steps ; as the foot-soldier, who hears nothing of the councils that determine the course of the great battle he is in, hears plainly enough the word of command which he must himself obey.
                              GEORGE ELIOT

*He leadeth me beside the still waters. He re-
storeth my soul ; He leadeth me in the paths of
righteousness for His name's sake.*—PS. xxiii. 2, 3.

HE leads me where the waters glide,
The waters soft and still,
And homeward He will gently guide
My wandering heart and will.

J. KEBLE

OUT of obedience and devotion arises an
habitual faith, which makes Him, though
unseen, a part of all our life. He will guide
us in a sure path, though it be a rough one :
though shadows hang upon it, yet He will be
with us. He will bring us home at last.
Through much trial it may be, and weariness,
in much fear and fainting of heart, in much
sadness and loneliness, in griefs that the world
never knows, and under burdens that the
nearest never suspect. Yet He will suffice for
all. By His eye or by His voice He will guide
us, if we be docile and gentle ; by His staff
and by His rod, if we wander or are wilful : any
how, and by all means, He will bring us to His
rest.

H. E. MANNING

I was afraid, and went and hid thy talent in the earth : lo, there thou hast that is thine.—MATT. XXV. 25.

TIME was, I shrank from what was right,
  From fear of what was wrong ;
I would not brave the sacred fight,
  Because the foe was strong.

But now I cast that finer sense
  And sorer shame aside ;
Such dread of sin was indolence,
  Such aim at heaven was pride.

J. H. NEWMAN

IF he falls into some error, he does not fret over it, but rising up with a humble spirit, he goes on his way anew rejoicing. Were he to fall a hundred times in the day, he would not despair,—he would rather cry out lovingly to God, appealing to His tender pity. The really devout man has a horror of evil, but he has a still greater love of that which is good ; he is more set on doing what is right, than avoiding what is wrong. Generous, large-hearted, he is not afraid of danger in serving God, and would rather run the risk of doing His will imperfectly than not strive to serve Him lest he fail in the attempt.

JEAN NICOLAS GROU

*We have waited for Him, and He will save us :
this is the Lord ; we have waited for Him, we will
be glad in His salvation.*—ISA. xxv. 9.

> BLEST are the humble souls that wait
> With sweet submission to His will ;
> Harmonious all their passions move,
> And in the midst of storms are still.
>
> P. DODDRIDGE

DO not be discouraged at your faults ; bear
with yourself in correcting them, as you
would with your neighbour. Lay aside this
ardour of mind, which exhausts your body, and
leads you to commit errors. Accustom yourself
gradually to carry prayer into all your daily
occupations. Speak, move, work, in peace, as
if you were in prayer, as indeed you ought to
be. Do everything without excitement, by the
spirit of grace. As soon as you perceive your
natural impetuosity gliding in, retire quietly
within, where is the kingdom of God. Listen
to the leadings of grace, then say and do nothing
but what the Holy Spirit shall put in your
heart. You will find that you will become more
tranquil, that your words will be fewer and
more effectual, and that, with less effort, you
will accomplish more good.

FÉNELON

I have finished the work which Thou gavest me to do.—JOHN xvii. 4.

She hath done what she could.—MARK xiv. 8.

HE who God's will has borne and done,
    And his own restless longings stilled ;
What else he does, or has foregone,
    His mission he has well fulfilled.

FROM THE GERMAN

CHEERED by the presence of God, I will do at each moment, without anxiety, according to the strength which He shall give me, the work that His Providence assigns me. I will leave the rest without concern ; it is not my affair. I ought to consider the duty to which I am called each day, as the work that God has given me to do, and to apply myself to it in a manner worthy of His glory, that is to say, with exactness and in peace. I must neglect nothing ; I must be violent about nothing.

FÉNELON

IT is thy duty oftentimes to do what thou wouldst not ; thy duty, too, to leave undone what thou wouldst do.

THOMAS À KEMPIS

Blessed be the Lord, who daily loadeth us with benefits.—PS. lxviii. 19.

Nor trust in uncertain riches, but in the living God, who giveth us richly all things to enjoy.—I TIM. vi. 17.

SOURCE of my life's refreshing springs,
　Whose presence in my heart sustains me,
Thy love ordains me pleasant things,
　Thy mercy orders all that pains me.

A. L. WARING

AND to be true, and speak my soul, when I survey the occurrences of my life, and call into account the finger of God, I can perceive nothing but an abyss and mass of mercies, either in general to mankind, or in particular to myself ; and whether out of the prejudice of my affection, or an inverting and partial conceit of His mercies, I know not ; but those which others term crosses, afflictions, judgments, misfortunes, to me who inquire farther into them than their visible effects, they both appear, and in event have ever proved, the secret and dissembled favours of His affection.

SIR T. BROWNE

The will of the Lord be done.—ACTS xxi. 14.

Let Him do to me as seemeth good unto Him.—
2 SAM. xv. 26.

TO have, each day, the thing I wish,
  Lord, that seems best to me ;
But not to have the thing I wish,
  Lord, that seems best to Thee.
Most truly, then, Thy will is done,
  When mine, O Lord, is crossed,
'Tis good to see my plans o'erthrown,
  My ways in Thine all lost.

H. BONAR

O LORD, Thou knowest what is best for us ;
let this or that be done, as Thou shalt
please. Give what Thou wilt, and how much
Thou wilt, and when Thou wilt. Deal with me
as Thou thinkest good. Set me where Thou wilt,
and deal with me in all things just as Thou
wilt. Behold, I am Thy servant, prepared for
all things : for I desire not to live unto myself,
but unto Thee ; and oh, that I could do it
worthily and perfectly ! THOMAS À KEMPIS

DARE to look up to God, and say, ' Make use
of me for the future as Thou wilt. I am of the
same mind ; I am one with Thee. I refuse
nothing which seems good to Thee. Lead me
whither Thou wilt, clothe me in whatever dress
Thou wilt. Is it Thy will that I should be in a
public or a private condition, dwell here, or be
banished, be poor or rich ? Under all these
circumstances, I will testify unto Thee before
men.

EPICTETUS

I would have you without carefulness.—I COR.
vii. 32.

> O LORD, how happy should we be
> If we could cast our care on Thee,
> 　If we from self could rest ;
> And feel at heart that One above,
> In perfect wisdom, perfect love,
> 　Is working for the best.
>
> 　　　　　　　J. ANSTICE

CAST *all* thy care on God. See that all thy
cares be such as thou canst cast on God,
and then hold none back. Never brood over
thyself ; never stop short in thyself ; but cast
thy whole self, even this very care which dis-
tresseth thee, upon God. Be not anxious about
little things, if thou wouldst learn to trust God
with thine all. Act upon faith in little things ;
commit thy daily cares and anxieties to Him ;
and He will strengthen thy faith for any greater
trials.   Rather, give thy whole self into God's
hands, and so trust Him to take care of thee in
all lesser things, as being His, for His own sake,
whose thou art.

　　　　　　　E. B. PUSEY

If ye fulfil the royal law according to the Scripture, Thou shalt love thy neighbour as thyself, ye do well.—JAMES ii. 8.

COME, children, let us go !
  We travel hand in hand ;
Each in his brother finds his joy
  In this wild stranger land.
The strong be quick to raise
  The weaker when they fall ;
Let love and peace and patience bloom
  In ready help for all.

G. TERSTEEGEN

IT is a sad weakness in us, after all, that the thought of a man's death hallows him anew to us ; as if life were not sacred too,—as if it were comparatively a light thing to fail in love and reverence to the brother who has to climb the whole toilsome steep with us, and all our tears and tenderness were due to the one who is spared that hard journey.

GEORGE ELIOT

WOULD we codify the laws that should reign in households, and whose daily transgression annoys and mortifies us, and degrades our household life,—we must learn to adorn every day with sacrifices. Good manners are made up of petty sacrifices. Temperance, courage, love, are made up of the same jewels. Listen to every prompting of honour.

R. W. EMERSON

Serve Him with a perfect heart, and with a willing mind.—I CHRON. xxviii. 9.

AND if some things I do not ask,
　In my cup of blessing be,
I would have my spirit filled the more
　With grateful love to Thee,—
More careful,—not to serve Thee much,
　But to please Thee perfectly.

A. L. WARING

LITTLE things come daily, hourly, within our reach, and they are not less calculated to set forward our growth in holiness, than are the greater occasions which occur but rarely. Moreover, fidelity in trifles, and an earnest seeking to please God in little matters, is a test of real devotion and love. Let your aim be to please our dear Lord perfectly in little things, and to attain a spirit of childlike simplicity and dependence. In proportion as self-love and self-confidence are weakened, and our will bowed to that of God, so will hindrances disappear, the internal troubles and contests which harassed the soul vanish, and it will be filled with peace and tranquillity.

JEAN NICOLAS GROU

My brethren, count it all joy when ye fall into divers temptations [or ' trials '], knowing this, that the trying of your faith worketh patience.—JAMES i. 2, 3.

FOR patience, when the rough winds blow !
For patience, when our hopes are fading,—
When visible things all backward go,
And nowhere seems the power of aiding !
God still enfolds thee with His viewless hand,
And leads thee surely to the Fatherland.

N. L. FROTHINGHAM, from the German

WE have need of patience with ourselves and with others ; with those below, and those above us, and with our own equals ; with those who love us and those who love us not ; for the greatest things and for the least ; against sudden inroads of trouble, and under our daily burdens ; disappointments as to the weather, or the breaking of the heart ; in the weariness of the body, or the wearing of the soul ; in our own failure of duty, or others' failure toward us ; in every-day wants, or in the aching of sickness or the decay of age ; in disappointment, bereavement, losses, injuries, reproaches ; in heaviness of the heart ; or its sickness amid delayed hopes. In all these things, from childhood's little troubles to the martyr's sufferings, patience is the grace of God, whereby we endure evil for the love of God.

E. B. PUSEY

It is good for me that I have been afflicted, that I might learn Thy statutes.—PS. cxix. 71.

But though He cause grief, yet will He have compassion, according to the multitude of His mercies.
—LAM. iii. 32.

And yet these days of dreariness are sent us from
    above ;
They do not come in anger, but in faithfulness and
    love ;
They come to teach us lessons which bright ones
    could not yield,
And to leave us blest and thankful when their
    purpose is fulfilled.

ANON‖

HEED not distressing thoughts when they rise ever so strongly in thee ; nay, though they have entered thee, fear them not, but be still awhile, not believing in the power which thou feelest they have over thee, and it will fall on a sudden. It is good for thy spirit, and greatly to thy advantage, to be much and variously exercised by the Lord. Thou dost not know what the Lord hath already done, and what He is yet doing for thee therein.

I. PENINGTON

WHY should I start at the plough of my Lord, that maketh deep furrows on my soul ? I know He is no idle husbandman, He purposeth a crop.

S. RUTHERFORD

My meat is to do the will of Him that sent me, and to finish His work.—JOHN iv. 34.

> I AM glad to think
> I am not bound to make the world go right ;
> But only to discover and to do,
> With cheerful heart, the work that God appoints.
> I will trust in Him,
> That He can hold His own ; and I will take
> His will, above the work He sendeth me,
> To be my chiefest good.
>
> J. INGELOW

DON'T object that your duties are so insignificant ; they are to be reckoned of infinite significance, and alone important to you. Were it but the more perfect regulation of your apartments, the sorting-away of your clothes and trinkets, the arranging of your papers,—' Whatsoever thy hand findeth to do, *do it* with all thy might', and all thy worth and constancy. Much more, if your duties are of evidently higher, wider scope ; if you have brothers, sisters, a father, a mother, weigh earnestly what claim does lie upon you, on behalf of each, and consider it as the one thing needful, to pay *them* more and more honestly and nobly what you owe. What matter how miserable one is, if one can do that ? That is the sure and steady disconnexion and extinction of whatsoever miseries one has in this world.

T. CARLYLE

Let us not therefore judge one another any more : but judge this rather, that no man put a stumblingblock, or an occasion to fall, in his brother's way.—ROM. xiv. 13.

Them that were entering in, ye hindered.—LUKE xi. 52.

MY mind was ruffled with small cares to-day,
And I said pettish words, and did not keep
Long-suffering patience well, and now how deep
My trouble for this sin ! in vain I weep
For foolish words I never can unsay.

H. S. SUTTON

A VEXATION arises, and our expressions of impatience hinder others from taking it patiently. Disappointment, ailment, or even weather depresses us ; and our look or tone of depression hinders others from maintaining a cheerful and thankful spirit. We say an unkind thing, and another is hindered in learning the holy lesson of charity that thinketh no evil. We say a provoking thing, and our sister or brother is hindered in that day's effort to be meek. How sadly, too, we may hinder without word or act ! For wrong feeling is more infectious than wrong doing ; especially the various phases of ill temper,—gloominess, touchiness, discontent, irritability,—do we not know how catching these are ?

F. R. HAVERGAL

If ye then, being evil, know how to give good gifts unto your children, how much more shall your Father which is in heaven give good gifts to them that ask Him.—MATT. vii. 11.

FOR His great love has compassed
  Our nature, and our need
We know not ; but He knoweth,
  And He will bless indeed.
Therefore, O heavenly Father,
  Give what is best to me ;
And take the wants unanswered,
  As offerings made to Thee.

                                ANON.

WHATSOEVER we ask which is not for our good, He will keep it back from us. And surely in this there is no less of love than in the granting what we desire as we ought. Will not the same love which prompts you to give a good, prompt you to keep back an evil, thing ? If, in our blindness, not knowing what to ask, we pray for things which would turn in our hands to sorrow and death, will not our Father, out of His very love, deny us ? How awful would be our lot, if our wishes should straightway pass into realities ; if we were endowed with a power to bring about all that we desire ; if the inclinations of our will were followed by fulfilment of our hasty wishes, and sudden longings were always granted. One day we shall bless Him, not more for what He has granted than for what He has denied.

                        H. E. MANNING

Be careful for nothing ; but in everything by prayer and supplication with thanksgiving let your requests be made known unto God.—PHIL. iv. 6.

WE tell Thee of our care,
Of the sore burden, pressing day by day,
And in the light and pity of Thy face,
    The burden melts away.

We breathe our secret wish,
The importunate longing which no man may see ;
We ask it humbly, or, more restful still,
    We leave it all to Thee.

SUSAN COOLIDGE

THAT prayer which does not succeed in moderating our wish, in changing the passionate desire into still submission, the anxious, tumultuous expectation into silent surrender, is no true prayer, and proves that we have not the spirit of true prayer. That life is most holy in which there is least of petition and desire, and most of waiting upon God ; that in which petition most often passes into thanksgiving. Pray till prayer makes you forget your own wish, and leave it or merge it in God's will. The Divine wisdom has given us prayer, not as a means whereby to obtain the good things of earth, but as a means whereby we learn to do without them ; not as a means whereby we escape evil, but as a means whereby we become strong to meet it.

F. W. ROBERTSON

Let the Lord do that which is good in His sight.
—1 CHRON. xix. 13.

*Let Thy mercy, O Lord, be upon us, according as
we hope in Thee.*—PS. xxxiii. 22.

        I CANNOT feel
That all is well, when darkening clouds conceal
      The shining sun ;
      But then, I know
He lives and loves ; and say, since it is so,
      Thy will be done.

S. G. BROWNING

NO felt evil or defect becomes divine until it
is inevitable ; and only when resistance to
it is exhausted and hope has fled, does surrender
cease to be premature. The hardness of our
task lies *here* ; that we have to strive against the
grievous things of life, while hope remains, as if
they were evil ; and then, when the stroke has
fallen, to accept them from the hand of God,
and doubt not they are good. But to the loving,
trusting heart all things are possible ; and even
this instant change, from overstrained will to
sorrowful repose, from fullest resistance to com-
plete surrender, is realized without convulsion.

MARTINEAU

*These things I have spoken unto you that in me
ye might have peace. In the world ye shall have
tribulation : but be of good cheer ; I have over-
come the world.*—JOHN xvi. 33.

O THOU, the primal fount of life and peace,
  Who shedd'st Thy breathing quiet all around,
In me command that pain and conflict cease,
  And turn to music every jarring sound.

J. STERLING

ACCUSTOM yourself to unreasonableness
and injustice. Abide in peace in the pres-
ence of God, who sees all these evils more
clearly than you do, and who permits them. Be
content with doing with calmness the little
which depends upon yourself, and let all else
be to you as if it were not.

FÉNELON

IT is rare when injustice, or slights patiently
borne, do not leave the heart at the close of the
day filled with marvellous joy and peace.

GOLD DUST

But now thus saith the Lord that created thee, O Jacob, and He that formed thee, O Israel, Fear not ; for I have redeemed thee, I have called thee by thy name ; thou art mine.—ISA. xliii. 1.

THOU art as much His care as if beside
   Nor man nor angel lived in heaven or earth ;
Thus sunbeams pour alike their glorious tide,
   To light up worlds, or wake an insect's mirth.
J. KEBLE

GOD beholds thee individually, whoever thou art. ' He calls thee by thy name.' He sees thee, and understands thee. He knows what is in thee, all thy own peculiar feelings and thoughts, thy dispositions and likings, thy strength and thy weakness. He views thee in thy day of rejoicing and thy day of sorrow. He sympathizes in thy hopes and in thy temptations ; He interests himself in all thy anxieties and thy remembrances, in all the risings and fallings of thy spirit. He compasses thee round, and bears thee in His arms ; He takes thee up and sets thee down. Thou dost not love thyself better than He loves thee. Thou canst not shrink from pain more than He dislikes thy bearing it ; and if He puts it on thee, it is as thou wilt put it on thyself, if thou art wise, for a greater good afterwards.

J. H. NEWMAN

The Lord is nigh unto all them that call upon Him, to all that call upon Him in truth.—PS. cxlv. 18.

I sought the Lord, and He heard me, and delivered me from all my fears.—PS. xxxiv. 4.

BE Thou, O Rock of Ages, nigh !
　So shall each murmuring thought be gone ;
And grief and fear and care shall fly,
　As clouds before the mid-day sun.

C. WESLEY

TAKE courage, and turn your troubles, which are without remedy, into material for spiritual progress. Often turn to our Lord, who is watching you, poor frail little being as you are, amid your labours and distractions. He sends you help, and blesses your affliction. This thought should enable you to bear your troubles patiently and gently, for love of Him who only allows you to be tried for your own good. Raise your heart continually to God, seek His aid, and let the foundation stone of your consolation be your happiness in being His. All vexations and annoyances will be comparatively unimportant while you know that you have such a Friend, such a Stay, such a Refuge. May God be ever in your heart.

FRANCIS DE SALES

Trust in the Lord, and do good ; so shalt thou dwell in the land, and verily thou shalt be fed.—
PS. xxxvii. 3.

BUILD a little fence of trust
   Around to-day ;
Fill the space with loving work,
   And therein stay ;
Look not through the sheltering bars
   Upon to-morrow,
God will help thee bear what comes,
   Of joy or sorrow.

MARY FRANCES BUTTS

LET us bow our souls and say, ' Behold the handmaid of the Lord ! ' Let us lift up our hearts and ask, ' Lord, what wouldst thou have me to do ? ' Then light from the opened heaven shall stream on our daily task, revealing the grains of gold, where yesterday all seemed dust ; a hand shall sustain us and our daily burden, so that, smiling at yesterday's fears, we shall say, ' *This is easy, this is light* ' ; every ' lion in the way ', as we come up to it, shall be seen chained, and leave open the gates of the Palace Beautiful ; and to us, even to us, feeble and fluctuating as we are, ministries shall be assigned, and through our hands blessings shall be conveyed in which the spirits of just men made perfect might delight.

ELIZABETH CHARLES

Beloved, let us love one another : for love is of God ; and every one that loveth is born of God, and knoweth God.—1 JOHN iv. 7.

so to the calmly gathered thought
The innermost of life is taught,
The mystery, dimly understood,
That love of God is love of good ;
That to be saved is only this,—
Salvation from our selfishness.

J. G. WHITTIER

THE Spirit of Love, wherever it is, is its own blessing and happiness, because it is the truth and reality of God in the soul ; and therefore is in the same joy of life, and is the same good to itself everywhere and on every occasion. Would you know the blessing of all blessings ? It is this God of Love dwelling in your soul, and killing every root of bitterness, which is the pain and torment of every earthly, selfish love. For all wants are satisfied, all disorders of nature are removed, no life is any longer a burden, every day is a day of peace, everything you meet becomes a help to you, because everything you see or do is all done in the sweet, gentle element of Love.

WM. LAW

3

Unto you that fear my name shall the Sun of Righteousness arise with healing in his wings.— MAL. iv. 2.

O send out Thy light and Thy truth ; let them lead me.— PS. xliii. 3.

OPEN our eyes, thou Sun of life and gladness,
    That we may see that glorious world of Thine !
It shines for us in vain, while drooping sadness
    Enfolds us here like mist ; come, Power benign,
        Touch our chilled hearts with vernal smile,
        Our wintry course do Thou beguile.
Nor by the wayside ruins let us mourn,
Who have th' eternal towers for our appointed bourn.
J. KEBLE

BECAUSE all those scattered rays of beauty and loveliness which we behold spread up and down over all the world, are only the emanations of that inexhausted light which is above ; therefore should we love them all in that, and climb up always by those sunbeams unto the eternal Father of lights : we should look upon Him, and take from Him the pattern of our lives, and always eyeing Him, should, as Hierocles speaks, ' polish and shape our souls into the clearest resemblance of Him ' ; and in all our behaviour in this world (that great temple of His) deport ourselves decently and reverently, with that humility, meekness, and modesty that becomes His house.

DR. JOHN SMITH, d. 1652

*Take no thought for your life, what ye shall eat,
or what ye shall drink, nor yet for your body, what
ye shall put on.*—MATT. vi. 25.

ONE there lives whose guardian eye
Guides our earthly destiny ;
One there lives, who, Lord of all,
Keeps His children lest they fall ;
Pass we, then, in love and praise
Trusting Him through all our days,
Free from doubt and faithless sorrow,—
God provideth for the morrow.

R. HEBER

IT has been well said that no man ever sank
under the burden of the day. It is when
to-morrow's burden is added to the burden of
to-day that the weight is more than a man can
bear. Never load yourselves so, my friends.
If you find yourselves so loaded, at least re-
member this : it is your own doing, not God's.
He begs you to leave the future to Him, and
mind the present.

G. MACDONALD

*But to do good and to communicate forget not :
for with such sacrifices God is well pleased.*—HEB.
xiii. 16.

*For this is the message that ye heard from the
beginning, that we should love one another.*—
I JOHN iii. 11.

BE useful where thou livest, that they may
Both want and wish thy pleasing presence still.
    . . . Find out men's wants and will,
And meet them there. All worldly joys go less
To the one joy of doing kindnesses.

G. HERBERT

LET the weakest, let the humblest remember, that in his daily course he can, if he will, shed around him almost a heaven. Kindly words, sympathizing attentions, watchfulness against wounding men's sensitiveness,—these cost very little, but they are priceless in their value. Are they not almost the staple of our daily happiness ? From hour to hour, from moment to moment, we are supported, blest, by small kindnesses.

F. W. ROBERTSON

SMALL kindnesses, small courtesies, small considerations, habitually practised in our social intercourse, give a greater charm to the character than the display of great talents and accomplishments.

M. A. KELTY

I made haste, and delayed not to keep Thy commandments.—PS. cxix. 60.

Ye know not what shall be on the morrow.—JAMES iv. 14.

> NEVER delay
> To do the duty which the hour brings,
> Whether it be in great or smaller things ;
> For who doth know
> What he shall do the coming day ?
>
> ANON.

IT is quite impossible that an idle, floating spirit can ever look up with clear eye to God ; spreading its miserable anarchy before the symmetry of the creative Mind ; in the midst of a disorderly being, that has neither centre nor circumference, kneeling beneath the glorious sky, that everywhere has both ; and for a life that is *all* failure, turning to the Lord of the silent stars, of whose punctual thought it is, that ' not one faileth '. The heavens, with their everlasting faithfulness, look down on no sadder contradiction, than the sluggard and the slattern in their prayers.

J. MARTINEAU

But the souls of the righteous are in the hand of God, and there shall no torment touch them. In the sight of the unwise they seemed to die : and their departure is taken for misery, and their going from us to be utter destruction : but they are in peace.—WISDOM OF SOLOMON iii. 1–3.

BUT souls that of His own good life partake,
He loves as His own self ; dear as His eye
They are to Him : He'll never them forsake :
When they shall die, then God Himself shall die ;
They live, they live in blest eternity.

HENRY MORE

THOUGH every good man is not so logically subtile as to be able by fit mediums to demonstrate his own immortality, yet he sees it in a higher light : his soul, being purged and enlightened by true sanctity, is more capable of those divine irradiations, whereby it feels itself in conjunction with God. It knows that God will never forsake His own life which He hath quickened in it ; He will never deny those ardent desires of a blissful fruition of Himself, which the lively sense of His own goodness hath excited within it : those breathings and gaspings after an eternal participation of Him are but the energy of His own breath within us ; if He had had any mind to destroy it, He would never have shown it such things as He hath done.

DR. JOHN SMITH

And every man that hath this hope in him puri-fieth himself, even as He is pure.—1 JOHN iii. 3.

> NOW, Lord, what wait I for?
>   On Thee alone
> My hope is all rested,—
>   Lord, seal me Thine own!
> Only Thine own to be,
> Only to live to Thee.
>   Thine, with each day begun,
>   Thine, with each set of sun,
>   Thine, till my work is done.
>   ANNA WARNER

NOW, believe me, God hides some ideal in every human soul. At some time in our life we feel a trembling, fearful longing to do some good thing. Life finds its noblest spring of excellence in this hidden impulse to do our best. There is a time when we are not content to be such merchants or doctors or lawyers as we see on the dead level or below it. The woman longs to glorify her womanhood as sister, wife, or mother. . . . Here is God,— God standing silently at the door all day long,— God whispering to the soul, that to be pure and true is to succeed in life, and whatever we get short of that will burn up like stubble, though the whole world try to save it.

ROBERT COLLYER

The shadow of a great rock in a weary land.—
ISA. xxxii. 2.

*In returning and rest shall ye be saved ; in
quietness and in confidence shall be your strength.—*
ISA. xxx. 15.

> O SHADOW in a sultry land !
>   We gather to Thy breast,
> Whose love, enfolding like the night,
>   Brings quietude and rest,
> Glimpse of the fairer life to be,
>   In foretaste here possessed.
>
> C. M. PACKARD

STRIVE to see God in all things without ex-
ception, and acquiesce in His will with
absolute submission. Do everything for God,
uniting yourself to Him by a mere upward
glance, or by the overflowing of your heart
towards Him. Never be in a hurry ; do every-
thing quietly and in a calm spirit. Do not lose
your inward peace for anything whatsoever,
even if your whole world seems upset. Com-
mend all to God, and then lie still and be at
rest in His bosom. Whatever happens, abide
steadfast in a determination to cling simply to
God, trusting to His eternal love for you ; and
if you find that you have wandered forth from
this shelter, recall your heart quietly and simply.
Maintain a holy simplicity of mind, and do
not smother yourself with a host of cares,
wishes, or longings, under any pretext.

FRANCIS DE SALES

There are diversities of operations, but it is the same God which worketh all in all.—I COR. xii. 6.

I form the light, and create darkness ; I make peace, and create evil ; I the Lord do all these things.—ISA. xlv. 7.

' ALL is of God that is, and is to be ;
And God is good.' Let this suffice us still,
Resting in childlike trust upon His will,
Who moves to His great ends, unthwarted by the ill.
                                        J. G. WHITTIER

THIS, then, is of faith, that everything, the very least, or what seemed to us great, every change in the seasons, everything which touches us in mind, body, or estate, whether brought about through this outward senseless nature, or by the will of man, good or bad, is overruled to each of us by the all-holy and all-loving will of God. Whatever befalls us, however it befalls us, we must receive as the will of God. If it befalls us through man's negligence, or ill-will, or anger, still it is, in every the least circumstance, to *us* the will of God. For if the least thing could happen to us without God's permission, it would be something out of God's control. God's providence or His love would not be what they are. Almighty God Himself would not be the same God ; not the God whom we believe, adore, and love.

                                        E. B. PUSEY

Study to show thyself approved unto God, a workman that needeth not to be ashamed.—2 TIM. ii. 15.

And let us not be weary in well-doing ; for in due season we shall reap if we faint not.—GAL. vi. 9.

THE task Thy wisdom hath assigned,
    Oh, let me cheerfully fulfil ;
In all my works Thy presence find,
    And prove Thine acceptable will.

C. WESLEY

'WHAT is my next duty ? What is the thing that lies nearest to me ? ' ' That belongs to your every-day history. No one can answer that question but yourself. Your next duty is just to determine what your next duty is. Is there nothing you neglect ? Is there nothing you know you ought not to do ? You would know your duty, if you thought in earnest about it, and were not ambitious of great things.' ' Ah, then,' responded she, ' I suppose it is something very commonplace, which will make life more dreary than ever. That cannot help me.' ' It will, if it be as dreary as reading the newspapers to an old deaf aunt. It will soon lead you to something more. Your duty will begin to comfort you at once, but will at length open the unknown fountain of life in your heart.'

G. MACDONALD

Thou shalt rejoice before the Lord thy God, in all that thou puttest thine hands unto.—DEUT. xii. 18.

Be ye thankful.—COL. iii. 15.

THOU that hast given so much to me,
Give one thing more, a grateful heart.
Not thankful when it pleaseth me,
As if thy blessings had spare days ;
But such a heart, whose pulse may be
           Thy praise.

              G. HERBERT

IF any one would tell you the shortest, surest way to all happiness and all perfection, he must tell you to make it a rule to yourself to thank and praise God for everything that happens to you. For it is certain that whatever seeming calamity happens to you, if you thank and praise God for it, you turn it into a blessing. Could you, therefore, work miracles, you could not do more for yourself than by this thankful spirit ; for it heals with a word speaking, and turns all that it touches into happiness.

              WM. LAW

When thou passest through the waters, I will be with thee ; and through the rivers, they shall not overflow thee : when thou walkest through the fire, thou shalt not be burned ; neither shall the flame kindle upon thee.—ISA. xliii 2.

I am with thee to deliver thee.—JER. i. 8.

WHEN through the deep waters I call thee to go,
The rivers of sorrow shall not overflow ;
For I will be with thee thy troubles to bless,
And sanctity to thee thy deepest distress.

ANON.

TURN it as thou wilt, thou must give thyself to suffer what is appointed thee. But if we did that, God would bear us up at all times in all our sorrows and troubles, and God would lay His shoulder under our burdens, and help us to bear them. For if, with a cheerful courage, we submitted ourselves to God, no suffering would be unbearable.

J. TAULER

LEARN to be as the angel, who could descend among the miseries of Bethesda without losing his heavenly purity or his perfect happiness. Gain healing from troubled waters. Make up your mind to the prospect of sustaining a certain measure of pain and trouble in your passage through life. By the blessing of God this will prepare you for it ; it will make you thoughtful and resigned without interfering with your cheerfulness.

J. H. NEWMAN

Cast thy burden upon the Lord, and He shall sustain thee ; He shall never suffer the righteous to be moved.—PS. lv. 22.

> NOW our wants and burdens leaving,
> To His care, who cares for all,
> Cease we fearing, cease we grieving,
> At His touch our burdens fall.
>
> S. LONGFELLOW

THE circumstances of her life she could not alter, but she took them to the Lord, and handed them over into His management ; and then she believed that He took it, and she left all the responsibility and the worry and anxiety with Him. As often as the anxieties returned she took them back ; and the result was that, although the circumstances remained unchanged, her soul was kept in perfect peace in the midst of them. And the secret she found so effectual in her outward affairs, she found to be still more effectual in her inward ones, which were in truth even more utterly unmanageable. She abandoned her whole self to the Lord, with all that she was and all that she had ; and, believing that He took that which she had committed to Him, she ceased to fret and worry, and her life became all sunshine in the gladness of belonging to Him.

H. W. S.

The Lord bless thee, and keep thee ; the Lord make His face shine upon thee, and be gracious unto thee ; the Lord lift up His countenance upon thee, and give thee peace.—NUM. vi. 24–26.

O LOVE, how cheering is Thy ray !
   All pain before Thy presence flies ;
Care, anguish, sorrow, melt away,
   Where'er Thy healing beams arise.
O Father, nothing may I see,
Nothing desire, or seek, but Thee.
P. GERHARDT

THERE is a faith in God, and a clear perception of His will and designs, and providence, and glory, which gives to its possessor a confidence and patience and sweet composure, under every varied and troubling aspect of events, such as no man can realize who has not felt its influences in his own heart. There is a communion with God, in which the soul feels the presence of the unseen One, in the profound depths of its being, with a vivid distinctness and a holy reverence, such as no words can describe. There is a state of union with God, I do not say often reached, yet it has been attained in this world, in which all the past and present and future seem reconciled, and eternity is won and enjoyed ; and God and man, earth and heaven, with all their mysteries, are apprehended in truth as they lie in the mind of the Infinite.

SAMUEL D. ROBBINS

He that abideth in me, and I in him, bringeth forth much fruit.—JOHN xv. 5.

Let the beauty of the Lord our God be upon us.—PS. xc. 17.

AS some rare perfume in a vase of clay
  Pervades it with a fragrance not its own,
So, when Thou dwellest in a mortal soul,
  All Heaven's own sweetness seems around it
    thrown.

H. B. STOWE

SOME glances of real beauty may be seen in their faces, who dwell in true meekness. There is a harmony in the sound of that voice to which Divine love gives utterance, and some appearance of right order in their temper and conduct whose passions are regulated.

JOHN WOOLMAN

I BELIEVE that no Divine truth can truly dwell in any heart, without an external testimony in manner, bearing, and appearance, that must reach the witness within the heart of the beholder, and bear an unmistakable, though silent, evidence to the eternal principle from which it emanates.

M. A. SCHIMMELPENNINCK

*I have called upon Thee, for Thou wilt hear me,
O God : incline Thine ear unto me, and hear my
speech.*—PS. xvii. 6.

*Ye people, pour out your heart before Him :
God is a refuge for us.*—PS. lxii. 8.

WHATE'ER the care which breaks thy rest,
Whate'er the wish that swells thy breast ;
Spread before God that wish, that care,
And change anxiety to prayer.

ANON.

TROUBLE and perplexity drive us to
prayer, and prayer driveth away trouble
and perplexity.

P. MELANCHTHON

WHATSOEVER it is that presses thee, go tell
thy Father ; put over the matter into His hand,
and so thou shalt be freed from that dividing,
perplexing care that the world is full of. When
thou art either to do or suffer anything, when
thou art about any purpose or business, go tell
God of it, and acquaint Him with it ; yea,
burden Him with it, and thou hast done for
matter of caring ; no more care, but quiet,
sweet diligence in thy duty, and dependence on
Him for the carriage of thy matters. Roll thy
cares, and thyself with them, as one burden,
all on thy God.

R. LEIGHTON

Hear me, O Lord, for Thy loving-kindness is good : turn unto me according to the multitude of Thy tender mercies.—PS. lxix. 16.

Let, I pray Thee, Thy merciful kindness be for my comfort, according to Thy word unto Thy servant..—PS. cxix. 76.

LOVE divine has seen and counted
　　Every tear it caused to fall ;
And the storm which Love appointed
　　Was its choicest gift of all.

ANON.

O THAT thou couldst dwell in the knowledge and sense of this ! even, that the Lord beholds thy sufferings with an eye of pity ; and is able, not only to uphold thee under them, but also to do thee good by them. Therefore, grieve not at thy lot, be not discontented, look not out at the hardness of thy condition ; but, when the storm and matters of vexation are sharp, look up to Him who can give meekness and patience, can lift up thy head over all, and cause thy life to grow, and be a gainer by all. If the Lord God help thee proportionably to thy condition of affliction and distress, thou wilt have no cause to complain, but to bless His Name.

I. PENINGTON

Whether therefore ye eat, or drink, or whatsoever ye do, do all to the glory of God.—1 COR. X. 31.

With good will doing service, as to the Lord and not unto men.—EPH. vi. 7.

> A SERVANT, with this clause,
> Makes drudgery divine :
> Who sweeps a room, as for Thy laws,
> Makes that and th' action fine.
>
> G. HERBERT

SURELY the truth must be, that whatsoever in our daily life is lawful and right for us to be engaged in, is in itself a part of our obedience to God ; a part, that is, of our very religion. Whensoever we hear people complaining of obstructions and hindrances put by the duties of life in the way of devoting themselves to God, we may be sure they are under some false view or other. They do not look upon their daily work as the task God has set them, and as obedience due to Him. We may go farther ; and say, not only that the duties of life, be they never so toilsome and distracting, are no obstructions to a life of any degree of inward holiness ; but that they are even direct means, when rightly used, to promote our sanctification.

H. E. MANNING

Where hast thou gleaned to-day ?—RUTH ii. 19

WHAT have I learnt where'er I've been,
From all I've heard, from all I've seen ?
What know I more that's worth the knowing ?
What have I done that's worth the doing ?
What have I sought that I should shun ?
What duties have I left undone ?

PYTHAGORAS

ALL of this world will soon have passed away. But God will remain, and thou, whatever thou hast become, good or bad. Thy deeds now are the seed-corn of eternity. Each single act, in each several day, good or bad, is a portion of that seed. Each day adds some line, making thee more or less like Him, more or less capable of His love.

E. B. PUSEY

THERE is something very solemn in the thought that that part of our work which we have left undone may first be revealed to us at the end of a life filled up, as we had fondly hoped, with useful and necessary employments.

ANNA, OR PASSAGES FROM HOME LIFE

Finally, be ye all of one mind, having compassion one of another ; love as brethren, be pitiful, be courteous.—I PETER iii. 8.

MAKE us of one heart and mind ;
Courteous, pitiful, and kind ;
Lowly, meek, in thought and word,
Altogether like our Lord.

C. WESLEY

A LITTLE thought will show you how vastly your own happiness depends on the way other people bear themselves toward you. The looks and tones at your breakfast-table, the conduct of your fellow-workers or employers, the faithful or unreliable men you deal with, what people say to you on the street, the way your cook and housemaid do their work, the letters you get, the friends or foes you meet,— these things make up very much of the pleasure or misery of your day. Turn the idea around, and remember that just so much are you adding to the pleasure or the misery of other people's days. And this is the half of the matter which you can control. Whether any particular day shall bring to you more of happiness or of suffering is largely beyond your power to determine. Whether each day of your life shall *give* happiness or suffering rests with yourself.

GEORGE S. MERRIAM

Showing all good fidelity, that they may adorn the doctrine of God our Saviour in all things.—
TITUS ii. 10.

> IF on our daily course our mind
> Be set to hallow all we find,
> New treasures still, of countless price,
> God will provide for sacrifice.
>
> J. KEBLE

IF content and thankfulness, if the patient bearing of evil, be duties to God, they are the duties of every day, and in every circumstance of our life. If we are to follow Christ, it must be in our common way of spending every day.

WM. LAW

HE who is faithful over a few things is a lord of cities. It does not matter whether you preach in Westminster Abbey, or teach a ragged class, so you be faithful. The faithfulness is all.

G. MACDONALD

I WOULD have you invoke God often through the day, asking Him to kindle a love for your vocation within you, and saying with St. Paul, ' " Lord, what wouldst Thou have me to do ? " Wouldst Thou have me serve Thee in the lowest ministries of Thy house ? too happy if I may but serve Thee anyhow.' And when any special thing goes against you, ask ' Wouldst Thou have me do it ? Then, unworthy though I be, I will do it gladly.'

FRANCIS DE SALES

Thou shalt worship the Lord thy God, and Him only shalt thou serve.—MATT. iv. 10.

Blessed are they that keep His testimonies, and that seek Him with the whole heart.—PS. cxix. 2.

THE comfort of a mind at rest
From every care Thou hast not blest ;
A heart from all the world set free,
To worship and to wait on Thee.

A. L. WARING

RESIGN every forbidden joy ; restrain every wish that is not referred to His will ; banish all eager desires, all anxiety. Desire only the will of God ; seek Him alone, and you will find peace.

FÉNELON

' I'VE been a great deal happier since I have given up thinking about what is easy and pleasant, and being discontented because I couldn't have my own will. Our life is determined for us ; and it makes the mind very free when we give up wishing, and only think of bearing what is laid upon us, and doing what is given us to do.'

GEORGE ELIOT

Your heavenly Father knoweth that ye have need of all these things.—MATT. vi. 32.

ALL as God wills, who wisely heeds
  To give or to withhold ;
And knoweth more of all my needs
  Than all my prayers have told.

J. G. WHITTIER

LORD, I know not what I ought to ask of Thee ; Thou only knowest what we need ; Thou lovest me better than I know how to love myself. O Father ! give to Thy child that which he himself knows not how to ask. I dare not ask either for crosses or consolations ; I simply present myself before Thee ; I open my heart to Thee. Behold my needs which I know not myself ; see, and do according to Thy tender mercy. Smite, or heal ; depress me, or raise me up ; I adore all Thy purposes without knowing them ; I am silent ; I offer myself in sacrifice ; I yield myself to Thee ; I would have no other desire than to accomplish Thy will. Teach me to pray ; pray Thyself in me.

FÉNELON

He that contemneth small things shall fall by little and little.—ECCLUS. xix. 1.

ONE finger's-breadth at hand will mar
A world of light in heaven afar,
A mote eclipse a glorious star,
　　An eyelid hide the sky.

J. KEBLE

A SINGLE sin, however apparently trifling, however hidden in some obscure corner of our consciousness,—a sin *which we do not intend to renounce*,—is enough to render real prayer impracticable. A course of action not wholly upright and honourable, feelings not entirely kind and loving, habits not spotlessly chaste and temperate,—any of these are impassable obstacles. If we know of a kind act which we might, but do not intend to, perform,—if we be aware that our moral health requires the abandonment of some pleasure which yet we do not intend to abandon, here is cause enough for the loss of all spiritual power.

F. P. COBBE

IT is astonishing how soon the whole conscience begins to unravel, if a single stitch drops ; one little sin indulged makes a hole you could put your head through.

CHARLES BUXTON

Beloved, thou doest faithfully whatsoever thou doest.—3 JOHN 5.

And this also we wish, even your perfection.— 2 COR. xiii. 9.

> IN all the little things of life,
>   Thyself, Lord, may I see ;
> In little and in great alike
>   Reveal Thy love to me.
>
> So shall my undivided life
>   To Thee, my God, be given ;
> And all this earthly course below
>   Be one dear path to heaven.
>
> H. BONAR

IN order to mould thee into entire conformity to His will, He must have thee pliable in His hands, and this pliability is more quickly reached by yielding in the little things than even by the greater. Thy one great desire is to follow Him fully ; canst thou not say then a continual ' yes ' to all His sweet commands, whether small or great, and trust Him to lead thee by the shortest road to thy fullest blessedness ?

H. W. S.

WITH meekness, humility, and diligence, apply yourself to the duties of your condition. They are the seemingly little things which make no noise that do the business.

HENRY MORE

I will both lay me down in peace, and sleep ; for Thou, Lord, only makest me dwell in safety.—PS. iv. 8.

He giveth His beloved sleep.—PS. cxxvii. 2.

HE guides our feet, He guards our way,
His morning smiles bless all the day ;
He spreads the evening veil, and keeps
The silent hours while Israel sleeps.

I. WATTS

WE sleep in peace in the arms of God, when we yield ourselves up to His providence, in a delightful consciousness of His tender mercies ; no more restless uncertainties, no more anxious desires, no more impatience at the place we are in ; for it is God who has put us there, and who holds us in His arms. Can we be unsafe where He has placed us ?

FÉNELON

ONE evening when Luther saw a little bird perched on a tree, to roost there for the night, he said, ' This little bird has had its supper, and now it is getting ready to go to sleep here, quite secure and content, never troubling itself what its food will be, or where its lodging on the morrow. Like David, it " abides under the shadow of the Almighty ". It sits on its little twig content, and lets God take care.'

I will hear what God the Lord will speak : for He will speak peace unto His people.—PS. lxxxv. 8.

THERE is a voice, ' a still, small voice ' of love,
       Heard from above ;
But not amidst the din of earthly sounds,
       Which here confounds ;
By those withdrawn apart it best is heard,
And peace, sweet peace, breathes in each gentle
    word.

                    ANONYMOUS

HE speaketh, but it is with us to hearken or no. It is much, yea, it is everything, not to turn away the ear, to be willing to hearken, not to drown His voice. ' The secret of the Lord is with them that fear Him.' It is a secret, hushed voice, a gentle intercourse of heart to heart, a still, small voice, whispering to the inner ear. How should we hear it, if we fill our ears and our hearts with the din of this world, its empty tumult, its excitement, its fretting vanities, or cares, or passions, or anxieties, or show, or rivalries, and its whirl of emptinesses ?

                    E. B. PUSEY

Are they not all ministering spirits?—HEB. i. 14.

> MAY I reach
> That purest heaven, be to other souls
> The cup of strength in some great agony,
> Enkindle generous ardour, feed pure love,
> Be the sweet presence of a good diffused,
> And in diffusion ever more intense !
> So shall I join the choir invisible
> Whose music is the gladness of the world.
>
> GEORGE ELIOT

CERTAINLY, in our own little sphere, it is not the most active people to whom we owe the most. Among the common people whom we know, it is not necessarily those who are busiest, not those who, meteor-like, are ever on the rush after some visible charge and work. It is the lives, like the stars, which simply pour down on us the calm light of their bright and faithful being, up to which we look and out of which we gather the deepest calm and courage. It seems to me that there is reassurance here for many of us who seem to have no chance for active usefulness. We can do nothing for our fellow-men. But still it is good to know that we can be something for them ; to know (and this we may know surely) that no man or woman of the humblest sort can really be strong, gentle, pure, and good, without the world being better for it, without somebody being helped and comforted by the very existence of that goodness.

PHILLIPS BROOKS

If we love one another, God dwelleth in us, and His love is perfected in us.—I JOHN iv. 12.

And he that keepeth His commandments dwelleth in Him, and He in him. And hereby we know that He abideth in us, by the Spirit which He hath given us.—I JOHN iii. 24.

ABIDE in me ; o'ershadow by Thy love
Each half-formed purpose and dark thought of sin ;
Quench, ere it rise, each selfish, low desire,
And keep my soul as Thine, calm and divine.

H. B. STOWE

THE Spirit of Love must work the works, and speak the tones, of Love. It cannot exist and give no sign, or a false sign. It cannot be a spirit of Love, and mantle into irritable and selfish impatience. It cannot be a spirit of Love, and at the same time make self the prominent object. It cannot rejoice to lend itself to the happiness of others, and at the same time be seeking its own. It cannot be generous, and envious. It cannot be sympathizing, and unseemly ; self-forgetful, and vain-glorious. It cannot delight in the rectitude and purity of other hearts, as the spiritual elements of their peace, and yet unnecessarily suspect them.

J. H. THOM

Giving thanks always for all things unto God.—
EPH. V. 20.

FOR blessings of the fruitful season,
  For work and rest, for friends and home,
For the great gifts of thought and reason,—
  To praise and bless Thee, Lord, we come.

Yes, and for weeping and for wailing,
  For bitter hail and blighting frost,
For high hopes on the low earth trailing,
  For sweet joys missed, for pure aims crossed.
                                    E. SCUDDER

NOTWITHSTANDING all that I have suffered, notwithstanding all the pain and weariness and anxiety and sorrow that necessarily enter into life, and the inward errings that are worse than all, I would end my record with a devout thanksgiving to the great Author of my being. For more and more am I unwilling to make my gratitude to Him what is commonly called 'a thanksgiving for mercies', —for any benefits or blessings that are peculiar to myself, or my friends, or indeed to any man. Instead of this, I would have it to be gratitude for *all* that belongs to my life and being,—for joy and sorrow, for health and sickness, for success and disappointment, for virtue and for temptation, for life and death ; because I believe that all is meant for good.

ORVILLE DEWEY

There shall no evil befall thee.—PS. xci. 10.

Whoso hearkeneth unto me shall dwell safely, and shall be quiet from fear of evil.—PROV. i. 33.

I ASK not, ' Take away this weight of care ' ;
No, for that love I pray that all can bear,
   And for the faith that whatsoe'er befall
Must needs be good, and for my profit prove,
Since from my Father's heart most rich in love,
   And from His bounteous hands it cometh all.
C. J. P. SPITTA

BE like the promontory, against which the waves continually break ; but it stands firm, and tames the fury of the water around it. Unhappy am I, because this has happened to me ? Not so, but happy am I, though this has happened to me, because I continue free from pain, neither crushed by the present, nor fearing the future. Will then this which has happened prevent thee from being just, magnanimous, temperate, prudent, secure against inconsiderate opinions and falsehood ? Remember, too, on every occasion which leads thee to vexation to apply this principle : that this is not a misfortune, but that to bear it nobly is good fortune.

MARCUS ANTONINUS

Thou shalt guide me with Thy counsel, and afterward receive me to glory.—PS. lxxiii. 24.

There remaineth therefore a rest to the people of God.—HEB. iv. 9.

> GUIDE us through life ; and when at last
>   We enter into rest,
> Thy tender arms around us cast,
>   And fold us to Thy breast.
>
> H. F. LYTE

GO forth to meet the solemnities and to conquer the trials of existence, believing in a Shepherd of your souls. Then faith in Him will support you in duty, and duty firmly done will strengthen faith ; till at last, when all is over here, and the noise and strife of the earthly battle fades upon your dying ear, and you hear, instead thereof, the deep and musical sound of the ocean of eternity, and see the lights of heaven shining on its waters still and fair in their radiant rest, your faith will raise the song of conquest, and in its retrospect of the life which has ended, and its forward glance upon the life to come, take up the poetic inspiration of the Hebrew king, ' Surely goodness and mercy have followed me all the days of my life, and I will dwell in the house of the Lord forever.'

STOPFORD A. BROOKE

Thou shalt be in league with the stones of the field, and the beasts of the field shall be at peace with thee. And thou shalt know that thy tabernacle shall be in peace.—JOB v. 23, 24.

LOVE had he found in huts where poor men lie ;
His daily teachers had been woods and ills,
The silence that is in the starry sky,
The sleep that is among the lonely hills.

W. WORDSWORTH

THAT spirit which suffices quiet hearts, which seems to come forth to such from every dry knoll of sere grass, from every pine-stump, and half-embedded stone, on which the dull March sun shines, comes forth to the poor and hungry, and to such as are of simple taste. If thou fill thy brain with Boston and New York, with fashion and covetousness, and wilt stimulate thy jaded senses with wine and French coffee, thou shalt find no radiance of wisdom in the lonely waste of the pine-woods.

R. W. EMERSON

For Thou lovest all the things that are, and ab-horrest nothing which Thou hast made : for never wouldest Thou have made any thing, if Thou hadst hated it.   But Thou sparest all : for they are Thine, O Lord, Thou lover of souls.—WISDOM OF SOLOMON xi. 24, 26.

HE prayeth best who loveth best
    All things both great and small ;
For the dear God who loveth us,
    He made and loveth all.

S. T. COLERIDGE

TO know that Love alone was the beginning of nature and creature, that nothing but Love encompasses the whole universe of things, that the governing Hand that overrules all, the watchful Eye that sees through all, is nothing but omnipotent and omniscient Love, using an infinity of wisdom, to save every misguided creature from the miserable works of his own hands, and make happiness and glory the perpetual inheritance of all the creation, is a reflection that must be quite ravishing to every intelligent creature that is sensible of it.

WM. LAW

Know ye not that ye are the temple of God, and that the Spirit of God dwelleth in you?—1 COR. iii. 16.

> FATHER ! replenish with Thy grace
> This longing heart of mine ;
> Make it Thy quiet dwelling-place,
> Thy sacred inmost shrine !
>
> ANGELUS SILESIUS

NOT man's manifold labours, but his manifold cares, hinder the presence of God. . . . Whatsoever thou doest, hush thyself to thine own feverish vanities, and busy thoughts, and cares ; in silence seek thy Father's face, and the light of His countenance will stream down upon thee. He will make a secret cell in thine heart, and when thou enterest there, there shalt thou find Him. And if thou hast found Him there, all around shall reflect Him, all shall speak to Him, and He will speak through all. Outwardly thou mayest be doing the work of thy calling ; inwardly, if thou commend thy work to God, thou mayest be with Him in the third Heaven.

E. B. PUSEY

As for thee, the Lord thy God hath not suffered thee so to do.—DEUT. xviii. 14.

> LORD, for the erring thought
> Not into evil wrought ;
> Lord, for the wicked will
> Betrayed and baffled still :
> For the heart from itself kept,
> Our Thanksgiving accept.
>
> W. D. HOWELLS

WHAT an amazing, what a blessed dispro-portion between the evil we do, and the evil we are capable of doing, and seem some-times on the very verge of doing ! If my soul has grown tares, when it was full of the seeds of nightshade, how happy ought I to be ! And that the tares have not wholly strangled the wheat, what a wonder it is ! We ought to thank God daily for the sins we have not committed.

F. W. FABER

WE give thanks often with a tearful, doubtful voice, for our spiritual mercies *positive* ; but what an almost infinite field there is for mercies negative ! We cannot even imagine all that God has suffered us *not* to do, *not* to be.

F. R. HAVERGAL

YOU are surprised at your imperfections—why ? I should infer from that, that your self-knowledge is small. Surely, you might rather be astonished that you do not fall into more frequent and more grievous faults, and thank God for His upholding grace.

JEAN NICOLAS GROU

Well done, good and faithful servant : thou hast been faithful over a few things, I will make thee ruler over many things : enter thou into the joy of thy Lord.—MATT. XXV. 23.

O FATHER ! help us to resign
  Our hearts, our strength, our wills to Thee ;
Then even lowliest work of Thine
  Most noble, blest, and sweet will be.
                              H. M. KIMBALL

NOTHING is too little to be ordered by our Father ; nothing too little in which to see His hand ; nothing, which touches our souls, too little to accept from Him ; nothing too little to be done to Him.

                              E. B. PUSEY

A SOUL occupied with great ideas best performs small duties ; the divinest views of life penetrate most clearly into the meanest emergencies ; so far from petty principles being best proportioned to petty trials, a heavenly spirit taking up its abode with us can alone sustain well the daily toils, and tranquilly pass the humiliations of our condition.

                              J. MARTINEAU

WHOSO neglects a thing which he suspects he ought to do, because it seems to him too small a thing, is deceiving himself ; it is not too little, but too great for him, that he doeth it not.

                              E. B. PUSEY

Yet I have left me seven thousand in Israel, all the knees which have not bowed unto Baal, and every mouth which hath not kissed him.—1 KINGS xix. 18.

BACK then, complainer ; loathe thy life no more,
Nor deem thyself upon a desert shore,
 Because the rocks the nearer prospect close.
Yet in fallen Israel are there hearts and eyes
That day by day in prayer like thine arise :
 Thou know'st them not, but their Creator knows.

J. KEBLE

HE went down to the great school with a glimmering of another lesson in his heart, —the lesson that he who has conquered his own coward spirit has conquered the whole outward world ; and that other one which the old prophet learnt in the cave in Mount Horeb, when he hid his face, and the still, small voice asked, ' What doest thou here, Elijah ? ' that however we may fancy ourselves alone on the side of good, the King and Lord of men is nowhere without His witnesses ; for in every society, however seemingly corrupt and godless, there are those who have not bowed the knee to Baal.

THOMAS HUGHES

so, then, Elijah's life had been no failure, after all. Seven thousand at least in Israel had been braced and encouraged by his example, and silently blessed him, perhaps, for the courage which they felt. In God's world, for those who are in earnest there is no failure. No work truly done, no word earnestly spoken, no sacrifice freely made, was ever made in vain.

F. W. ROBERTSON

In the multitude of my thoughts within me Thy comforts delight my soul.—PS. xciv. 19.

Perplexed, but not in despair ; cast down, but not destroyed.—2 COR. iv. 8, 9.

DISCOURAGED in the work of life,
  Disheartened by its load,
Shamed by its failures or its fears,
  I sink beside the road ;—
But let me only think of Thee,
And then new heart springs up in me.
                        S. LONGFELLOW

DISCOURAGEMENT is an inclination to give up all attempts after the devout life, in consequence of the difficulties by which it is beset, and our already numerous failures in it. We lose heart ; and partly in ill-temper, partly in real doubt of our own ability to persevere, we first grow querulous and peevish with God, and then relax in our efforts to mortify ourselves and to please Him. It is a sort of shadow of despair, and will lead us into numberless venial sins the first half-hour we give way to it.

                        F. W. FABER

NEVER let us be discouraged with ourselves ; it is not when we are conscious of our faults that we are the most wicked ; on the contrary, we are less so. We see by a brighter light ; and let us remember, for our consolation, that we never perceive our sins till we begin to cure them.

                        FÉNELON

*That ye may prove what is that good, and accept-
able, and perfect will of God.*—ROM. xii. 2.

THOU knowest what is best ;
   And who but Thee, O God, hath power to know ?
In Thy great will my trusting heart shall rest ;
   Beneath that will my humble head shall bow.
                                        T. C. UPHAM

TO those who are His, all things are not only
   easy to be borne, but even to be gladly
chosen. Their will is united to that will which
moves heaven and earth, which gives laws to
angels, and rules the courses of the world. It is
a wonderful gift of God to man, of which we
that know so little must needs speak little. To
be at the centre of that motion, where is ever-
lasting rest ; to be sheltered in the peace of
God ; even now to dwell in heaven, where all
hearts are stayed, and all hopes fulfilled. ' Thou
shalt keep him in perfect peace whose mind is
stayed on Thee.'

                                   H. E. MANNING

STUDY to follow His will in all, to have no will
but His. This is thy duty, and thy wisdom.
Nothing is gained by spurning and struggling
but to hurt and vex thyself ; but by complying
all is gained—sweet peace. It is the very secret,
the mystery of solid peace within, to resign all
to His will, to be disposed of at His pleasure,
without the least contrary thought.

                                   R. LEIGHTON

The Lord is my Shepherd ; I shall not want.—PS. xxiii. 1.

They that seek the Lord shall not want any good thing.—PS. xxxiv. 10.

GOD, who the universe doth hold
    In his fold,
Is my shepherd kind and heedful.
Is my shepherd, and doth keep
    Me, his sheep,
Still supplied with all things needful.

        F. DAVISON

WHO is it that is your shepherd ? The Lord ! Oh, my friends, what a wonderful announcement ! The Lord God of heaven and earth, the almighty Creator of all things, He who holds the universe in His hand as though it were a very little thing,—HE is your shepherd, and has charged Himself with the care and keeping of you, as a shepherd is charged with the care and keeping of his sheep. If your hearts could really take in this thought, you would never have a fear or a care again ; for with such a shepherd, how could it be possible for you ever to want any good thing ?

        H. W. S.

Watch and pray, that ye enter not into tempta-tion.—MATT. xxvi. 41.

I WANT a sober mind,
  A self-renouncing will,
That tramples down and casts behind
  The baits of pleasing ill ;
A spirit still prepared,
  And armed with jealous care,
Forever standing on its guard,
  And watching unto prayer.

C. WESLEY

WHEN you say, ' Lead us not into tempta-tion,' you must in good earnest mean to avoid in your daily conduct those temptations which you have already suffered from. When you say, ' Deliver us from evil,' you must mean to struggle against that evil in your hearts, which are you conscious of, and which you pray to be forgiven. . . . To watch and pray are surely in our power, and by these means we are certain of getting strength. You feel your weak-ness ; you fear to be overcome by temptation : then keep out of the way of it. This is watch-ing. Avoid society which is likely to mislead you ; flee from the very shadow of evil ; you cannot be too careful ; better be a little too strict than a little too easy,—it is the safer side. Abstain from reading books which are danger-ous to you. Turn from bad thoughts when they arise.

J. H. NEWMAN

*Whatsoever ye do, do it heartily, as to the Lord,
and not unto men.*—COL. iii. 23.

*Not with eye-service, as men-pleasers ; but in
singleness of heart, fearing God.*—COL. iii. 22.

> TEACH me, my God and King,
>   In all things Thee to see,
> And what I do in anything,
>   To do it as for Thee.
>
> G. HERBERT

THERE is no action so slight nor so mean
but it may be done to a great purpose, and
ennobled therefore ; nor is any purpose so
great but that slight actions may help it, and
may be so done as to help it much, most
especially, that chief of all purposes—the
pleasing of God.

> J. RUSKIN

EVERY duty, even the least duty, involves the
whole principle of obedience. And little duties
make the will *dutiful*, that is, supple and
prompt to obey. Little obediences lead into
great. The daily round of duty is full of proba-
tion and of discipline ; it trains the will, heart,
and conscience. We need not to be prophets
or apostles. The commonest life may be full
of perfection. The duties of home are a dis-
cipline for the ministries of heaven.

> H. E. MANNING

Wherefore, beloved . . . be diligent that ye may be found of Him in peace, without spot, and blameless.—2 PETER iii. 14.

HIS conscience knows no secret stings,
　While grace and joy combine
To form a life whose holy springs
　Are hidden and divine.

I. WATTS

EVEN the smallest discontent of conscience may render turbid the whole temper of the mind ; but only produce the effort that restores its peace, and over the whole atmosphere a breath of unexpected purity is spread ; doubt and irritability pass as clouds away ; the withered sympathies of earth and home open their leaves and live ; and through the clearest blue the deep is seen of the heaven where God resides.

J. MARTINEAU

THE state of mind which is described as meekness, or quietness of spirit, is characterized in a high degree by inward harmony. There is not, as formerly, that inward jarring of thought contending with thought, and conscience asserting rights which it could not maintain.

T. C. UPHAM

Be perfect, be of good comfort, be of one mind, live in peace ; and the God of love and peace shall be with you.—2 COR. xiii. 11.

He that loveth not his brother whom he hath seen, how can he love God whom he hath not seen ?—1 JOHN iv. 20.

> LORD ! subdue our selfish will ;
>   Each to each our tempers suit,
> By Thy modulating skill,
>   Heart to heart, as lute to lute.
>
> C. WESLEY

IT requires far more of the constraining love of Christ to love our cousins and neighbours as members of the heavenly family, than to feel the heart warm to our suffering brethren in Tuscany or Madeira. To love the whole Church is one thing ; to love—that is, to delight in the graces and veil the defects—of the person who misunderstood me and opposed my plans yesterday, whose peculiar infirmities grate on my most sensitive feelings, or whose natural faults are precisely those from which my natural character most revolts, is quite another.

ELIZABETH CHARLES

In all these things we are more than conquerors through Him that loved us.—ROM. viii. 37.

THUS my soul before her God
  Lieth still, nor speaketh more,
Conqueror thus o'er pain and wrong,
  That once smote her to the core ;
Like a silent ocean, bright
With her God's great praise and light.

WINKLER, 1713

MY mind is forever closed against embarrassment and perplexity, against uncertainty, doubt, and anxiety ; my heart against grief and desire. Calm and unmoved, I look down on all things, for I know that I cannot explain a single event, nor comprehend its connexion with that which alone concerns me. In His world all things prosper ; this satisfies me, and in this belief I stand fast as a rock. . . . My breast is steeled against annoyance on account of personal offences and vexations, or exultation in personal merit ; for my whole personality has disappeared in the contemplation of the purpose of my being.

J. G. FICHTE

All things are yours ; whether Paul, or Apollos, or Cephas, or the world, or life, or death, or things present, or things to come ; all are yours.—1 COR. iii. 21, 22.

As having nothing, and yet possessing all things. —2 COR. vi. 10.

OLD friends, old scenes, will lovelier be,
As more of Heaven in each we see :
Some softening gleam of love and prayer
Shall dawn on every cross and care.

J. KEBLE

OUT of love and hatred, out of earnings, and borrowings, and lendings, and losses ; out of sickness and pain ; out of wooing and worshipping ; out of travelling, and voting, and watching, and caring ; out of disgrace and contempt, comes our tuition in the serene and beautiful laws. Let him not slur his lesson ; let him learn it by heart. Let him endeavour exactly, bravely, and cheerfully, to solve the problem of that life which is set before *him*. And this, by punctual action, and not by promises or dreams. Believing, as in God, in the presence and favour of the grandest influences, let him deserve that favour, and learn how to receive and use it, by fidelity also to the lower observances.

R. W. EMERSON

We know that all things work together for good to them that love God.—ROM. viii. 28.

As for you, ye thought evil against me ; but God meant it unto good.—GEN. l. 20.

ILL that He blesses is our good,
    And unblest good is ill ;
And all is right that seems most wrong,
    If it be His sweet Will.

F. W. FABER

TO those who know themselves, all things work together for good, and all things seem to be, as they are to them, good. The goods which God gives seem ' very good ', and God Himself in them, because they know that they deserve them not. The evils which God allows and overrules seem also ' very good ', because they see in them His loving hand, put forth to heal them of what shuts out God from the soul. They love God intensely, in that He is so good to them in each, and every, the least good, because it is more than they deserve : how much more in the greatest ! They love God for every, and each, the very greatest of what seem evils, knowing them to be, from His love, real goods. For He by whom ' all the hairs of our head are numbered ', and who ' knoweth whereof we are made ', directs everything which befalls us in life, in perfect wisdom and love, to the well-being of our souls.

E. B. PUSEY

The very God of peace sanctify you wholly, and I pray God your whole spirit, and soul, and body, be preserved blameless. Faithful is He that calleth you, who also will do it.—1 THESS. V. 23, 24.

BE still, my soul !—the Lord is on thy side ;
  Bear patiently the cross of grief and pain ;
Leave to thy God to order and provide,—
  In every change He faithful will remain.
    HYMNS FROM THE LAND OF LUTHER

IT was no relief from temporal evils that the Apostle promised. . . . No ; the mercy of God might send them to the stake, or the lions ; it was still His mercy, if it but kept them ' unspotted from the world '. It might expose them to insult, calumny, and wrong ; they received it still as mercy, if it ' established them in every good word and work '. O brethren ! how many of *you* are content with *such* faithfulness as this on the part of your heavenly Father ? Is this, indeed, the tone and tenor of your prayers ?

WM. ARCHER BUTLER

Blessed is that man that maketh the Lord his trust.—PS. xl. 4.

That we may lead a quiet and peaceable life.— I TIM. ii. 2.

> JUST to let thy Father do
>   What He will ;
> Just to know that He is true,
>   And be still ;
> Just to trust Him, this is all !
>   Then the day will surely be
> Peaceful, whatsoe'er befall,
>   Bright and blessèd, calm and free.

F. R. HAVERGAL

EVERY morning compose your soul for a tranquil day, and all through it be careful often to recall your resolution, and bring yourself back to it, so to say. If something discomposes you, do not be upset, or troubled ; but having discovered the fact, humble yourself gently before God, and try to bring your mind into a quiet attitude. Say to yourself, ' Well, I have made a false step ; now I must go more carefully and watchfully.' Do this each time, however frequently you fall. When you are at peace use it profitably, making constant acts of meekness, and seeking to be ca m even in the most trifling things. Above all, do not be discouraged ; be patient ; wait ; strive to attain a calm, gentle spirit.

FRANCIS DE SALES

What doth the Lord thy God require of thee, but to fear the Lord thy God, to walk in all His ways, and to love Him, and to serve the Lord thy God with all thy heart and with all thy soul ?—DEUT. x. 12.

WHAT asks our Father of His children save
  Justice and mercy and humility,
  A reasonable service of good deeds,
  Pure living, tenderness to human needs,
Reverence, and trust, and prayer for light to see
  The Master's footprints in our daily ways ?
    No knotted scourge, nor sacrificial knife,
    But the calm beauty of an ordered life
Whose every breathing is unworded praise.
                J. G. WHITTIER

GIVE up yourself to God without reserve ; in singleness of heart, meeting everything that every day brings forth, as something that comes from God, and is to be received and gone through by you, in such an heavenly use of it, as you would suppose the holy Jesus would have done, in such occurrences. This is an attainable degree of perfection.

                WM. LAW

WE ought to measure our actual lot, and to fulfil it ; to be with all our strength that which our lot requires and allows. What is beyond it, is no calling of ours. How much peace, quiet, confidence, and strength, would people attain, if they would go by this plain rule.

              H. E. MANNING

The hand of our God is upon all them for good that seek Him.—EZRA viii. 22.

Into Thy hand I commit my spirit.—PS. xxxi. 5.

THOU layest Thy hand on the fluttering heart,
    And sayest, ' Be still ! '
The silence and shadow are only a part
    Of Thy sweet will ;
Thy presence is with me, and where Thou art
    I fear no ill.

F. R. HAVERGAL

BE still and cool in thy own mind and spirit from thy own thoughts, and then thou wilt feel the principle of God, to turn thy mind to the Lord God, from whom life comes ; whereby thou mayest receive His strength, and power to allay all blustering storms and tempests. That is it which works up into patience, into innocency, into soberness, into stillness, into stayedness, into quietness, up to God with His power. . . . Therefore be still awhile from thy own thoughts, searching, seeking, desires, and imaginations, and be stayed in the principle of God in thee, that it may raise thy mind up to God, and stay it upon God ; and thou wilt find strength from Him, and find Him to be a God at hand, a present help in the time of trouble and need.

GEORGE FOX

I waited patiently for the Lord ; and He inclined unto me, and heard my cry.—PS. xl. 1.

Tribulation worketh patience ; and patience. experience ; and experience, hope.—ROM. v. 3, 4

LORD, we have wandered forth through doubt and
    sorrow,
And Thou hast made each step an onward one ;
And we will ever trust each unknown morrow,—
Thou wilt sustain us till its work is done.

S. JOHNSON

IT is possible, when the future is dim, when our depressed faculties can form no bright ideas of the perfection and happiness of a better world,—it is possible still to cling to the conviction of God's merciful purpose towards His creatures, of His parental goodness even in suffering ; still to feel that the path of duty, though trodden with a heavy heart, leads to peace ; still to be true to conscience ; still to do our work, to resist temptation, to be useful, though with diminished energy, to give up our wills when we cannot rejoice under God's mysterious providence. In this patient, though uncheered obedience, we become prepared for light. The soul gathers force.

WM. E. CHANNING

Whom having not seen, ye love ; in whom, though now ye see Him not, ye rejoice with joy unspeakable, and full of glory.—1 PETER i. 8.

If ye love me, keep my commandments.—JOHN xiv. 15.

> BLEST be Thy love, dear Lord,
> That taught us this sweet way,
> Only to love Thee for Thyself,
> And for that love obey.
>
> J. AUSTIN

TO love God is to love His character. For instance, God is Purity. And to be pure in thought and look, to turn away from unhallowed books and conversation, to abhor the moments in which we have not been pure, is to love God. God is Love ; and to love men till private attachments have expanded into a philanthropy which embraces all,—at last even the evil and enemies with compassion,—that is to love God. God is Truth. To be true, to hate every form of falsehood, to live a brave, true, real life,—that is to love God. God is Infinite ; and to love the boundless, reaching on from grace to grace, adding charity to faith, and rising upwards ever to see the Ideal still above us, and to die with it unattained, aiming insatiably to be perfect even as the Father is perfect,—that is to love God.

F. W. ROBERTSON

Enter thou into the joy of thy Lord.—MATT. xxv. 23.

Serving the Lord ; rejoicing in hope.—ROM. xii. 11, 12.

IF our love were but more simple,
  We should take Him at His word ;
And our lives would be all sunshine
  In the sweetness of our Lord.

F. W. FABER

WHAT would it be to love absolutely a Being absolutely lovely,—to be able to give our whole existence, every thought, every act, every desire, to that adored One,—to know that He accepts it all, and loves us in return as God alone can love ? . . . This happiness grows forever. The larger our natures become, the wider our scope of thought, the stronger our will, the more fervent our affections, the deeper must be the rapture of such God-granted prayer. Every sacrifice *resolved on* opens wide the gate ; every sacrifice *accomplished* is a step towards the paradise within. Soon it will be no transitory glimpse, no rapture of a day, to be followed by clouds and coldness. Let us but labour, and pray, and wait, and the intervals of human frailty shall grow shorter and less dark, the days of our delight in God longer and brighter, till at last life shall be nought but His love ; our eyes shall never grow dim, His smile never turn away.

F. P. COBBE

These were the potters, and those that dwelt among plants and hedges : there they dwelt with the king for his work.—I CHRON. iv. 23.

A LOWLIER task on them is laid,
   With love to make the labour light ;
And there their beauty they must shed
   On quiet homes, and lost to sight.
Changed are their visions high and fair,
Yet, calm and still, they labour there.

HYMNS OF THE AGES

ANYWHERE and everywhere we may dwell ' with the King for His work '. We may be in a very unlikely or unfavourable place for this ; it may be in a literal country life, with little enough to be seen of the 'goings' of the King around us ; it may be among hedges of all sorts, hindrances in all directions ; it may be, furthermore, with our hands full of all manner of pottery for our daily task. No matter ! The King who placed us ' there ' will come and dwell there with us ; the hedges are all right, or He would soon do away with them ; and it does not follow that what seems to hinder our way may not be for its very protection ; and as for the pottery, why, that is just exactly what He has seen fit to put into our hands, and therefore it is, for the present, ' His work '.

F. R. HAVERGAL

Bear ye one another's burdens, and so fulfil the law of Christ.—GAL. vi. 2.

IS thy cruse of comfort wasting ?
  Rise and share it with another,
And through all the years of famine,
  It shall serve thee and thy brother.
Is thy burden hard and heavy ?
  Do thy steps drag heavily ?
Help to bear thy brother's burden ;
  God will bear both it and thee.

ELIZABETH CHARLES

HOWEVER perplexed you may at any hour become about some question of truth, one refuge and resource is always at hand : you can do something for some one besides yourself. When your own burden is heaviest, you can always lighten a little some other burden. At the times when you cannot see God, there is still open to you this sacred possibility, to *show* God ; for it is the love and kindness of human hearts through which the divine reality comes home to men, whether they name it or not. Let this thought, then, stay with you ; there may be times when you cannot find help, but there is no time when you cannot give help.

GEORGE S. MERRIAM

Surely, I have behaved and quieted myself, as a child that is weaned of his mother ; my soul is even as a weanèd child.—PS. cxxxi. 2.

QUIET, Lord, my froward heart,
Make me teachable and mild,
Upright, simple, free from art,
Make me as a weanèd child ;
From distrust and envy free,
Pleased with all that pleaseth Thee.
J. NEWTON

OH ! look not after great things : small breathings, small desires after the Lord, if true and pure, are sweet beginnings of life. Take heed of despising ' the day of small things ', by looking after some great visitation, proportionable to thy distress, according to thy eye. Nay, thou must become a child ; thou must lose thy own will quite by degrees. Thou must wait for life to be measured out by the Father, and be content with what proportion, and at what time, He shall please to measure.

I. PENINGTON

' WHEN Israel was a child, then I loved him ' (Hosea xi. 1). Aim to be ever this little child, contented with what the Father gives of pleasure or of play ; and when restrained from pleasure or from play, and led for a season into the chamber of sorrow, rest quiet on His bosom, and be patient, and smile, as one who is nestled in a sweet and secure asylum.

ANON.

If we hope for that we see not, then do we with patience wait for it.—ROM. viii. 25.

One day is with the Lord as a thousand years, and a thousand years as one day.—2 PETER iii. 8.

> LORD ! who Thy thousand years dost wait
>   To work the thousandth part
> Of Thy vast plan, for us create
>   With zeal a patient heart.
>
>   **J. H. NEWMAN**

I BELIEVE that if we could only see beforehand what it is that our heavenly Father means us to be,—the *soul* beauty and perfection and glory, the glorious and lovely spiritual body that this soul is to dwell in through all eternity,—if we could have a glimpse of *this*, we should not grudge all the trouble and pains He is taking with us now, to bring us up to that ideal, which is His thought of us. We know that it is God's way to work slowly, so we must not be surprised if He takes a great many years of discipline to turn a mortal being into an immortal, glorious angel.

                 ANNIE KEARY

Speak ye every man the truth to his neighbour.—
ZECH. viii. 16.

*For our rejoicing is this, the testimony of our con-
science, that in simplicity and godly sincerity . . .
we have had our conversation in the world.*—2 COR.
i. 12.

APPEAR I always what I am ?
And am I what I am pretending ?
Know I what way my course is bending ?
And sound my word and thought the same ?
ANON.

AM I acting in simplicity, from a germ of the
Divine life within, or am I shaping my
path to obtain some immediate result of ex-
pediency ? Am I endeavouring to compass
effects, amidst a tangled web of foreign influ-
ences I cannot calculate ; or am I seeking
simply to do what is right, and leaving the
consequences to the good providence of God ?

M. A. SCHIMMELPENNINCK

LET it not be in any man's power to say truly
of thee that thou art not simple, or that thou
art not good ; but let him be a liar whoever shall
think anything of this kind about thee ; and this
is altogether in thy power. For who is he that
shall hinder thee from being good and simple ?

MARCUS ANTONINUS

The Lord is thy keeper ; the Lord is thy shade upon thy right hand.—PS. cxxi. 5.

Great peace have they which love Thy law ; and nothing shall offend them.—PS. cxix. 165.

I REST beneath the Almighty's shade,
  My griefs expire, my troubles cease ;
Thou, Lord, on whom my soul is stayed,
  Wilt keep me still in perfect peace.

C. WESLEY

ONE great sign of the practical recognition of the ' divine moment ', and of our finding God's habitation in it, is constant calmness and peace of mind. Events and things come with the moment ; but God comes with them too. So that if He comes in the sunshine, we find rest and joy ; and if He comes in the storm, we know He is King of the storms, and our hearts are not troubled. God Himself, though possessing a heart filled with the tenderest feelings, is, nevertheless, an everlasting tranquillity ; and when we enter into His holy tabernacle, our souls necessarily enter into the tabernacle of rest.

T. C. UPHAM

MY soul was not only brought into harmony with itself and with God, but with God's providences. In the exercise of faith and love, I endured and performed whatever came in God's providence, in submission, in thankfulness, and silence.

MADAME GUYON

I will arise and go to my Father.—LUKE xv. 18.

O MY God, my Father ! hear,
  And help me to believe ;
Weak and weary I draw near ;
  Thy child, O God, receive.
I so oft have gone astray ;
  To the perfect Guide I flee ;
Thou wilt turn me not away,
  Thy love is pledged to me.

HYMNS OF THE SPIRIT

O CHILD, hast thou fallen ? arise, and go,
with childlike trust, to thy Father, like the
prodigal son, and humbly say, with heart and
mouth, ' Father, I have sinned against heaven,
and before Thee, and am no more worthy to
be called Thy son ; make me as one of Thy
hired servants.' And what will thy heavenly
Father do but what that father did in the
parable ? Assuredly He will not change His
essence, which is love, for the sake of thy
misdoings. Is it not His own precious treasure,
and a small thing with Him to forgive thee thy
trespasses, if thou believe in Him ? for His
hand is not shortened that it cannot make
thee fit to be saved.

JOHN TAULER

Speak unto the children of Israel, that they go forward.—EX. xiv. 15.

No man, having put his hand to the plough, and looking back, is fit for the kingdom of God.—LUKE ix. 62.

BE trustful, be steadfast, whatever betide thee,
   Only one thing do thou ask of the Lord,—
Grace to go forward wherever He guide thee,
   Simply believing the truth of His word.

                      ANON.

THE soul ceases to weary itself with planning and foreseeing, giving itself up to God's Holy Spirit within, and to the teachings of His providence without. . . . He is not forever fretting as to his progress, or looking back to see how far he is getting on ; rather he goes steadily and quietly on, and makes all the more progress because it is unconscious. So he never gets troubled and discouraged ; if he falls he humbles himself, but gets up at once, and goes on with renewed earnestness.

                JEAN NICOLAS GROU

I will bless the Lord at all times : His praise shall continually be in my mouth.—PS. XXXIV. 1.

I will praise Thee, O Lord, with my whole heart ; I will show forth all Thy marvellous works.—PS. IX. 1.

THRICE blest will all our blessings be,
When we can look through them to Thee ;
When each glad heart its tribute pays
Of love and gratitude and praise.

M. J. COTTERILL

THAT which befits us, embosomed in beauty and wonder as we are, is cheerfulness, and courage, and the endeavour to realize our aspirations. Shall not the heart which has received so much, trust the Power by which it lives ? May it not quit other leadings, and listen to the Soul that has guided it so gently, and taught it so much, secure that the future will be worthy of the past ?

R. W. EMERSON

I HAVE experienced that the habit of taking out of the hand of our Lord every little blessing and brightness on our path, confirms us, in an especial manner, in communion with His love.

M. A. SCHIMMELPENNINCK

The ornament of a meek and quiet spirit, which is in the sight of God of great price.—I PETER iii. 4.

To present you holy, and unblameable, and unreproveable in His sight.—COL. i. 22.

THY sinless mind in us reveal,
  Thy spirit's plenitude impart !
Till all my spotless life shall tell
  The abundance of a loving heart.

                                        C. WESLEY

HOLINESS appeared to me to be of a sweet, pleasant, charming, serene, calm nature. It seemed to me, it brought an inexpressible purity, brightness, peacefulness, and ravishment to the soul ; and that it made the soul like a field or garden of God, with all manner of pleasant flowers, that is all pleasant, delightful, and undisturbed ; enjoying a sweet calm, and the gently vivifying beams of the sun. The soul of a true Christian appeared like such a little white flower, as we see in the spring of the year, low and humble on the ground, opening its bosom to receive the pleasant beams of the sun's glory ; rejoicing, as it were, in a calm rapture ; diffusing around a sweet fragrancy ; standing peacefully and lovingly in the midst of other flowers round about, all in like manner opening their bosoms to drink in the light of the sun.

                                        JONATHAN EDWARDS

The Lord is good, a strong-hold in the day of trouble ; and He knoweth them that trust in Him.
—NAHUM i. 7.

> LEAVE God to order all thy ways,
> And hope in Him, whate'er betide.
> Thou 'lt find Him in the evil days
> Thy all-sufficient strength and guide ;
> Who trusts in God's unchanging love,
> Builds on the rock that nought can move.
> G. NEUMARCK

OUR whole trouble in our lot in this world rises from the disagreement of our mind therewith. Let the mind be brought to the lot, and the whole tumult is instantly hushed ; let it be kept in that disposition, and the man shall stand at ease, in his affliction, like a rock unmoved with waters beating upon it.

T. BOSTON

HOW does our will become sanctified ? By conforming itself unreservedly to that of God. We will all that He wills, and will nothing that He does not will ; we attach our feeble will to that all-powerful will which performs everything. Thus, nothing can ever come to pass against our will ; for nothing can happen save that which God wills, and we find in His good pleasure an inexhaustible source of peace and consolation.

FÉNELON

Who through faith subdued kingdoms, wrought righteousness, obtained promises, stopped the mouths of lions, out of weakness were made strong.
—HEB. xi. 33, 34.

SHE met the hosts of Sorrow with a look
   That altered not beneath the frown they wore,
And soon the lowering brood were tamed, and took,
   Meekly, her gentle rule, and frowned no more.
Her soft hand put aside the assaults of wrath,
     And calmly broke in twain
     The fiery shafts of pain,
And rent the nets of passion from her path.
   By that victorious hand despair was slain ;
With love she vanquished hate, and overcame
   Evil with good, in her great Master's name.

                    W. C. BRYANT

AS to what may befall us outwardly, in this confused state of things, shall we not trust our tender Father, and rest satisfied in His will ? Shall anything hurt us ? Can tribulation, distress, persecution, famine, nakedness, peril, or sword, come between the love of the Father to the child, or the child's rest, content, and delight in His love ? And doth not the love, the rest, the peace, the joy felt, swallow up all the bitterness and sorrow of the outward condition ?

                    I. PENINGTON

If thou hast run with the footmen, and they have wearied thee, then how canst thou contend with horses? and if in the land of peace wherein thou trustedst, they wearied thee, then how wilt thou do in the swelling of Jordan?—JER. xii. 5.

> HOW couldst thou hang upon the cross,
> To whom a weary hour is loss?
> Or how the thorns and scourging brook,
> Who shrinkest from a scornful look?
>
> J. KEBLE

A HEART unloving among kindred has no love towards God's saints and angels. If we have a cold heart towards a servant or a friend, why should we wonder if we have no fervour towards God? If we are cold in our private prayers, we should be earthly and dull in the most devout religious order; if we cannot bear the vexations of a companion, how should we bear the contradiction of sinners? if a little pain overcomes us, how could we endure a cross? if we have no tender, cheerful, affectionate love to those with whom our daily hours are spent, how should we feel the pulse and ardour of love to the unknown and the evil, the ungrateful and repulsive?

H. E. MANNING

Be kindly affectioned one to another with brotherly love.—ROM. xii. 10.

In her tongue is the law of kindness.—PROV. xxxi. 26.

SINCE trifles make the sum of human things,
And half our misery from our foibles springs ;
Since life's best joys consist in peace and ease,
And though but few can serve, yet all can please ;
Oh, let the ungentle spirit learn from hence,
A small unkindness is a great offence.

HANNAH MORE

ALL usefulness and all comfort may be prevented by an unkind, a sour, crabbed temper of mind,—a man that can bear with no difference of opinion or temperament. A spirit of fault-finding ; an unsatisfied temper ; a constant irritability ; little inequalities in the look, the temper, or the manner ; a brow cloudy and dissatisfied—your husband or your wife cannot tell why—will more than neutralize all the good you can do, and render life anything but a blessing.

ALBERT BARNES

YOU have not fulfilled every duty, unless you have fulfilled that of being pleasant.

CHARLES BUXTON

*He healeth the broken in heart, and bindeth up
their wounds.   He telleth the number of the stars ;
He calleth them all by their names.*—PS. cxlvii. **3, 4.**

TEACH me your mood, O patient stars !
  Who climb each night the ancient sky,
Leaving on space no shade, no scars,
  No trace of age, no fear to die.

R. W. EMERSON

I LOOKED up to the heavens once more, and
the quietness of the stars seemed to reproach
me. ' We are safe up here ', they seemed to say;
' we shine, fearless and confident, for the God
who gave the primrose its rough leaves to hide
it from the blast of uneven spring, hangs us in
the awful hollows of space. We cannot fall out
of His safety. Lift up your eyes on high, and
behold ! Who hath created these things—that
bringeth out their host by number ? He calleth
them all by names. By the greatness of His
might, for that He is strong in power, not one
faileth. Why sayest thou, O Jacob ! and speak-
est, O Israel ! my way is hid from the Lord, and
my judgment is passed over from my God ? '

G. MACDONALD

This is the day which the Lord hath made ; we will rejoice and be glad in it.—PS. cxviii. 24.

Why stand ye here all the day idle ?—MATT. xx. 6.

so here hath been dawning another blue day ;
Think, wilt thou let it slip useless away ?
Out of eternity this new day is born ;
Into eternity at night will return.

T. CARLYLE

SMALL cares, some deficiencies in the mere arrangement and ordering of our lives, daily fret our hearts, and cross the clearness of our faculties ; and these entanglements hang around us, and leave us no free soul able to give itself up, in power and gladness, to the true work of life. The severest training and self-denial,—a superiority to the servitude of indulgence,—are the indispensable conditions even of genial spirits, of unclouded energies, of tempers free from morbidness,—much more of the practised and vigorous mind, ready at every call, and thoroughly furnished unto all good works.

J. H. THOM

TRUE, we can never be at peace till we have performed the highest duty of all,—till we have arisen, and gone to our Father ; but the performance of smaller duties, yes, even of the smallest, will do more to give us temporary repose, will act more as healthful anodynes, than the greatest joys that can come to us from any other quarter.

G. MACDONALD

The Lord gave, and the Lord hath taken away ; blessed be the name of the Lord.—JOB. i. 21.

WHAT Thou hast given, Thou canst take,
And when Thou wilt new gifts can make.
All flows from Thee alone ;
When Thou didst give it, it was Thine ;
When Thou retook'st it, 'twas not mine.
Thy will in all be done.

JOHN AUSTIN

WE are ready to praise when all shines fair; but when life is overcast, when all things seem to be against us, when we are in fear for some cherished happiness, or in the depths of sorrow, or in the solitude of a life which has no visible support, or in a season of sickness, and with the shadow of death approaching,—then to praise God ; then to say, This fear, loneliness, affliction, pain, and trembling awe are as sure token of love, as life, health, joy, and the gifts of home : ' The Lord gave, and the Lord hath taken away ' ; on either side it is He, and all is love alike ; ' blessed be the name of the Lord ',—this is the true sacrifice of praise. What can come amiss to a soul which is so in accord with God ? What can make so much as one jarring tone in all its harmony ? In all the changes of this fitful life, it ever dwells in praise.

H. E. MANNING

The Lord redeemeth the soul of His servants ; and none of them that trust in Him shall be desolate.
—PS. xxxiv. 22.

Though He slay me, yet will I trust in Him.—
JOB xiii. 15.

I PRAISE Thee while my days go on ;
I love Thee while my days go on :
Through dark and dearth, through fire and frost,
With emptied arms and treasure lost,
I thank Thee while my days go on.

> E. B. BROWNING

THE sickness of the last week was fine medicine ; pain disintegrated the spirit, or became spiritual. I rose,—I felt that I had given to God more perhaps than an angel could,—had promised Him in youth that to be a blot on this fair world, at His command, would be acceptable. Constantly offer myself to continue the obscurest and loneliest thing ever heard of, with one proviso,—His agency. Yes, love Thee, and all Thou dost, while Thou sheddest frost and darkness on every path of mine.

> MARY MOODY EMERSON

Shall we receive good at the hand of God, and shall we not receive evil ?—JOB ii. 10.

Thou hast dealt well with Thy servant, O Lord, according to Thy word.—PS. cxix. 65.

WHATSOE'ER our lot may be,
  Calmly in this thought we'll rest,—
Could we see as Thou dost see,
  We should choose it as the best.

WM. GASKELL

IT is a proverbial saying, that every one makes his own destiny ; and this is usually interpreted, that every one, by his wise or unwise conduct, prepares good or evil for himself : but we may also understand it, that whatever it be that he receives from the hand of Providence, he may so accommodate himself to it, that he will find his lot good for him, however much may seem to others to be wanting.

WM. VON HUMBOLDT

EVIL, once manfully fronted, ceases to be evil ; there is generous battle-hope in place of dead, passive misery ; the evil itself has become a kind of good.

T. CARLYLE

Fear none of those things which thou shalt suffer : . . . ye shall have tribulation ten days : be thou faithful unto death, and I will give thee a crown of life.—REV. ii. 10.

> THEN, O my soul, be ne'er afraid,
> On Him who thee and all things made
>   Do thou all calmly rest ;
> Whate'er may come, where'er we go,
> Our Father in the heavens must know
>   In all things what is best.
>
> PAUL FLEMMING

GUIDE me, O Lord, in all the changes and varieties of the world ; that in all things that shall happen, I may have an evenness and tranquillity of spirit ; that my soul may be wholly resigned to Thy divinest will and pleasure, never murmuring at Thy gentle chastisements and fatherly correction. Amen.

JEREMY TAYLOR

THOU art never at any time nearer to God than when under tribulation ; which He permits for the purification and beautifying of thy soul.

M. MOLINOS

PRIZE inward exercises, griefs, and troubles ; and let faith and patience have their perfect work in them.

I. PENINGTON

I pray not that Thou shouldest take them out of the world, but that Thou shouldest keep them from the evil.—JOHN xvii. 15.

> IN busy mart and crowded street,
> No less than in the still retreat,
> Thou, Lord, art near, our souls to bless,
> With all a Father's tenderness.
>
> I. WILLIAMS

ONLY the individual conscience, and He who is greater than the conscience, can tell where worldliness prevails. Each heart must answer for itself, and at its own risk. That our souls are committed to our own keeping, at our own peril, in a world so mixed as this, is the last reason we should slumber over the charge, or betray the trust. If only that outlet to the Infinite is kept open, the inner bond with eternal life preserved, while not one movement of this world's business is interfered with, nor one pulse-beat of its happiness repressed, with all natural associations dear and cherished, with all human sympathies fresh and warm, we shall yet be near to the kingdom of heaven, within the order of the Kosmos of God—in the world, but not of the world—not taken out of it, but kept from its evil.

J. H. THOM

And what doth the Lord require of thee, but to do justly, and to love mercy, and to walk humbly with thy God?—MICAH vi. 8.

Put on therefore . . . kindness, humbleness of mind, meekness, long-suffering.—COL. iii. 12.

> PLANT in us an humble mind,
> Patient, pitiful, and kind ;
> Meek and lowly let us be,
> Full of goodness, full of Thee.
>
> C. WESLEY

THERE is no true and constant gentleness without humility ; while we are so fond of ourselves, we are easily offended with others. Let us be persuaded that nothing is due to us, and then nothing will disturb us. Let us often think of our own infirmities, and we shall become indulgent towards those of others.

FÉNELON

ENDEAVOUR to be patient in bearing with the defects and infirmities of others, of what sort soever they be ; for that thyself also hast many failings which must be borne with by others. If thou canst not make thyself such an one as thou wouldest, how canst thou expect to have another in all things to thy liking ?

THOMAS À KEMPIS

My presence shall go with thee, and I will give thee rest.—EX. xxxiii. 14.

Thou wilt show me the path of life : in Thy presence is fulness of joy ; at Thy right hand there are pleasures for evermore.—PS. xvi. 11.

THY presence fills my mind with peace,
　Brightens the thoughts so dark erewhile,
Bids cares and sad forebodings cease,
　Makes all things smile.

CHARLOTTE ELLIOTT

HOW shall we rest in God ? By giving our- selves wholly to Him. If you give your- self by halves, you cannot find full rest ; there will ever be a lurking disquiet in that half which is withheld. Martyrs, confessors, and saints have tasted this rest, and ' counted themselves happy in that they endured '. A countless host of God's faithful servants have drunk deeply of it under the daily burden of a weary life,—dull, commonplace, painful, or desolate. All that God has been to them He is ready to be to you. The heart once fairly given to God, with a clear conscience, a fitting rule of life, and a steadfast purpose of obedience, you will find a wonderful sense of rest coming over you.

JEAN NICOLAS GROU

Finally, my brethren, be strong in the Lord, and in the power of His might.—EPH. vi. 10.

No man can serve two masters.—MATT. vi. 24.

OH, there are heavenly heights to reach
   In many a fearful place,
Where the poor timid heir of God
   Lies blindly on his face ;
Lies languishing for grace divine
   That he shall never see
Till he go forward at Thy sign,
   And trust himself to Thee.

A. L. WARING

RESERVATIONS lie latent in the mind concerning some unhallowed sentiments or habits in the present, some possibly impending temptations in the future ; and thus do we cheat ourselves of inward and outward joys together. We give up many an indulgence for conscience' sake, but stop short at that point of entire faithfulness wherein conscience could reward us. If we would but give ourselves wholly to God,—give up, for the present and the future, every act, and, above all, every thought and every feeling, to be all purified to the uttermost, and rendered the best, noblest, holiest we can conceive,—then would sacrifice bear with it a peace rendering itself, I truly believe, far *easier* than before.

F. P. COBBE

Wherefore comfort yourselves together, and edify one another, even as also ye do.—I THESS. V. 11.

Thou shalt love thy neighbour as thyself.—MATT. xix. 19.

so others shall
Take patience, labour, to their heart and hand,
From thy hand, and thy heart, and thy brave cheer,
And God's grace fructify through thee to all.
The least flower with a brimming cup may stand,
And share its dewdrop with another near.

E. B. BROWNING

WHAT is meant by our neighbour we cannot doubt ; it is every one with whom we are brought into contact. First of all, he is literally our neighbour who is next to us in our own family and household ; husband to wife, wife to husband, parent to child, brother to sister, master to servant, servant to master. Then it is he who is close to us in our own neighbourhood, in our own town, in our own parish, in our own street. With these all true charity begins. To love and be kind to these is the very beginning of all true religion. But, besides these, as our Lord teaches, it is every one who is thrown across our path by the changes and chances of life ; he or she, whosoever it be, whom we have any means of helping,—the unfortunate stranger whom we may meet in travelling, the deserted friend whom no one else cares to look after.

A. P. STANLEY

We know that we have passed from death unto life, because we love the brethren.—1 JOHN iii. 14.

He that loveth not knoweth not God ; for God is love.—1 JOHN iv. 8.

> MUTUAL love the token be,
> Lord, that we belong to Thee ;
> Love, Thine image, love impart ;
> Stamp it on our face and heart ;
> Only love to us be given ;
> Lord, we ask no other heaven.
>
> C. WESLEY

OH, how many times we can most of us remember when we would gladly have made any compromise with our consciences, would gladly have made the most costly sacrifices to God, if He would only have excused us from this duty of loving, of which our nature seemed utterly incapable. It is far easier to feel kindly, to act kindly, toward those with whom we are seldom brought into contact, whose tempers and prejudices do not rub against ours, whose interests do not clash with ours, than to keep up an habitual, steady, self-sacrificing love towards those whose weaknesses and faults are always forcing themselves upon us, and are stirring up our own. A man may pass good muster as a philanthropist who makes but a poor master to his servants, or father to his children.

F. D. MAURICE

Rest in the Lord, and wait patiently for Him.—
PS. xxxvii. 7.

Trust in Him at all times.—PS. lxii. 8.

> DOST thou ask when comes His hour ?
> Then, when it shall aid thee best.
> Trust His faithfulness and power,
> Trust in Him, and quiet rest.
>
> ANON.

I HAD found [communion with God] to consist, not only in the silencing of the outward man, but in the silencing also of every thought, and in the concentration of the soul and all its powers into a simple, quiet watching and waiting for the food which its heavenly Father might see fit either to give or to withhold. In no case could it be sent empty away ; for, if comfort, light, or joy were withheld, the act of humble waiting at the gate of heavenly wisdom could not but work patience in it, and thus render it, by humility and obedience, more ' meet to be a partaker of the inheritance of the saints in light ', and also more blessed in itself.

M. A. KELTY

' REST IN THE LORD ; WAIT PATIENTLY FOR HIM.' In Hebrew, ' be silent to God, and let Him mould thee.' Keep still, and He will mould thee to the right shape.

MARTIN LUTHER

To be spiritually minded is life and peace.—ROM. viii. 6.

> STILLED now be every anxious care ;
> See God's great goodness everywhere ;
> Leave all to Him in perfect rest :
> He will do all things for the best.
>
> FROM THE GERMAN

WE should all endeavour and labour for a calmer spirit, that we may the better serve God in praying to Him and praising Him ; and serve one another in love, that we may be fitted to do and receive good ; that we may make our passage to heaven more easy and cheerful, without drooping and hanging the wing. So much as we are quiet and cheerful upon good ground, so much we live, and are, as it were, in heaven.

R. SIBBES

POSSESS yourself as much as you possibly can in peace ; not by any effort, but by letting all things fall to the ground which trouble or excite you. This is no work, but is, as it were, a setting down a fluid to settle that has become turbid through agitation.

MADAME GUYON

The beloved of the Lord shall dwell in safety by Him ; and the Lord shall cover him all the day long.—DEUT. xxxiii. 12.

WHATE'ER events betide,
　Thy will they all perform ;
Safe in Thy breast my head I hide,
　Nor fear the coming storm.

H. F. LYTE

I HAVE seemed to see a need of everything God gives me, and want nothing that He denies me. There is no dispensation, though afflictive, but either in it, or after it, I find that I could not be without it. Whether it be taken from or not given me, sooner or later God quiets me in Himself without it. I cast all my concerns on the Lord, and live securely on the care and wisdom of my heavenly Father. My ways, you know, are, in a sense, hedged up with thorns, and grow darker and darker daily ; but yet I distrust not my good God in the least, and live more quietly in the absence of all by faith, than I should do, I am persuaded, if I possessed them.

ANON., 1810

He that dwelleth in the secret place of the Most High shall abide under the shadow of the Almighty. —PS. xci. 1.

> THEY who on the Lord rely,
> Safely dwell though danger's nigh;
> Lo! His sheltering wings are spread
> O'er each faithful servant's head.
> When they wake, or when they sleep,
> Angel guards their vigils keep;
> Death and danger may be near,
> Faith and love have nought to fear.
>
> HARRIET AUBER

'THERE shall no evil befall thee, neither shall any plague come nigh thy dwelling', is a promise to the fullest extent verified in the case of all 'who dwell in the secret place of the Most High'. To them sorrows are not 'evils', sicknesses are not 'plagues'; the shadow of the Almighty extending far around those who abide under it, alters the character of all things which come within its influence.

ANON.

IT is faith's work to claim and challenge loving-kindness out of all the roughest strokes of God.

S. RUTHERFORD

Be content with such things as ye have.—HEB. xiii. 5.

I have learned, in whatsoever state I am, therewith to be content.—PHIL. iv. 11.

> NO longer forward nor behind
> I look in hope or fear ;
> But, grateful, take the good I find,
> The best of now and here.
>
> J. G. WHITTIER

IF we wished to gain contentment, we might try such rules as these :

1. Allow thyself to complain of nothing, not even of the weather.

2. Never picture thyself to thyself under any circumstances in which thou art not.

3. Never compare thine own lot with that of another.

4. Never allow thyself to dwell on the wish that this or that had been, or were, otherwise than it was, or is. God Almighty loves thee better and more wisely than thou dost thyself.

5. Never dwell on the morrow. Remember that it is God's, not thine. The heaviest part of sorrow often is to look forward to it. ' The Lord will provide.'

E. B. PUSEY

Now no chastening for the present seemeth to be joyous, but grievous : nevertheless afterward it yieldeth the peaceable fruit of righteousness unto them which are exercised thereby.—HEB. xii. 11.

I CANNOT say,
Beneath the pressure of life's cares to-day,
ᵀ joy in these ;
But I can say
That I had rather walk this rugged way,
If Him it please.

S. G. BROWNING

THE particular annoyance which befell you this morning ; the vexatious words which met your ear and ' grieved ' your spirit ; the disappointment which was His appointment for to-day ; the slight but hindering ailment ; the presence of some one who is ' a grief of mind ' to you,—whatever this day seemeth not joyous, but grievous, is linked in ' the good pleasure of His goodness ' with a corresponding afterward of ' peaceable fruit ', the very seed from which, if you only do not choke it, this shall spring and ripen.

F. R. HAVERGAL

O my Father, if it be possible, let this cup pass from me ; nevertheless not as I will, but as Thou wilt.—MATT. xxvi. 39.

o LORD my God, do Thou Thy holy will,—
    I will lie still.
I will not stir, lest I forsake Thine arm,
    And break the charm
Which lulls me, clinging to my Father's breast,
    In perfect rest.

J. KEBLE

RESIGNATION to the will of God is the whole of piety ; it includes in it all that is good ; and is a source of the most settled quiet and composure of mind. Our resignation to the will of God may be said to be perfect, when our will is lost and resolved up into His ; when we rest in His will as our end, as being itself most just, and right, and good. And where is the impossibility of such an affection to what is just and right and good, such a loyalty of heart to the Governor of the universe, as shall prevail over all sinister indirect desires of our own ?

JOSEPH BUTLER

THERE are no disappointments to those whose wills are buried in the will of God.

F. W. FABER

LORD, Thy will be done in father, mother, child, in everything and everywhere ; without a reserve, without a BUT, an IF, or a limit.

FRANCIS DE SALES

The Lord heareth your murmurings, which ye murmur against Him.—EX. xvi. 8.

WITHOUT murmur, uncomplaining,
In His hand,
Leave whatever things thou canst not
Understand.

K. R. HAGENBACH

ONE great characteristic of holiness is never to be exacting—never to complain. Each complaint drags us down a degree, in our upward course. If you would discern in whom God's spirit dwells, watch that person, and notice whether you ever hear him murmur.

GOLD DUST

WHEN we wish things to be otherwise than they are, we lose sight of the great practical parts of the life of godliness. We wish, and wish —when, if we have done all that lies on us, we should fall quietly into the hands of God. Such wishing cuts the very sinews of our privileges and consolations. You are leaving me for a time ; and you say that you wish you could leave me better, or leave me with some assistance ; but, if it is right for you to go, it is right for me to meet what lies on me, without a wish that I had less to meet, or were better able to meet it.

R. CECIL

He that is faithful in that which is least is faithful also in much.—LUKE xvi. 10.

The Lord preserveth the faithful.—PS. xxxi. 23.

THE trivial round, the common task,
Would furnish all we ought to ask ;
Room to deny ourselves ; a road
To bring us, daily, nearer God.

J. KEBLE

EXACTNESS in little duties is a wonderful source of cheerfulness.

F. W. FABER

THE unremitting retention of simple and high sentiments in obscure duties is hardening the character to that temper which will work with honour, if need be, in the tumult or on the scaffold.

R. W. EMERSON

WE are too fond of our own will. We want to be doing what we fancy mighty things ; but the great point is, to do small things, when called to them, in a right spirit.

R. CECIL

IT is not on great occasions only that we are required to be faithful to the will of God ; occasions constantly occur, and we should be surprised to perceive how much our spiritual advancement depends on small obediences.

MADAME SWETCHIN

Strengthened with all might, according to His glorious power, unto all patience and long-suffering with joyfulness. —COL. i. 11.

                    GOD doth not need
Either man's works or His own gifts ; who best
Bear His mild yoke, they serve Him best ; His state
Is kingly ; thousands at His bidding speed,
And post o'er land and ocean without rest ;
They also serve who only stand and wait.

J. MILTON

WE cannot always be doing a great work, but we can always be doing something that belongs to our condition. To be silent, to suffer, to pray when we cannot act, is acceptable to God. A disappointment, a contradiction, a harsh word, an annoyance, a wrong received and endured as in His presence, is worth more than a long prayer ; and we do not lose time if we bear its loss with gentleness and patience, provided the loss was inevitable, and was not caused by our own fault.

FÉNELON

Be not slothful, but followers of them who through faith and patience inherit the promises.— HEB. vi. 12.

WHERE now with pain thou treadest, trod
The whitest of the saints of God !
To show thee where their feet were set,
The light which led them shineth yet.

J. G. WHITTIER

LET us learn from this communion of saints to live in hope. Those who are now at rest were once like ourselves. They were once weak, faulty, sinful ; they had their burdens and hindrances, their slumbering and weariness, their failures and their falls. But now they have overcome. Their life was once homely and commonplace. Their day ran out as ours. Morning and noon and night came and went to them as to us. Their life, too, was as lonely and sad as yours. Little fretful circumstances and frequent disturbing changes wasted away their hours as yours. There is nothing in your life that was not in theirs ; there was nothing in theirs but may be also in your own. They have overcome, each one, and one by one ; each in his turn, when the day came, and God called him to the trial. And so shall you likewise.

H. E. MANNING

And thus this man died, leaving his death for an example of a noble courage, and a memorial of virtue, not only unto young men, but unto all his nation.—2 MAC. vi. 31.

Zebulun and Naphtali were a people that jeoparded their lives unto the death in the high places of the field.—JUDGES v. 18.

THOUGH Love repine, and Reason chafe,
　There came a voice without reply,—
'Tis man's perdition to be safe,
　When for the truth he ought to die.

R. W. EMERSON

SOME say that the age of chivalry is past. The age of chivalry is never past, so long as there is a wrong left unredressed on earth, or a man or woman left to say, ' I will redress that wrong, or spend my life in the attempt.' The age of chivalry is never past, so long as we have faith enough to say, ' God will help me to redress that wrong ; or, if not me, He will help those that come after me, for His eternal Will is to overcome evil with good.'

C. KINGSLEY

THUS man is made equal to every event. He can face danger for the right. A poor, tender, painful body, he can run into flame or bullets or pestilence, with duty for his guide.

R. W. EMERSON

Let all those that put their trust in Thee rejoice :
. . . let them also that love Thy name be joyful in
Thee.—PS. V. II.

He maketh me to lie down in green pastures.—
PS. xxiii. 2.

> I CAN hear these violets chorus
>   To the sky's benediction above ;
> And we all are together lying
>   On the bosom of Infinite Love.
>
> Oh, the peace at the heart of Nature !
>   Oh, the light that is not of day !
> Why seek it afar forever,
>   When it cannot be lifted away ?
>   W. C. GANNETT

WHAT inexpressible joy for me, to look up through the apple-blossom and the fluttering leaves, and to see God's love there ; to listen to the thrush that has built his nest among them, and to feel God's love, who cares for the birds, in every note that swells his little throat ; to look beyond to the bright blue depths of the sky, and feel they are a canopy of blessing,— the roof of the house of my Father ; that if clouds pass over it, it is the unchangeable light they veil ; that, even when the day itself passes, I shall see that the night itself only unveils new worlds of light ; and to know that if I could unwrap fold after fold of God's universe, I should only unfold more and more blessing, and see deeper and deeper into the love which is at the heart of all.

                      ELIZABETH CHARLES

*One thing have I desired of the Lord, that will I
seek after ; that I may dwell in the house of the
Lord all the days of my life, to behold the beauty
of the Lord, and to enquire in His temple.*—PS.
xxvii. 4.

THY beauty, O my Father ! All is Thine ;
   But there is beauty in Thyself, from whence
The beauty Thou hast made doth ever flow
   In streams of never-failing affluence.

Thou art the Temple ! and though I am lame,—
   Lame from my birth, and shall be till I die,—
I enter through the Gate called Beautiful,
   And am alone with Thee, O Thou Most High !
                    J. W. CHADWICK

CONSIDER that all which appears beautiful outwardly, is solely derived from the invisible Spirit which is the source of that external beauty, and say joyfully, ' Behold, these are streamlets from the uncreated Fountain ; behold, these are drops from the infinite Ocean of all good ! Oh ! how does my inmost heart rejoice at the thought of that eternal, infinite Beauty, which is the source and origin of all created beauty ! '

                    L. SCUPOLI

We all, with open face, beholding as in a glass the glory of the Lord, are changed into the same image, from glory to glory, even as by the Spirit of the Lord.—2 COR. iii. 18.

> THEN every tempting form of sin,
>   Shamed in Thy presence, disappears,
> And all the glowing, raptured soul
>   The likeness it contemplates wears.
>
> P. DODDRIDGE

THEN does a good man become the tabernacle of God, wherein the divine Shechinah does rest, and which the divine glory fills, when the frame of his mind and life is wholly according to that idea and pattern which he receives from the mount. We best glorify Him when we grow most like to Him : and we then act most for His glory, when a true spirit of sanctity, justice, meekness, etc., runs through all our actions ; when we so live in the world as becomes those that converse with the great Mind and Wisdom of the whole world, with that Almighty Spirit that made, supports, and governs all things, with that Being from whence all good flows, and in which there is no spot, stain, or shadow of evil ; and so being captivated and overcome by the sense of the Divine loveliness and goodness, endeavour to be like Him, and conform ourselves, as much as may be, to Him.

DR. JOHN SMITH

The righteous shall be glad in the Lord, and shall trust in Him.—PS. lxiv. 10.

Whoso trusteth in the Lord, happy is he.—PROV. xvi. 20.

> THE heart that trusts forever sings,
> And feels as light as it had wings,
> A well of peace within it springs,—
>   Come good or ill,
> Whate'er to-day, to-morrow brings,
>   It is His will.
>
> I. WILLIAMS

HE will weave no longer a spotted life of shreds and patches, but he will live with a divine unity. He will cease from what is base and frivolous in his life, and be content with all places, and with any service he can render. He will calmly front the morrow, in the negligency of that trust which carries God with it, and so hath already the whole future in the bottom of the heart.

R. W. EMERSON

HE who believes in God is not careful for the morrow, but labours joyfully and with a great heart. ' For He giveth His beloved, as in sleep.' They must work and watch, yet never be careful or anxious, but commit all to Him, and live in serene tranquillity ; with a quiet heart, as one who sleeps safely and quietly.

MARTIN LUTHER

Therefore, my beloved brethren, be ye stedfast, unmoveable, always abounding in the work of the Lord, forasmuch as ye know that your labour is not in vain in the Lord.—1 COR. XV. 58.

SAY not, 'Twas all in vain,
   The anguish and the darkness and the strife ;
Love thrown upon the waters comes again
   In quenchless yearnings for a nobler life.

ANNA SHIPTON

DID you ever hear of a man who had striven all his life faithfully and singly toward an object and in no measure obtained it ? If a man constantly aspires, is he not elevated ? Did ever a man try heroism, magnanimity, truth, sincerity, and find that there was no advantage in them,—that it was a vain endeavour ?

H. D. THOREAU

DO right, and God's recompense to you will be the power of doing more right. Give, and God's reward to you will be the spirit of giving more : a blessed spirit, for it is the Spirit of God himself, whose Life is the blessedness of giving. Love, and God will pay you with the capacity of more love ; for love is Heaven— love is God within you.

F. W. ROBERTSON

Speak, Lord : for Thy servant heareth.— I SAM. iii. 9.

> THOUGH heralded with nought of fear
>   Or outward sign or show :
> Though only to the inward ear
>   It whispers soft and low ;
> Though dropping, as the manna fell,
>   Unseen, yet from above,
> Noiseless as dew-fall, heed it well,—
>   Thy Father's call of love.
>
> J. G. WHITTIER

THIS is one result of the attitude into which we are put by humility, by disinterestedness, by purity, by calmness, that we have the opportunity, the disengagement, the silence in which we may watch what is the will of God concerning us. If we think no more of ourselves than we ought to think, if we seek not our own but others' welfare, if we are prepared to take all things as God's dealings with us, then we may have a chance of catching from time to time what God has to tell us. In the Mussulman devotions one constant gesture is to put the hands to the ears, as if to listen for the messages from the other world. This is the attitude, the posture which our minds assume, if we have a standing-place above and beyond the stir and confusion and dissipation of this mortal world.

A. P. STANLEY

Him that overcometh will I make a pillar in the temple of my God.—REV. iii. 12.

In whom ye also are builded together for an habitation of God through the Spirit.—EPH. ii. 22.

NONE the place ordained refuseth,
They are one, and they are all,
Living stones, the Builder chooseth
For the courses of his wall.
JEAN INGELOW

SLOWLY, through all the universe, that temple of God is being built. Wherever, in any world, a soul, by free-willed obedience, catches the fire of God's likeness, it is set into the growing walls, a living stone. When, in your hard fight, in your tiresome drudgery, or in your terrible temptation, you catch the purpose of your being, and give yourself to God, and so give Him the chance to give Himself to you, your life, a living stone, is taken up and set into that growing wall. . . . Wherever souls are being tried and ripened, in whatever commonplace and homely ways;—there God is hewing out the pillars for His temple. Oh, if the stone can only have some vision of the temple of which it is to lie a part forever, what patience must fill it as it feels the blows of the hammer, and knows that success for it is simply to let itself be wrought into what shape the Master wills.

PHILLIPS BROOKS

Ye are the children of light, and the children of the day.—1 THESS. V. 5.

Light is sown for the righteous, and gladness for the upright in heart.—PS. xcvii. 11.

> SERENE will be our days and bright,
>   And happy will our nature be,
> When love is an unerring light,
>   And joy its own security.
>
>   W. WORDSWORTH

NOTHING can produce so great a serenity of life, as a mind free from guilt, and kept untainted, not only from actions, but purposes that are wicked. By this means the soul will be not only unpolluted, but not disturbed ; the fountain will run clear and unsullied, and the streams that flow from it will be just and honest deeds, ecstasies of satisfaction, a brisk energy of spirit, which makes a man an enthusiast in his joy, and a tenacious memory, sweeter than hope. For as shrubs which are cut down with the morning dew upon them do for a long time after retain their fragrancy, so the good actions of a wise man perfume his mind, and leave a rich scent behind them. So that joy is, as it were, watered with these essences, and owes its flourishing to them.

PLUTARCH

Who hath despised the day of small things ?—
ZECH. iv. 10.

LITTLE things
On little wings
Bear little souls to heaven.

ANON.

AN occasional effort even of an ordinary holiness may accomplish great acts of sacrifice, or bear severe pressure of unwonted trial, specially if it be the subject of observation. But constant discipline in unnoticed ways, and the spirit's silent unselfishness, becoming the hidden habit of the life, give to it its true saintly beauty, and this is the result of care and lowly love in little things. Perfection is attained most readily by this constancy of religious faithfulness in all minor details of life, consecrating the daily efforts of self-forgetting love.

T. T. CARTER

LOVE'S secret is to be always doing things for God, and not to mind because they are such very little ones.

F. W. FABER

THERE may be living and habitual conversation in heaven, under the aspect of the most simple, ordinary life. Let us always remember that holiness does not consist in doing uncommon things, but in doing everything with purity of heart.

H. E. MANNING

He that is slow to anger is better than the mighty ; and he that ruleth his spirit than he that taketh a city.—PROV. xvi. 32.

PURGE from our hearts the stains so deep and foul,
  Of wrath and pride and care ;
Send Thine own holy calm upon the soul,
  And bid it settle there !

ANON.

LET this truth be present to thee in the excitement of anger,—that to be moved by passion is not manly, but that mildness and gentleness, as they are more agreeable to human nature, so also are they more manly. . . . For in the same degree in which a man's mind is nearer to freedom from all passion, in the same degree also is it nearer to strength.

MARCUS ANTONINUS

IT is no great matter to associate with the good and gentle, for this is naturally pleasing to all, and every one willingly enjoyeth peace, and loveth those best that agree with him. But to be able to live peaceably with hard and perverse persons, or with the disorderly, or with such as go contrary to us, is a great grace, and a most commendable and manly thing.

THOMAS À KEMPIS

Who is among you that feareth the Lord, that obeyeth the voice of His servant, that walketh in darkness, and hath no light? let him trust in the name of the Lord, and stay upon his God.—ISA. l. 10.

The Lord my God will enlighten my darkness.—PS. xviii. 28.

WHEN we in darkness walk,
Nor feel the heavenly flame,
Then is the time to trust our God,
And rest upon His name.

A. M. TOPLADY

HE has an especial tenderness of love towards thee for that thou art in the dark and hast no light, and His heart is glad when thou dost arise and say, ' I will go to my Father.' For He sees thee through all the gloom through which thou canst not see Him. Say to Him, ' My God, I am very dull and low and hard ; but Thou art wise and high and tender, and Thou art my God. I am Thy child. Forsake me not.' Then fold the arms of thy faith, and wait in quietness until light goes up in the darkness. Fold the arms of thy Faith, I say, but not of thy Action : bethink thee of something that thou oughtest to do, and go and do it, if it be but the sweeping of a room, or the preparing of a meal, or a visit to a friend ; heed not thy feelings : do thy work.

G. MACDONALD

*In the day when I cried Thou answeredst me
and strengthenedst me with strength in my soul.—*
PS. CXXXVIII. 3.

IT is not that I feel less weak, but Thou
Wilt be my strength ; it is not that I see
Less sin ; but more of pardoning love with Thee,
  And all-sufficient grace. Enough ! And now
All fluttering thought is stilled ; I only rest,
And feel that Thou art near, and know that I am
    blest.

F. R. HAVERGAL

YEA, though thou canst not believe, yet be
not dismayed thereat ; only do thou sink
into, or at least pant after the hidden measure
of life, which is not in that which distresseth,
disturbeth, and filleth thee with thoughts, fears,
troubles, anguish, darknesses, terrors, and the
like ; no, no ! but in that which inclines to the
patience, to the stillness, to the hope, to the
waiting, to the silence before the Father.

I. PENINGTON

WE have only to be patient, to pray, and to
do His will, according to our present light and
strength, and the growth of the soul will go on.
The plant grows in the mist and under clouds as
truly as under sunshine. So does the heavenly
principle within.

W. E. CHANNING

Then answered he me, and said, This is the condition of the battle which man that is born upon the earth shall fight ; that, if he be overcome, he shall suffer as thou hast said : but if he get the victory, he shall receive the thing that I say.—2 ESDRAS vii. 57, 58.

> ONE holy Church, one army strong,
> One steadfast high intent,
> One working band, one harvest-song,
> One King omnipotent.
>
>   S. JOHNSON

WE listened to a man whom we felt to be, with all his heart and soul and strength, striving against whatever was mean and unmanly and unrighteous in our little world. It was not the cold clear voice of one giving advice and warning from serene heights to those who were struggling and sinning below, but the warm living voice of one who was fighting for us and by our sides, and calling on us to help him and ourselves and one another. And so, wearily and little by little, but surely and steadily on the whole, was brought home to the young boy, for the first time, the meaning of his life ; that it was no fool's or sluggard's paradise into which he had wandered by chance, but a battle-field ordained from of old, where there are no spectators, but the youngest must take his side, and the stakes are life and death.

       THOMAS HUGHES

If we walk in the light as He is in the light, we have followship one with another.—I JOHN i. 7.

God is not unrighteous to forget your work and labour of love, which ye have showed toward His name, in that he have ministered to the saints, and do minister.—HEB. vi. 10.

WHEREVER in the world I am,
  In whatsoe'er estate,
I have a fellowship with hearts,
  To keep and cultivate,
And a work of lowly love to do
  For the Lord on whom I wait.

A. L. WARING

WE do not always perceive that even the writing of a note of congratulation, the fabrication of something intended as an offering of affection, our necessary intercourse with characters which have no congeniality with our own, or hours apparently trifled away in the domestic circle, may be made by us the performance of a most sacred and blessed work ; even the carrying out, after our feeble measure, of the design of God for the increase of happiness.

ANNA, OR PASSAGES FROM HOME LIFE

DEFINITE work is not always that which is cut and squared for us, but that which comes as a claim upon the conscience, whether it's nursing in a hospital, or hemming a handkerchief.

ELIZABETH M. SEWELL

*The Lord shall give thee rest from thy sorrow,
and from thy fear, and from the hard bondage
wherein thou wast made to serve.*—ISA. xiv. 3.

TO-DAY, beneath Thy chastening eye,
I crave alone for peace and rest ;
Submissive in Thy hand to lie,
    And feel that it is best.

J. G. WHITTIER

O LORD, who art as the Shadow of a great
Rock in a weary land, who beholdest Thy
weak creatures weary of labour, weary of
pleasure, weary of hope deferred, weary of self ;
in Thine abundant compassion, and unutter-
able tenderness, bring us, I pray Thee, unto
Thy rest.   Amen.

CHRISTINA G. ROSSETTI

GRANT to me above all things that can be de-
sired, to rest in Thee, and in Thee to have my
heart at peace.   Thou art the true peace of
the heart, Thou its only rest ; out of Thee all
things are hard and restless.   In this very peace,
that is, in Thee, the One Chiefest Eternal Good,
I will sleep and rest.   Amen.

THOMAS À KEMPIS

THOU hast made us for Thyself, O Lord ; and
our heart is restless until it rests in Thee.

ST. AUGUSTINE

God is our refuge and strength, a very present help in trouble. Therefore will not we fear, though the earth be removed, and though the mountains be carried into the midst of the sea.—PS. xlvi. 1, 2.

THOUGH waves and storms go o'er my head,
  Though strength and health and friends be gone,
Though joys be withered all, and dead,
  Though every comfort be withdrawn,
On this my steadfast soul relies,—
  Father! Thy mercy never dies.
                        JOHANN A. RÖTHE

YOUR external circumstances may change, toil may take the place of rest, sickness of health, trials may thicken within and without. Externally, you are the prey of such circumstances; but if your heart is stayed on God, no changes or chances can touch it, and all that may befall you will but draw you closer to Him. Whatever the present moment may bring, your knowledge that it is His will, and that your future heavenly life will be influenced by it, will make all not only tolerable, but welcome to you, while no vicissitudes can affect you greatly, knowing that He who holds you in His powerful hand cannot change, but abideth forever.
                        JEAN NICOLAS GROU

Now unto Him that is able to do exceeding abund-
antly above all that we ask or think, according to
the power that worketh in us, unto Him be glory,
throughout all ages, world without end. Amen.—
EPH. iii. 20, 21.

WE would not meagre gifts down-call
When Thou dost yearn to yield us all ;
But for this life, this little hour,
Ask all Thy love and care and power.

J. INGELOW

GOD so loveth us that He would make all
things channels to us and messengers of
His love. Do for His sake deeds of love, and
He will give thee His love. Still thyself, thy
own cares, thy own thoughts for Him, and He
will speak to thy heart. Ask for Himself, and
He will give thee Himself. Truly, a secret
hidden thing is the love of God, known only to
them who seek it, and to them also secret, for
what man can have of it here is how slight a
foretaste of that endless ocean of His love !

E. B. PUSEY

Consider the lilies of the field, how they grow.—
MATT. vi. 28.

> THEY do not toil :
> Content with their allotted task
> They do but grow ; they do not ask
> A richer lot, a higher sphere,
> But in their loveliness appear,
> And grow, and smile, and do their best,
> And unto God they leave the rest.
>
> MARIANNE FARNINGHAM

INTERPOSE no barrier to His mighty life-giving power, working in you all the good pleasure of His will. Yield yourself up utterly to His sweet control. Put your growing into His hands as completely as you have put all your other affairs. Suffer Him to manage it as He will. Do not concern yourself about it, nor even think of it. Trust Him absolutely and always. Accept each moment's dispensation as it comes to you from His dear hands, as being the needed sunshine or dew for that moment's growth. Say a continual ' yes ' to your Father's will.

H. W. S.

THINE own self-will and anxiety, thy hurry and labour, disturb thy peace and prevent Me from working in thee. Look at the little flowers, in the serene summer days ; they quietly open their petals, and the sun shines into them with his gentle influences. So will I do for thee, if thou wilt yield thyself to Me.

G. TERSTEEGEN

Wherefore, if God so clothe the grass of the field, which to-day is, and to-morrow is cast into the oven, shall He not much more clothe you, O ye of little faith ?—MATT. vi. 30.

I trust in the mercy of God for ever and ever.—PS. lii. 8.

CALMLY we look behind us, on joys and sorrows past,
We know that all is mercy now, and shall be well at
   last ;
Calmly we look before us,—we fear no future ill,
Enough for safety and for peace, if Thou art with
   us still.

JANE BORTHWICK

NEITHER go back in fear and misgiving to the past, nor in anxiety and forecasting to the future ; but lie quiet under His hand, having no will but His.

H. E. MANNING

I SAW a delicate flower had grown up two feet high, between the horses' path and the wheel-track. An inch more to right or left had sealed its fate, or an inch higher ; and yet it lived to flourish as much as if it had a thousand acres of untrodden space around it, and never knew the danger it incurred. It did not borrow trouble, nor invite an evil fate by apprehending it.

HENRY D. THOREAU

The Lord shall preserve thee from all evil : He shall preserve thy soul.—PS. cxxi. 7.

UNDER Thy wings, my God, I rest,
  Under Thy shadow safely lie ;
By Thy own strength in peace possessed,
  While dreaded evils pass me by.

A. L. WARING

A HEART rejoicing in God delights in all His will, and is surely provided with the most firm joy in all estates ; for if nothing can come to pass beside or against His will, then cannot that soul be vexed which delights in Him and hath no will but His, but follows Him in all times, in all estates ; not only when He shines bright on them, but when they are clouded. That flower which follows the sun doth so even in dark and cloudy days : when it doth not shine forth, yet it follows the hidden course and motion of it. So the soul that moves after God keeps that course when He hides His face ; is content, yea, even glad at His will in all estates or conditions or events.

R. LEIGHTON

LET God do with me what He will, anything He will ; whatever it be, it will be either heaven itself or some beginning of it.

WM. MOUNTFORD

Be merciful unto me, O God, be merciful unto me : for my soul trusteth in Thee : yea, in the shadow of Thy wings will I make my refuge, until these calamities be overpast.—PS. lvii. 1.

MY God ! in whom are all the springs
　Of boundless love and grace unknown,
Hide me beneath Thy spreading wings,
　Till the dark cloud is overblown.

I. WATTS

IN time of trouble go not out of yourself to seek for aid ; for the whole benefit of trial consists in silence, patience, rest, and resignation. In this condition divine strength is found for the hard warfare, because God Himself fights for the soul.

M. MOLINOS

IN vain will you let your mind run out after help in times of trouble ; it is like putting to sea in a storm. Sit still, and *feel after* your principles ; and, if you find none that furnish you with somewhat of a stay and prop, and which point you to quietness and silent submission, depend upon it you have never yet learned Truth from the Spirit of Truth, whatever notions thereof you may have picked up from this and the other description of it.

M. A. KELTY

Thou calledst in trouble, and I delivered thee.—
PS. lxxxi. 7.

*Be strong, and of good courage ; dread not, nor
be dismayed.—*I CHRON. xxii. 13.

> THOU canst calm the troubled mind,
>   Thou its dread canst still ;
> Teach me to be all resigned
>   To my Father's will.
>
> HEINRICH PUCHTA

THOUGH this patient, meek resignation is
to be exercised with regard to all outward
things and occurrences of life, yet it chiefly
respects our own inward state, the troubles, per-
plexities, weaknesses, and disorders of our own
souls. And to stand turned to a patient, meek,
humble resignation to God, when your own
impatience, wrath, pride, and irresignation
attack yourself, is a higher and more beneficial
performance of this duty, than when you
stand turned to meekness and patience, when
attacked by the pride, or wrath, or disorderly
passions of other people.

WM. LAW

There hath no temptation taken you, but such as is common to man : but God is faithful, who will not suffer you to be tempted above that ye are able ; but will with the temptation also make a way to escape, that ye may be able to bear it.—I COR. x. 13, 14.

NOT so, not so, no load of woe
  Need bring despairing frown ;
For while we bear it, we can bear,
  Past that, we lay it down

SARAH WILLIAMS

EVERYTHING which happens, either happens in such wise that thou art formed by nature to bear it, or that thou art not formed by nature to bear it. If then, it happens to thee in such way that thou art formed by nature to bear it, do not complain, but bear it as thou art formed by nature to bear it. But, if it happens in such wise that thou art not able to bear it, do not complain ; for it will perish after it has consumed thee. Remember, however, that thou art formed by nature to bear everything, with respect to which it depends on thy own opinion to make it endurable and tolerable, by thinking that it is either thy interest or thy duty to do this.

MARCUS ANTONINUS

Why art thou cast down, O my soul? and why art thou disquieted within me? hope thou in God; for I shall yet praise Him, who is the health of my countenance, and my God.—PS. xlii. 11.

AH! why by passing clouds oppressed,
Should vexing thoughts distract thy breast?
Turn thou to Him in every pain,
Whom never suppliant sought in vain;
Thy strength in joy's ecstatic day,
Thy hope, when joy has passed away.

H. F. LYTE

BEWARE of letting your care degenerate into anxiety and unrest; tossed as you are amid the winds and waves of sundry troubles, keep your eyes fixed on the Lord, and say, ' Oh, my God, I look to Thee alone; be Thou my guide, my pilot'; and then be comforted. When the shore is gained, who will heed the toil and the storm? And we shall steer safely through every storm, so long as our heart is right, our intention fervent, our courage steadfast, and our trust fixed on God. If at times we are somewhat stunned by the tempest, never fear; let us take breath, and go on afresh. Do not be disconcerted by the fits of vexation and uneasiness which are sometimes produced by the multiplicity of your domestic worries. No indeed, dearest child, all these are but opportunities of strengthening yourself in the loving, forbearing graces which our dear Lord sets before us.

FRANCIS DE SALES

Even so, Father, for so it seemed good in Thy sight.—MATT. xi. 26.

> LET nothing make thee sad or fretful,
> Or too regretful ;
> Be still ;
> What God hath ordered must be right,
> Then find in it thine own delight,
> My will.
>
> P. FLEMMING

IF we listen to our self-love, we shall estimate our lot less by what it is, than by what it is not ; shall dwell on its hindrances, and be blind to its possibilities ; and, comparing it only with imaginary lives, shall indulge in flattering dreams of what we should do, if we had but power ; and give, if we had but wealth ; and be, if we had no temptations. We shall be forever querulously pleading our difficulties and privations as excuses for our unloving temper and unfruitful life ; and fancying ourselves injured beings, virtually frowning at the dear Providence that loves us, and chafing with a self-torture which invites no pity. If we yield ourselves unto God, and sincerely accept our lot as assigned by Him, we shall count up its contents, and disregard its omissions ; and be it as feeble as a cripple's, and as narrow as a child's, shall find in it resources of good surpassing our best economy, and sacred claims that may keep awake our highest will.

J. MARTINEAU

My times are in Thy hand.—PS. xxxi. 15.

Every purpose of the Lord shall be performed.— JER. li. 29.

I AM so glad ! It is such rest to know
That Thou hast ordered and appointed all,
And wilt yet order and appoint my lot.
For though so much I cannot understand,
And would not choose, has been, and yet may be,
Thou choosest, Thou performest, THOU, my Lord,
This is enough for me.

F. R. HAVERGAL

' WE mustn't be in a hurry to fix and choose our own lot ; we must wait to be guided. We are led on, like the little children, by a way that we know not. It is a vain thought to flee from the work that God appoints us, for the sake of finding a greater blessing to our own souls ; as if we could choose for ourselves where we shall find the fullness of the Divine Presence, instead of seeking it where alone it is to be found, in loving obedience.'

GEORGE ELIOT

EVERYWHERE and at all times it is in thy power piously to acquiesce in thy present condition, and to behave justly to those who are about thee.

MARCUS ANTONINUS

And when ye stand praying, forgive, if ye have aught against any ; that your Father also which is in heaven may forgive you your trespasses. But if ye do not forgive, neither will your Father which is in heaven forgive your trespasses.—MARK xi. 25, 26.

'TIS not enough to weep my sins,
  'Tis but one step to heaven ;—
When I am kind to others,—then
  I know myself forgiven.

F. W. FABER

EVERY relation to mankind, of hate or scorn or neglect, is full of vexation and torment. There is nothing to do with men but to love them ; to contemplate their virtues with admiration, their faults with pity and forbearance, and their injuries with forgiveness. Task all the ingenuity of your mind to devise some other thing, but you never can find it. To hate your adversary will not help you ; to kill him will not help you ; nothing within the compass of the universe can help you, but to love him. But let that love flow out upon all around you, and what could harm you ? How many a knot of mystery and misunderstanding would be untied by one word spoken in simple and confiding truth of heart ! How many a solitary place would be made glad if love were there ; and how many a dark dwelling would be filled with light !

ORVILLE DEWEY

The kingdom of God is within you.—LUKE xvii. 21.

> OH, take this heart that I would give
> Forever to be all Thine own ;
> I to myself no more would live,—
> Come, Lord, be Thou my King alone.
>
> G. TERSTEEGEN

HEREIN is the work assigned to the individual soul, to have life in itself, to make our sphere, whatever it is, sufficient for a reign of God within ourselves, for a true and full reign of our Father's abounding spirit,—thankful, unutterably thankful, if with the place and the companionship assigned to us we are permitted to build an earthly tabernacle of grace and goodness and holy love, a home like a temple ; but, should this be denied us, resolved for our own souls that God shall reign there, for ourselves at least that we will not, by sin or disobedience or impious distrust, break with our own wills our filial connexion with our Father, —that whether joyful or sorrowing, struggling with the perplexity and foulness of circumstance, or in an atmosphere of peace, whether in dear fellowship or alone, our desire and prayer shall be that God may have in us a realm where His will is law, and where obedience and submission spring, not from calculating prudence or ungodly fear, but from communion of spirit, ever humble aspiration, and ever loving trust.

J. H. THOM

The Lord preserveth the simple.—PS. cxvi. 6.

THY home is with the humble, Lord !
  The simple are Thy rest ;
Thy lodging is in childlike hearts ;
  Thou makest there Thy nest.

F. W. FABER

THIS deliverance of the soul from all useless and selfish and unquiet cares, brings to it an unspeakable peace and freedom ; this is true simplicity. This state of entire resignation and perpetual acquiescence produces true liberty ; and this liberty brings perfect simplicity. The soul which knows no self-seeking, no interested ends, is thoroughly candid ; it goes straight forward without hindrance ; its path opens daily more and more to ' perfect day ', in proportion as its self-renunciation and its self-forgetfulness increase ; and its peace, amid whatever troubles beset it, will be as boundless as the depths of the sea.

FÉNELON

Let not him that girdeth on his harness boast himself as he that putteth it off.—I KINGS xx. 11.

Put on the whole armour of God.—EPH. vi. 11.

WAS I not girded for the battle-field ?
Bore I not helm of pride and glittering sword ?
Behold the fragments of my broken shield,
And lend to me Thy heavenly armour, Lord !

ANON.

OH, be at least able to say in that day,—
Lord, I am no hero. I have been careless, cowardly, sometimes all but mutinous. Punishment I have deserved, I deny it not. But a traitor I have never been ; a deserter I have never been. I have tried to fight on Thy side in Thy battle against evil. I have tried to do the duty which lay nearest me ; and to leave whatever Thou didst commit to my charge a little better than I found it. I have not been good, but I have at least tried to be good. Take the will for the deed, good Lord. Strike not my unworthy name off the roll-call of the noble and victorious army, which is the blessed company of all faithful people ; and let me, too, be found written in the Book of Life ; even though I stand the lowest and last upon its list. Amen.

C. KINGSLEY

And the work of righteousness shall be peace ; and the effect of righteousness, quietness and assurance forever.—ISA. xxxii. 17.

THE heart that ministers for Thee
In Thy own work will rest ;
And the subject spirit of a child
Can serve Thy children best.

A. L. WARING

IT matters not where or what we are, so we be His servants. They are happy who have a wide field and great strength to fulfil His missions of compassion ; and they, too, are blessed who, in sheltered homes and narrow ways of duty, wait upon Him in lowly services of love. Wise or simple, gifted or slender in knowledge, in the world's gaze or in hidden paths, high or low, encompassed by affections and joys of home, or lonely and content in God alone, what matters, so that they bear the seal of the living God? Blessed company, unknown to each other, unknowing even themselves !

H. E. MANNING

In the morning, then ye shall see the glory of the Lord.—EX. xvi. 7.

Serving the Lord ; rejoicing in hope.—ROM. xii. 11, 12.

EVERY day is a fresh beginning,
 Every morn is the world made new.
You who are weary of sorrow and sinning,
Here is a beautiful hope for you ;
 A hope for me and a hope for you.
SUSAN COLLIDGE

BE patient with every one, but above all with yourself. I mean, do not be disturbed because of your imperfections, and always rise up bravely from a fall. I am glad that you make a daily new beginning ; there is no better means of progress in the spiritual life than to be continually beginning afresh, and never to think that we have done enough.

FRANCIS DE SALES

BECAUSE perseverance is so difficult, even when supported by the grace of God, thence is the value of new beginnings. For new beginnings are the life of perseverance.

E. B. PUSEY

Herein do I exercise myself, to have always a conscience void of offence toward God, and toward men.—ACTS xxiv. 6.

I will instruct thee and teach thee in the way which thou shalt go ; I will guide thee with mine eye.—PS. xxxii. 8.

> OH, keep thy conscience sensitive ;
>   No inward token miss ;
> And go where grace entices thee ;—
>   Perfection lies in this.
>
>   F. W. FABER

WE need only obey. There is guidance for each of us, and by lowly listening we shall hear the right word.

                          R. W. EMERSON

THE heights of Christian perfection can only be reached by faithfully each moment following the Guide who is to lead you there, and He reveals your way to you one step at a time, in the little things of your daily lives, asking only on your part that you yield yourselves up to His guidance. If then, in anything you feel doubtful or troubled, be sure that it is the voice of your Lord, and surrender it at once to His bidding, rejoicing with a great joy that He has begun thus to lead and guide you.

                          H. W. S

He shall redeem Israel from all his iniquities.—
PS. CXXX. 8.

> BE it according to Thy word ;
> Redeem me from all sin ;
> My heart would now receive Thee, Lord,
> Come in, my Lord, come in !
>
> C. WESLEY

WHEN you wake, or as soon as you are dressed, offer up your whole self to God, soul and body, thoughts and purposes and desires, to be for that day what He wills. Think of the occasions of the sin likely to befall you, and go, as a child, to your Father which is in heaven, and tell Him in childlike, simple words, your trials—in some such simple words as these—' Thou knowest, good Lord, that I am tempted to—[*then name the temptations to it, and the ways in which you sin, as well as you know them*]. But, good Lord, for love of Thee, I would this day keep wholly from all [*naming the sin*] and be very [*naming the opposite grace*]. I will not, by Thy grace, do one [N.] act, or speak one [N.] word, or give one [N.] look, or harbour one [N.] thought in my soul. If Thou allow any of these temptations to come upon me this day, I desire to think, speak, and do only what Thou willest. Lord, without Thee I can do nothing ; with Thee I can do all.'

E. B. PUSEY

Look at the generations of old, and see ; did ever any trust in the Lord, and was confounded? or did any abide in His fear, and was forsaken? or whom did He ever despise, that called upon Him?
—ECCLUS. ii. 10.

Remember, O Lord, Thy tender mercies, and Thy loving-kindnesses ; for they have been ever of old.
—PS. XXV. 6.

> MY Father ! see
> I trust the faithfulness displayed of old,
> I trust the love that never can grow cold—
> I trust in Thee.
>
> CHRISTIAN INTELLIGENCER

BE not so much discouraged in the sight of what is yet to be done, as comforted in His good-will towards thee. 'Tis true, He hath chastened thee with rods and sore afflictions ; but did He ever take away His loving-kindness from thee ? or did His faithfulness ever fail in the sorest, blackest, thickest, darkest night that ever befell thee ?

I. PENINGTON

WE call Him the '*God of our fathers*' ; and we feel that there is some stability at centre, while we can tell our cares to One listening at our right hand, by whom theirs are remembered and removed.

J. MARTINEAU

He stayeth His rough wind in the day of the east wind.—ISA. xxvii. 8.

A bruised reed shall He not break.—ISA. xlii. 3.

ALL my life I still have found,
And I will forget it never ;
Every sorrow hath its bound,
And no cross endures forever.
All things else have but their day,
God's love only lasts for aye.

P. GERHARDT

WE never have more than we can bear. The present hour we are always able to endure. As our day, so is our strength. If the trials of many years were gathered into one, they would overwhelm us ; therefore, in pity to our little strength, He sends first one, then another, then removes both, and lays on a third, heavier, perhaps, than either ; but all is so wisely measured to our strength that the bruised reed is never broken. We do not enough look at our trials in this continuous and successive view. Each one is sent to teach us something, and altogether they have a lesson which is beyond the power of any to teach alone.

H. E. MANNING

*I the Lord have called thee in righteousness,
and will hold thine hand, and will keep thee.—*
ISA. xlii. 6.

*O keep my soul, and deliver me : for I put my
trust in Thee.*—PS. XXV. 20.

I DO not ask my cross to understand,
  My ways to see ;
Better in darkness just to feel Thy hand,
  And follow Thee.

ADELAIDE A. PROCTER

O LORD, if only my will may remain right
and firm towards Thee, do with me what-
soever it shall please Thee. For it cannot be
anything but good, whatsoever Thou shalt do
with me. If it be Thy will I should be in dark-
ness, be Thou blessed ; and, if it be Thy will
I should be in light, be Thou again blessed. If
Thou vouchsafe to comfort me, be Thou
blessed ; and, if Thou wilt have me afflicted,
be Thou equally blessed. O Lord ! for Thy
sake I will cheerfully suffer whatever shall
come on me with Thy permission.

THOMAS À KEMPIS

MY soul could not incline itself on the one side
or the other, since another will had taken the
place of its own ; but only nourished itself
with the daily providences of God.

MADAME GUYON

The Lord is my light and my salvation ; whom shall I fear ? The Lord is the strength of my life ; of whom shall I be afraid ?—PS. xxvii. 1.

THOU hidden Source of calm repose,
   Thou all-sufficient Love divine,
My Help and Refuge from my foes,
   Secure I am while Thou art mine.
And lo ! from sin, and grief, and shame,
I hide me, Father, in Thy name.

C. WESLEY

WHATEVER troubles come on you, of mind, body, or estate, from within or from without, from chance or from intent, from friends or foes—whatever your trouble be, though you be lonely, O children of a heavenly Father, be not afraid !

J. H. NEWMAN

WHATSOEVER befalleth thee, receive it not from the hand of any creature, but from Him alone, and render back all to Him, seeking in all things His pleasure and honour, the purifying and subduing of thyself. What can harm thee, when all must first touch God, within whom thou hast enclosed thyself ?

R. LEIGHTON

HOW God rejoices over a soul, which, surrounded on all sides by suffering and misery, does that upon earth which the angels do in heaven ; namely, loves, adores, and praises God !

G. TERSTEEGEN

Be ye kind one to another.—EPH. iv. 32.

SHE doeth little kindnesses
　　Which most leave undone or despise ;
For nought which sets one heart at ease,
And giveth happiness or peace,
　　Is low-esteemèd in her eyes.

J. R. LOWELL

WHAT was the secret of such a one's
power ? What had she done ? Abso-
lutely nothing ; but radiant smiles, beaming
good-humour, the tact of divining what every
one felt and every one wanted, told that she had
got out of self and learned to think of others ;
so that at one time it showed itself in depre-
cating the quarrel, which lowering brows and
raised tones already showed to be impending,
by sweet words ; at another, by smoothing an
invalid's pillow ; at another, by soothing a
sobbing child ; at another, by humouring and
softening a father who had returned weary and
ill-tempered from the irritating cares of busi-
ness. None but she saw those things. None
but a loving heart *could* see them. That was
the secret of her heavenly power. The one
who will be found in trial capable of great acts
of love, is ever the one who is always doing
considerate small ones.

F. W. ROBERTSON

Love is of God ; and every one that loveth is born of God, and knoweth God.—1 JOHN iv. 7.

Forbearing one another, and forgiving one another, if any man have a quarrel (or ' complaint ') against any.—COL. iii. 13.

> OH, might we all our lineage prove,
> Give and forgive, do good and love ;
> By soft endearments, in kind strife,
> Lightening the load of daily life.
>
> J. KEBLE

WE may, if we choose, make the worst of one another. Every one has his weak points ; every one has his faults ; we may make the worst of these ; we may fix our attention constantly upon these. But we may also make the best of one another. We may forgive, even as we hope to be forgiven. We may put ourselves in the place of others, and ask what we should wish to be done to us, and thought of us, were we in their place. By loving whatever is lovable in those around us, love will flow back from them to us, and life will become a pleasure instead of a pain ; and earth will become like heaven ; and we shall become not unworthy followers of Him whose name is Love.

A. P. STANLEY

The Lord will perfect that which concerneth me :
Thy mercy, O Lord, endureth forever ; forsake not
the works of Thine own hands.—PS. cxxxviii. 8.

AS God leads me, will I go,—
  Nor choose my way ;
Let Him choose the joy or woe
  Of every day :
They cannot hurt my soul,
Because in His control :
I leave to Him the whole,—
  His children may.

L. GEDICKE

WHY is it that we are so busy with the
future ? It is not *our* province ; and is
there not a criminal interference with *Him* to
whom it belongs, in our feverish, anxious at-
tempts to dispose of it, and in filling it up with
shadows of good and evil shaped· by our own
wild imaginations ? To do God's will as fast
as it is made known to us, to inquire hourly—
I had almost said each moment—what He
requires of us, and to leave ourselves, our
friends, and every interest at His control, with
a cheerful trust that the path which He marks
out leads to our perfection and to Himself,—
this is at once our duty and happiness ; and
why will we not walk in the plain, simple way ?

WILLIAM E. CHANNING

When He giveth quietness, who then can make trouble?—JOB xxxiv. 29.

None of these things move me.—ACTS xx. 24.

I'VE many a cross to take up now,
  And many left behind ;
But present troubles move me not,
  Nor shake my quiet mind.
And what may be to-morrow's cross
  I never seek to find ;
My Father says, ' Leave that to me,
  And keep a quiet mind.'

ANON.

LET us then think only of the present, and not even permit our minds to wander with curiosity into the future. This future is not yet ours ; perhaps it never will be. It is exposing ourselves to temptation to wish to anticipate God, and to prepare ourselves for things which He may not destine for us. If such things should come to pass, He will give us light and strength according to the need. Why should we desire to meet difficulties prematurely, when we have neither strength nor light as yet provided for them ? Let us give heed to the present, whose duties are pressing ; it is fidelity to the present which prepares us for fidelity in the future.

FÉNELON

EVERY hour comes with some little fagot of God's will fastened upon its back.

F. W. FABER

Be strong, and of a good courage, fear not, nor be afraid . . . for the Lord thy God, He it is that doth go with thee ; He will not fail thee, nor forsake thee.—DEUT. xxxi. 6.

THE timid it concerns to ask their way,
And fear what foe in caves and swamps can stray,
To make no step until the event is known,
And ills to come as evils past bemoan.
Not so the wise ; no coward watch he keeps
To spy what danger on his pathway creeps ;
Go where he will, the wise man is at home,
His hearth the earth,—his hall the azure dome ;
Where his clear spirit leads him, there's his road,
By God's own light illumined and foreshowed.

R. W. EMERSON

THOUGH I sympathize, I do not share in the least the feeling of being disheartened and cast down. It is not things of this sort that depress me, or ever will. The contrary things, praise, openings, the feeling of the greatness of my work, and my inability in relation to it, these things oppress and cast me down ; but little hindrances, and closing up of accustomed or expected avenues, and the presence of difficulties to be overcome,—I'm not going to be cast down by trifles such as these.

JAMES HINTON

And the Lord shall guide thee continually, and satisfy thy soul in drought.—ISA. lviii. 11.

WHEREVER He may guide me,
   No want shall turn me back ;
My Shepherd is beside me,
   And nothing can I lack.
His wisdom ever waketh,
   His sight is never dim,—
He knows the way He taketh,
   And I will walk with Him.

A. L. WARING

ABANDON yourself to His care and guidance, as a sheep in the care of a shepherd, and trust Him utterly. No matter though you may seem to yourself to be in the very midst of a desert, with nothing green about you, inwardly or outwardly, and may think you will have to make a long journey before you can get into the green pastures. Our Shepherd will turn that very place where you are into green pastures, for He has power to make the desert rejoice and blossom as a rose.

H. W. S.

*Be not conformed to this world ; but be ye trans-
formed by the renewing of your mind.*—ROM. xii. 2.

> FATHER, let our faithful mind
> Rest, on Thee alone inclined ;
> Every anxious thought repress,
> Keep our souls in perfect peace.
> C. WESLEY

RETIREMENT from anxieties of every
kind ; entering into no disputes ; avoiding
all frivolous talk ; and simplifying everything
we engage in, whether in a way of doing or
suffering ; denying the imagination its false
activities, and the intellect its false searchings
after what it cannot obtain,—these seem to be
some of the steps that lead to obedience to the
holy precept in our text.   JAMES P. GREAVES

RETIRE inwardly ; wait to feel somewhat of
God's Spirit, discovering and drawing away
from that which is contrary to His holy nature,
and leading into that which is acceptable to Him.
As the mind is joined to this, some true light
and life is received.   I. PENINGTON

ACT up faithfully to your convictions ; and
when you have been unfaithful, bear with your-
self, and resume always with calm simplicity
your little task. Suppress, as much as you
possibly can, all recurrence to yourself, and you
will suppress much vanity. Accustom yourself
to much calmness and an indifference to events.
MADAME GUYON

Lift up your heads, O ye gates, even lift them up, ye everlasting doors ; and the King of glory shall come in.—PS. xxiv. 9.

Ye are the temple of the living God.—2 COR. vi. 16.

> FLING wide the portals of your heart,
> Make it a temple set apart
> From earthly use for Heaven's employ,
> Adorned with prayer, and love, and joy.
> So shall your Sovereign enter in,
> And new and nobler life begin
>
>   WEISSEL

THOU art to know that thy soul is the centre, habitation, and kingdom of God. That, therefore, to the end the sovereign King may rest on that throne of thy soul, thou oughtest to take pains to keep it clean, quiet, and peaceable,—clean from guilt and defects ; quiet from fears ; and peaceable in temptations and tribulations. Thou oughtest always, then, to keep thine heart in peace, that thou mayest keep pure that temple of God ; and with a right and pure intention thou art to work, pray, obey, and suffer (without being in the least moved), whatever it pleases the Lord to send unto thee.

                        M. MOLINOS

Oh how great is Thy goodness, which Thou hast laid up for them that fear Thee ; which Thou hast wrought for them that trust in Thee.—PS. xxxi. 19.

I will sing unto the Lord, because He hath dealt bountifully with me.—PS. xiii. 6.

THY calmness bends serene above
　My restlessness to still ;
Around me flows Thy quickening life,
　To nerve my faltering will ;
Thy presence fills my solitude ;
Thy providence turns all to good.

S. LONGFELLOW

WITH a heart devoted to God and full of God, no longer seek Him in the heavens above or the earth beneath, or in the things under the earth, but recognize Him as the great fact of the universe, separate from no place or part, but revealed in all places and in all things and events, *moment by moment*. And as eternity alone will exhaust this momentary revelation, which has sometimes been called the ETERNAL Now, thou shalt thus find God ever present and ever new ; and thy soul shall adore Him and feed upon Him in the things and events which each new moment brings ; and thou shalt never be absent from Him, and He shall never be absent from thee.

T. C. UPHAM

For I reckon that the sufferings of this present time are not worthy to be compared with the glory which shall be revealed in us.—ROM. viii. 18.

The power of an endless life.—HEB. vii. 16.

BELIEV'ST thou in eternal things?
　Thou knowest, in thy inmost heart,
Thou art not clay ; thy soul hath wings,
　And what thou seest is but part.
Make this thy med'cine for the smart
　Of every day's distress ; be dumb,
In each new loss thou truly art
　Tasting the power of things that come.

T. W. PARSONS

EVERY contradiction of our will, every little ailment, every petty disappointment, will, if we take it patiently, become a blessing. So, walking on earth, we may be in heaven ; the ill-tempers of others, the slights and rudenesses of the world, ill-health, the daily accidents with which God has mercifully strewed our paths, instead of ruffling or disturbing our peace, may cause His peace to be shed abroad in our hearts abundantly.

E. B. PUSEY

A new commandment I give unto you, That ye love one another ; as I have loved you, that ye also love one another.—JOHN xiii. 34.

And the Lord make you to increase and abound in love, one toward another, and toward all men.—I THESS. iii. 12.

> LET love through all my conduct shine,
> An image fair, though faint, of Thine ;
> Thus let me his disciple prove,
> Who come to manifest Thy love.
>
> ANON.

WE should arrive at a fullness of love extending to the whole creation, a desire to impart, to pour out in full and copious streams the love and goodness we bear to all around us.

J. P. GREAVES

GOODNESS and love mould the form into their own image, and cause the joy and beauty of love to shine forth from every part of the face. When this form of love is seen, it appears ineffably beautiful, and affects with delight the inmost life of the soul.

SWEDENBORG

THE soul within had so often lighted up her countenance with its own full happiness and joy, that something of a permanent radiance remained upon it.

ANNA, OR PASSAGES FROM HOME LIFE

The Lord is good to all ; and His tender mercies are over all his works.—PS. cxlv. 9.

For every beast of the forest is Mine, and the cattle upon a thousand hills.—PS. l. 10.

MAKER of earth and sea and sky,
   Creation's sovereign Lord and King,
Who hung the starry worlds on high,
   And formed alike the sparrow's wing ;
Bless the dumb creatures of Thy care,
And listen to their voiceless prayer.
ANON.

I BELIEVE where the love of God is verily perfected, and the true spirit of government watchfully attended to, a tenderness towards all creatures made subject to us will be experienced ; and a care felt in us, that we do not lessen that sweetness of life in the animal creation, which the great Creator intends for them under our government. . . . To say we love God as unseen, and at the same time exercise cruelty toward the least creature moving by His life, or by life derived from Him, was a contradiction in itself.

JOHN WOOLMAN

I WOULD give nothing for that man's religion whose very dog and cat are not the better for it.

ROWLAND HILL

*Then I said, I have laboured in vain, I have
spent my strength for nought, and in vain.*—ISA.
xlix. 4.

BECAUSE I spent the strength Thou gavest me
In struggle which Thou never didst ordain,
And have but dregs of life to offer Thee—
    O Lord, I do repent.
                    SARAH WILLIAMS

MIND, it is our best work that He wants,
not the dregs of our exhaustion. I think
He must prefer quality to quantity.
                    GEORGE MACDONALD

IF the people about you are carrying on their
business or their benevolence at a pace which
drains the life out of you, resolutely take a
slower pace ; be called a laggard, make less
money, accomplish less work than they, but be
what you were meant to be and can be. You
have your natural limit of power as much as an
engine,—ten-horse power, or twenty, or a
hundred. You are fit to do certain kinds of
work, and you need a certain kind and amount
of fuel, and a certain kind of handling.
                    GEORGE S. MERRIAM

IN your occupations, try to possess your soul
in peace. It is not a good plan to be in haste
to perform any action that it may be the sooner
over. On the contrary, you should accustom
yourself to do whatever you have to do with
tranquillity, in order that you may retain the
possession of yourself and of settled peace.
                    MADAME GUYON

For which cause we faint not ; but, though our outward man perish, yet the inward man is renewed day by day.—2 COR. iv. 16.

> LET my soul beneath her load
> Faint not through the o'erwearied flesh ;
> Let me hourly drink afresh
> Love and peace from Thee, my God !
>
> RICHTER

IN my attempts to promote the comfort of my family, the quiet of my spirit has been disturbed. Some of this is doubtless owing to physical weakness ; but, with every temptation, there is a way of escape ; there is *never* any *need* to sin. Another thing I have suffered loss from,—entering into the business of the day without seeking to have my spirit quieted and directed. So many things press upon me, this is sometimes neglected ; shame to me that it should be so.

This is of great importance, to watch carefully,—now I am so weak—not to over-fatigue myself, because then I cannot contribute to the pleasure of others ; and a placid face and a gentle tone will make my family more happy than anything else I can do for them. Our own will gets sadly into the performance of our duties sometimes.

ELIZABETH T. KING, 1856

*Whoso is wise, and will observe these things,
even they shall understand the loving-kindness of
the Lord.*—PS. cvii. 43.

WHAT channel needs our faith, except the eyes ?
  God leaves no spot of earth unglorified ;
Profuse and wasteful, lovelinesses rise ;
  New beauties dawn before the old have died.

Trust thou thy joys in keeping of the Power
  Who holds these changing shadows in His hand ;
Believe and live, and know that hour by hour
  Will ripple newer beauty to thy strand.

T. W. HIGGINSON

I WONDERED over again for the hundredth
time what could be the principle which, in
the wildest, most lawless, fantastically chaotic,
apparently capricious work of nature, always
kept it beautiful. The beauty of holiness must
be at the heart of it somehow, I thought. Be-
cause our God is so free from stain, so loving, so
unselfish, so good, so altogether what He wants
us to be, so holy, therefore all His works declare
Him in beauty ; His fingers can touch nothing
but to mould it into loveliness ; and even the
play of His elements is in grace and tenderness
of form.

G. MACDONALD

Thou shalt love the Lord thy God with all thy heart, and with all thy soul, and with all thy strength, and with all thy mind.—LUKE X. 27.

> O GOD, what offering shall I give
>   To Thee, the Lord of earth and skies?
> My spirit, soul, and flesh receive,
>   A holy, living sacrifice.
>
> J. LANGE

TO love God 'with all our heart', is to know the spiritual passion of measureless gratitude for loving-kindness, and self-devotedness to goodness; to love Him 'with all our mind', is to know the passion for Truth that is the enthusiasm of Science, the passion for Beauty that inspires the poet and the artist, when all truth and beauty are regarded as the self-revealings of God; to love Him 'with all our soul', is to know the saint's rapture of devotion and gaze of penitential awe into the face of the All-holy, the saint's abhorrence of sin, and agony of desire to save a sinner's soul; and to love Him 'with all our strength', is the supreme spiritual passion that tests the rest; the passion for reality, for worship in spirit and in truth, for *being* what we adore, for *doing* what we know to be God's word; the lotalty that exacts the living sacrifice, the whole burnt-offering that is our reasonable service, and in our coldest hours keeps steadfast to what seemed good when we were aglow.

J. H. THOM

*Walk worthy of God, who hath called you unto
His kingdom and glory.*—I THESS. ii. 12.

*Surely the Lord is in this place ; and I knew it
not.*—GEN. xxviii. 16.

THOU camest not to thy place by accident,
It is the very place God meant for thee ;
And shouldst thou there small scope for action see,
Do not for this give room to discontent.

R. C. TRENCH

ACCEPT the place the divine providence
has found for you, the society of your
contemporaries, the connexion of events.

R. W. EMERSON

ADAPT thyself to the things with which thy lot
has been cast ; and love the men with whom it
is thy portion to live, and that with a sincere
affection. . . . No longer be either dissatisfied
with thy present lot, or shrink from the future.

MARCUS ANTONINUS

I LOVE best to have each thing in its season,
doing without it at all other times. I have never
got over my surprise that I should have been
born into the most estimable place in all the
world, and in the very nick of time too.

H. D. THOREAU

He knoweth the way that I take.—JOB xxiii. 10.

Man's goings are of the Lord ; how can a man then understand his own way ?—PROV. xx. 24.

> BE quiet, why this anxious heed
> About thy tangled ways ?
> God knows them all, He giveth speed,
> And He allows delays.
>
> E. W.

WE complain of the slow, dull life we are forced to lead, of our humble sphere of action, of our low position in the scale of society, of our having no room to make ourselves known, of our wasted energies, of our years of patience. So do we say that we have no Father who is directing our life ; so do we say that God has forgotten us ; so do we boldly judge what life is best for us ; and so by our complaining do we lose the use and profit of the quiet years. O men of little faith ! Because you are not sent out yet into your labour, do you think God has ceased to remember you ? Because you are forced to be outwardly inactive, do you think you, also, may not be, in your years of quiet, ' about your Father's business ' ? . . . It is a period given to us in which to mature ourselves for the work which God will give us to do.

STOPFORD A. BROOKE

They that trust in the Lord shall be as Mount Zion, which cannot be removed, but abideth for ever. As the mountains are round about Jerusalem, so the Lord is round about His people from henceforth even for ever.—PS. CXXV. I, 2.

HOW on a rock they stand,
Who watch His eye, and hold His guiding hand !
Not half so fixed amid her vassal hills,
Rises the holy pile that Kedron's valley fills.

J. KEBLE

THAT is the way to be immovable in the midst of troubles, as a rock amidst the waves. When God is in the midst of a kingdom or city, He makes it firm as Mount Sion, that cannot be removed. When He is in the midst of a soul, though calamities throng about it on all hands, and roar like the billows of the sea, yet there is a constant calm within, such a peace as the world can neither give nor take away. What is it but want of lodging God in the soul, and that in His stead the world is in men's hearts, that makes them shake like leaves at every blast of danger ?

R. LEIGHTON

He that received seed into the good ground is he that heareth the word, and understandeth it; which also beareth fruit, and bringeth forth, some an hundredfold, some sixty, some thirty.—MATT. xiii. 23.

THEN bless thy secret growth, nor catch
At noise, but thrive unseen and dumb ;
Keep clean, bear fruit, earn life, and watch
Till the white-wingèd reapers come.

H. VAUGHAN

HE does not need to transplant us into a different field, but right where we are, with just the circumstances that surround us. He makes His sun to shine and His dew to fall upon us, and transforms the very things that were before our greatest hindrances, into the chiefest and most blessed means of our growth. . . . No difficulties in your case can baffle Him. No dwarfing of your growth in years that are past, no apparent dryness of your inward springs of life, no crookedness or deformity in any of your past development, can in the least mar the perfect work that He will accomplish, if you will only put yourselves absolutely into His hands, and let Him have His own way with you.

H. W. S.

But I would not have you to be ignorant, brethren, concerning them which are asleep, that ye sorrow not, even as others which have no hope.— I THESS. iv. 13.

YET Love will dream, and Faith will trust
(Since He who knows our need is just),
That somehow, somewhere, meet we must.
Alas for him who never sees
The stars shine through his cypress trees ;
Who hath not learned in hours of faith,
The truth to flesh and sense unknown,
That life is ever Lord of Death,
And Love can never lose its own.

J. G. WHITTIER

WHILE we poor wayfarers still toil, with hot and bleeding feet, along the highway and the dust of life, our companions have but mounted the divergent path, to explore the more sacred streams, and visit the diviner vales, and wander amid the everlasting Alps, of God's upper province of creation. And so we keep up the courage of our hearts, and refresh ourselves with the memories of love, and travel forward in the ways of duty, with less weary step, feeling ever for the hand of God, and listening for the domestic voices of the immortals whose happy welcome waits us. Death, in short, under the Christian aspect, is but God's method of colonization ; the transition from this mother-country of our race to the fairer and newer world of our emigration.

J. MARTINEAU

But this I say, brethren, the time is short. —
I COR. vii. 29.

I SOMETIMES feel the thread of life is slender,
And soon with me the labour will be wrought ;
Then grows my heart to other hearts more tender.
The time is short.

D. M. CRAIK

OH, my dear friends, you who are letting miserable misunderstandings run on from year to year, meaning to clear them up some day ; you who are keeping wretched quarrels alive because you cannot quite make up your mind that now is the day to sacrifice your pride and kill them ; you who are passing men sullenly upon the street, not speaking to them out of some silly spite, and yet knowing that it would fill you with shame and remorse if you heard that one of those men were dead to-morrow morning ; you who are letting your neighbour starve, till you hear that he is dying of starvation ; or letting your friend's heart ache for a word of appreciation or sympathy, which you mean to give him some day,—if you only could know and see and feel, all of a sudden, that ' the time is short ', how it would break the spell ! How you would go instantly and do the thing which you might never have another chance to do.

PHILLIPS BROOKS

Remember not the sins of my youth, nor my transgressions ; according to Thy mercy remember Thou me, for Thy goodness' sake, O Lord.—PS. XXV. 7.

> WHEN on my aching, burdened heart
>   My sins lie heavily,
> My pardon speak, new peace impart,
>   In love remember me.
>
> T. HAWEIS

WE need to know that our sins are forgiven. And how shall we know this ? By feeling that we have peace with God,—by feeling that we are able so to trust in the divine compassion and infinite tenderness of our Father, as to arise and go to Him, whenever we commit sin, and say at once to Him, ' Father, I have sinned ; forgive me.' To know that we are forgiven, it is only necessary to look at our Father's love till it sinks into our heart, to open our soul to Him till He shall pour His love into it ; to wait on Him till we find peace, till our conscience no longer torments us, till the weight of responsibility ceases to be an oppressive burden to us, till we can feel that our sins, great as they are, cannot keep us away from our Heavenly Father.

J. F. CLARKE

*I have blotted out, as a thick cloud, thy trans-
gressions, and, as a cloud, thy sins : return unto
Me, for I have redeemed thee.*—ISA. xliv. 22.

*He will turn again, He will have compassion
upon us ; He will subdue our iniquities ; and Thou
wilt cast all their sins into the depths of the sea.*—
MICAH vii. 19.

IF my shut eyes should dare their lids to part,
I know how they must quail beneath the blaze
Of Thy Love's greatness. No ; I dare not raise
One prayer, to look aloft, lest it should gaze
On such forgiveness as would break my heart.

H. S. SUTTON

O LORD God gracious and merciful, give
us, I entreat Thee, a humble trust in Thy
mercy, and suffer not our heart to fail us.
Though our sins be seven, though our sins be
seventy times seven, though our sins be more
in number than the hairs of our head, yet give
us grace in loving penitence to cast ourselves
down into the depth of Thy compassion. Let
us fall into the hand of the Lord. Amen.

C. G. ROSSETTI

Be not hasty in thy spirit to be angry ; for anger resteth in the bosom of fools.—ECCLES. vii. 9.

Let not the sun go down upon your wrath.—EPH. iv. 26.

> QUENCH thou the fires of hate and strife,
> The wasting fever of the heart ;
> From perils guard our feeble life,
> And to our souls Thy peace impart.
>
>   J. H. NEWMAN, *Tr. from Latin*

WHEN thou art offended or annoyed by others, suffer not thy thoughts to dwell thereon, or on anything relating to them. For example, ' that they ought not so to have treated thee ; who they are, or whom they think themselves to be ' ; or the like ; for all this is fuel and kindling of wrath, anger, and hatred.

L. SCUPOLI

STRUGGLE diligently against your impatience, and strive to be amiable and gentle, in season and out of season, towards every one, however much they may vex and annoy you, and be sure God will bless your efforts.

FRANCIS DE SALES

*Behold, God is my salvation ; I will trust, and not be afraid : for the Lord Jehovah is my strength and my song ; He also is become my salvation.—*ISA. xii. 2.

*Why are ye so fearful ? How is it that ye have no faith ?—*MARK iv. 40.

STILL heavy is thy heart ?
  Still sink thy spirits down ;
Cast off the weight, let fear depart,
  And every care be gone.

P. GERHARDT

GO on in all simplicity ; do not be so anxious to win a quiet mind, and it will be all the quieter. Do not examine so closely into the progress of your soul. Do not crave so much to be perfect, but let your spiritual life be formed by your duties, and by the actions which are called forth by circumstances. Do not take overmuch thought for to-morrow. God, who has led you safely on so far, will lead you on to the end. Be altogether at rest in the loving holy confidence which you ought to have in His heavenly Providence.

FRANCIS DE SALES

Thou hast made him exceeding glad with Thy countenance.—PS. xxi. 6.

MY heart for gladness springs,
　It cannot more be sad,
For very joy it laughs and sings,
　Sees nought but sunshine glad.
P. GERHARDT

A NEW day rose upon me. It was as if another sun had risen into the sky; the heavens were indescribably brighter, and the earth fairer; and that day has gone on brightening to the present hour. I have known the other joys of life, I suppose, as much as most men; I have known art and beauty, music and gladness; I have known friendship and love and family ties; but it is certain that till we see GOD in the world—GOD in the bright and boundless universe—we never know the highest joy. It is far more than if one were translated to a world a thousand times fairer than this; for that supreme and central Light of Infinite Love and Wisdom, shining over this world and all worlds, alone can show us how noble and beautiful, how fair and glorious they are.

ORVILLE DEWEY

WHEN I look like this into the blue sky, it seems so deep, so peaceful, so full of a mysterious tenderness, that I could lie for centuries and wait for the dawning of the face of God out of the awful loving-kindness.

G. MACDONALD

He satisfieth the longing soul, and filleth the hungry soul with goodness.—PS. cvii. 9.

That ye might be filled with all the fulness of God.—EPH. iii. 19.

ENOUGH that He who made can fill the soul
  Here and hereafter till its deeps o'erflow ;
Enough that love and tenderness control
  Our fate where'er in joy or doubt we go.

ANON.

O GOD, the Life of the Faithful, the Bliss of the righteous, mercifully receive the prayers of Thy suppliants, that the souls which thirst for Thy promises may evermore be filled from Thy abundance. Amen.

GELASIAN, A.D. 49C

GOD makes every common thing serve, if thou wilt, to enlarge that capacity of bliss in His love. Not a prayer, not an act of faithfulness in your calling, not a self-denying or kind word or deed, done out of love for Himself ; not a weariness or painfulness endured patiently ; not a duty performed ; not a temptation resisted ; but it enlarges the whole soul for the endless capacity of the love of God.

E. B. PUSEY

O receive the gift that is given you, and be glad, giving thanks unto Him that hath called you to the heavenly kingdom.—2 ESDRAS ii. 37.

Thanks be unto God for His unspeakable gift.—2 COR. ix. 15.

> O GIVER of each perfect gift !
> This day our daily bread supply ;
> While from the Spirit's tranquil depths
> We drink unfailing draughts of joy.
> LYRA CATHOLICA

THE best way for a man rightly to enjoy himself, is to maintain a universal, ready, and cheerful compliance with the divine and uncreated Will in all things ; as knowing that nothing can issue and flow forth from the fountain of goodness but that which is good ; and therefore a good man is never offended with any piece of divine dispensation, nor hath he any reluctancy against that Will that dictates and determines all things by an eternal rule of goodness ; as knowing that there is an unbounded and almighty Love, that without any disdain or envy, freely communicates itself to everything He made ; that always enfolds those in His everlasting arms who are made partakers of His own image, perpetually nourishing and cherishing them with the fresh and vital influences of His grace.

DR. JOHN SMITH

Bless the Lord, O my soul, and forget not all His benefits.—PS. ciii. 2.

WISER it were to welcome and make ours
What'er of good, though small, the Present brings,—
Kind greetings, sunshine, song of birds, and flowers,
With a child's pure delight in little things.

R. C. TRENCH

INTO all our lives, in many simple, familiar, homely ways, God infuses this element of joy from the surprises of life, which unexpectedly brighten our days, and fill our eyes with light. He drops this added sweetness into his children's cup, and makes it to run over. The success we were not counting on, the blessing we were not trying after, the strain of music in the midst of drudgery, the beautiful morning picture or sunset glory thrown in as we pass to or from our daily business, the unsought word of encouragement or expression of sympathy, the sentence that meant for us more than the writer or speaker thought,— these and a hundred others that every one's experience can supply are instances of what I mean. You may call it accident or chance— it often is ; you may call it human goodness— it often is ; but always, always call it God's love. for that is always in it. These are the overflowing riches of His grace, these are His free gifts.

S. LONGFELLOW

If thou canst believe, all things are possible to him that believeth.—MARK ix. 23.

Nothing shall be impossible unto you.—MATT. xvii. 20.

> so nigh is grandeur to our dust,
>   So near is God to man,
> When Duty whispers low, *Thou must*,
>   The youth replies, *I can*.
>
> R. W. EMERSON

KNOW that 'impossible', where truth and mercy and the everlasting voice of nature order, has no place in the brave man's dictionary. That when all men have said 'Impossible', and tumbled noisily elsewhither, and thou alone art left, then first thy time and possibility have come. It is for thee now : **do** thou that, and ask no man's counsel, but **thy** own only and God's. Brother, thou hast possibility in thee for much : the possibility of writing on the eternal skies the record of a heroic life.

T. CARLYLE

IN the moral world there is nothing impossible, if we bring a thorough will to it. Man can do everything with himself ; but he must not attempt to do too much with others.

WM. VON HUMBOLDT

Stand fast therefore in the liberty wherewith Christ hath made us free, and be not entangled again with the yoke of bondage.—GAL. v. 1.

I believed, and therefore have I spoken.—2 COR. iv. 13.

> THEY are slaves who fear to speak
> For the fallen and the weak ;
> They are slaves who will not choose
> Hatred, scoffing, and abuse,
> Rather than in silence shrink
> From the truth they needs must think ;
> They are slaves who dare not be
> In the right with two or three.
>
> J. R. LOWELL

THE real corrupters of society may be, not the corrupt, but those who have held back the righteous leaven, the salt that has lost its savour, the innocent who have not even the moral courage to show what they think of the effrontery of impurity,—the serious, who yet timidly succumb before some loud-voiced scoffer,—the heart trembling all over with religious sensibilities that yet suffers itself through false shame to be beaten down into outward and practical acquiescence by some rude and worldly nature.

J. H. THOM

The things which are impossible with men are possible with God.—LUKE xviii. 27.

Unless the Lord had been my help, my soul had almost dwelt in silence.—PS. xciv. 17.

WHEN obstacles and trials seem
　　Like prison-walls to be,
I do the little I can do,
　　And leave the rest to Thee.

F. W. FABER

THE mind never puts forth greater power over itself than when, in great trials, it yields up calmly its desires, affections, interests to God. There are seasons when to be *still* demands immeasurably higher strength than to act. Composure is often the highest result of power. Think you it demands no power to calm the stormy elements of passion, to moderate the vehemence of desire, to throw off the load of dejection, to suppress every repining thought, when the dearest hopes are withered, and to turn the wounded spirit from dangerous reveries and wasting grief, to the quiet discharge of ordinary duties ? Is there no power put forth, when a man, stripped of his property, of the fruits of a life's labours, quells discontent and gloomy forebodings, and serenely and patiently returns to the tasks which Providence assigns ?

WM. E. CHANNING

The cup which my Father has given me, shall I not drink it ?—JOHN xviii. 11.

Whatsoever is brought upon thee, take cheerfully.—ECCLUS. ii. 4.

> EVERY sorrow, every smart,
> That the Eternal Father's heart
> Hath appointed me of yore,
> Or hath yet for me in store,
> As my life flows on, I'll take
> Calmly, gladly, for his sake,
> No more faithless murmurs make.
>
> P. GERHARDT

THE very least and the very greatest sorrows that God ever suffers to befall thee, proceed from the depths of His unspeakable love ; and such great love were better for thee than the highest and best gifts besides that He has given thee, or ever could give thee, if thou couldst but see it in this light. So that if your little finger only aches, if you are cold, if you are hungry or thirsty, if others vex you by their words or deeds, or whatever happens to you that causes you distress or pain, it will all help to fit you for a noble and blessed state.

J. TAULER

The Lord thy God shall bless thee in all thy works, and in all that thou puttest thine hand unto.
—DEUT. XV. 10.

MY place of lowly service, too,
　Beneath Thy sheltering wings I see ;
For all the work I have to do
　Is done through sheltering rest in Thee.
A. L. WARING

I THINK I find most help in trying to look on all interruptions and hindrances to work that one has planned out for oneself as discipline, trials sent by God to help one against getting selfish over one's work. Then one can feel that perhaps one's true work—one's work for God—consists in doing some trifling haphazard thing that has been thrown into one's day. It is not waste of time, as one is tempted to think, it is the most important part of the work of the day,—the part one can best offer to God. After such a hindrance, do not rush after the planned work ; trust that the time to finish it will be given sometime, and keep a quiet heart about it.

ANNIE KEARY

Master, what shall I do to inherit eternal life?
—LUKE X. 25.

Whatsoever thy hand findeth to do, do it with thy might.—ECCLES. ix. 10.

' WHAT shall I do to gain eternal life ? '
   ' Discharge aright
The simple dues with which each day is rife
   Yea, with thy might.'

               F. VON SCHILLER

A MAN is relieved and gay when he has put his heart into his work, and done his best ; but what he has said or done otherwise, shall give him no peace.

               R. W. EMERSON

BE diligent, after thy power, to do deeds of love. Think nothing too little, nothing too low, to do lovingly for the sake of God. Bear with infirmities, ungentle tempers, contradictions ; visit, if thou mayest, the sick ; relieve the poor ; forego thyself and thine own ways for love ; and He whom in them thou lovest, to whom in them thou ministerest, will own thy love, and will pour His own love into thee.

               E. B. PUSEY

In your patience possess ye your souls.—LUKE
xxi. 19.

> WHAT though thy way be dark, and earth
> With ceaseless care do cark, till mirth
>   To thee no sweet strain singeth ;
> Still hide thy life above, and still
> Believe that God is love ; fulfil
>   Whatever lot He bringeth.
>
> ALBERT E. EVANS

THE soul loses command of itself when it
is impatient. Whereas, when it submits
without a murmur it possesses itself in peace,
and possesses God. To be impatient, is to
desire what we have not, or not to desire what
we have. When we acquiesce in an evil, it is
no longer such. Why make a real calamity of
it by resistance ? Peace does not dwell in out-
ward things, but within the soul. We may
preserve it in the midst of the bitterest pain,
if our will remains firm and submissive. Peace
in this life springs from acquiescence even in
disagreeable things, not in an exemption from
bearing them.

FÉNELON

THE chief pang of most trials is not so much
the actual suffering itself, as our own spirit of
resistance to it.

JEAN NICOLAS GROU

I will lift up mine eyes unto the hills, from whence cometh my help.—PS. cxxi. 1.

My grace is sufficient for thee.—2 COR. xii. 9.

I LOOK to Thee in every need,
    And never look in vain ;
I feel Thy touch, Eternal Love,
    And all is well again :
The thought of Thee is mightier far
Than sin and pain and sorrow are.

S. LONGFELLOW

HOW can you live sweetly amid the vexatious things, the irritating things, the multitude of little worries and frets, which lie all along your way, and which you cannot evade ? You cannot at present change your surroundings. Whatever kind of life you are to live, must be lived amid precisely the experiences in which you are now moving. Here you must win your victories or suffer your defeats. No restlessness or discontent can change your lot. Others may have other circumstances surrounding them, but here are yours. You had better make up your mind to accept what you cannot alter. You *can* live a beautiful life in the midst of your present circumstances.

J. R. MILLER

STRIVE to realize a state of inward happiness, independent of circumstances.

J. P. GREAVES

God hath not given us the spirit of fear ; but of power, and of love, and of a sound mind.—2 TIM. i. 7.

WE cast behind fear, sin, and death ;
  With Thee we seek the things above ;
Our inmost souls Thy spirit breathe,
  Of power, of calmness, and of love.
                    HYMNS OF THE SPIRIT

I MUST conclude with a more delightful subject,—my most dear and blessed sister. I never saw a more perfect instance of the spirit of power and of love, and of a sound mind ; intense love, almost to the annihilation of selfishness—a daily martyrdom for twenty years, during which she adhered to her early-formed resolution of never talking about herself ; thoughtful about the very pins and ribands of my wife's dress, about the making of a doll's cap for a child,—but of herself, save only as regarded her ripening in all goodness, wholly thoughtless, enjoying everything lovely, graceful, beautiful, high-minded, whether in God's works or man's, with the keenest relish ; inheriting the earth to the very fullness of the promise, though never leaving her crib, nor changing her posture ; and preserved through the very valley of the shadow of death, from all fear or impatience, or from every cloud of impaired reason, which might mar the beauty of Christ's spirit's glorious work.

                    THOMAS ARNOLD

Whatsoever a man soweth, that shall he also reap.—GAL. vi. 7.

. . . .

THE life above, when this is past,
Is the ripe fruit of life below.

Sow love, and taste its fruitage pure ;
Sow peace, and reap its harvest bright
Sow sunbeams on the rock and moor,
And find a harvest-home of light.

H. BONAR

THE dispositions, affections, inclinations or soul, which shall issue hereafter in perfection, must be trained and nurtured in us throughout the whole course of this earthly life. When shall we bear in mind this plain truth, that the future perfection of the saints is not a translation from one state or disposition of soul into another, diverse from the former ; but the carrying out, and, as it were, the blossom and the fruitage of one and the same principle of spiritual life, which, through their whole career on earth, has been growing with an even strength, putting itself forth in the beginnings and promise of perfection, reaching upward with steadfast aspirations after perfect holiness ?

H. E. MANNING

O turn unto me, and have mercy upon me ; give Thy strength unto Thy servant, and save the son of Thy handmaid.—PS. lxxxvi. 16.

THOU art my King—
My King henceforth alone ;
And I, Thy servant, Lord, am all Thine own.
Give me Thy strength ; oh ! let Thy dwelling be
In this poor heart that pants, my Lord, for Thee !

G. TERSTEEGEN

WHEN it is the one ruling, never-ceasing desire of our hearts, that God may be the beginning and end, the reason and motive, the rule and measure, of our doing or not doing, from morning to night ; then everywhere, whether speaking or silent, whether inwardly or outwardly employed, we are equally offered up to the eternal Spirit, have our life in Him and from Him, and are united to Him by that Spirit of Prayer which is the comfort, the support, the strength and security of the soul, travelling, by the help of God, through the vanity of time into the riches of eternity. Let us have no thought or care, but how to be wholly His devoted instruments ; everywhere, and in everything, His adoring, joyful, and thankful servants.

Beloved, if our heart condemn us not, then have we confidence toward God.—1 JOHN iii. 21.

> O LORD, how happy is the time
>   When in Thy love I rest :
> When from my weariness I climb
>   E'en to Thy tender breast.
> The night of sorrow endeth there,
>   Thy rays outshine the sun ;
> And in Thy pardon and Thy care
>   The heaven of heavens is won.
>
> W. C. DESSLER

NOTHING doth so much establish the mind amidst the rollings and turbulency of present things, as both a look above them, and a look beyond them ; above them to the good and steady Hand by which they are ruled, and beyond them to the sweet and beautiful end to which, by that Hand, they shall be brought. . . . Study pure and holy walking, if you would have your confidence firm, and have boldness and joy in God. You will find that a little sin will shake your trust and disturb your peace more than the greatest sufferings : yea, in those sufferings, your assurance and joy in God will grow and abound most if sin be kept out. So much sin as gets in, so much peace will go out.

R. LEIGHTON

Teach me Thy way, O Lord, and lead me in a plain path.—PS. xxvii. 11.

LEAD, kindly Light, amid the encircling gloom,
    Lead Thou me on ;
The night is dark, and I am far from home,
    Lead Thou me on.
Keep Thou my feet ; I do not ask to see
The distant scene ; one step enough for me.
J. H. NEWMAN

GOD only is holy ; He alone knows how to lead His children in the paths of holiness. He knows every aspect of your soul, every thought of your heart, every secret of your character, its difficulties and hindrances ; He knows how to mould you to His will, and lead you onwards to perfect sanctification ; He knows exactly how each event, each trial, each temptation, will tell upon you, and He disposes all things accordingly. The consequences of this belief, if fully grasped, will influence your whole life. You will seek to give yourself up to God more and more unreservedly, asking nothing, refusing nothing, wishing nothing, but what He wills ; not seeking to bring things about for yourself, taking all He sends joyfully, and believing the ' one step ' set before you to be enough for you. You will be satisfied that even though there are clouds around, and your way seems dark, He is directing all, and that what seems a hindrance will prove a blessing, since He wills it.

JEAN NICOLAS GROU

Wait on the Lord : be of good courage, and He shall strengthen thine heart : wait, I say, on the Lord.—PS. xxvii. 14.

He giveth power to the faint ; and to them that have no might He increaseth strength.—ISA. xl. 29.

LEANING on Him, make with reverent meekness
His own thy will,
And with strength from Him shall thy utter weakness
Life's task fulfil.

J. G. WHITTIER

SHOULD we feel at times disheartened and discouraged, a confiding thought, a simple movement of heart towards God will renew our powers. Whatever he may demand of us, he will give us at the moment the strength and the courage that we need.

FÉNELON

WE require a certain firmness in all circumstances of life, even the happiest, and perhaps contradictions come in order to prove and exercise this ; and, if we can only determine so to use them, the very effort brings back tranquillity to the soul, which always enjoys having exercised its strength in conformity to duty.

WM. VON HUMBOLDT

We then that are strong ought to bear the infirmities of the weak, and not to please ourselves.—ROM. XV. I.

The Lord God hath given me the tongue of the learned, that I should know how to speak a word in season to him that is weary.—ISA. l. 4.

> IF there be some weaker one,
> Give me strength to help him on ;
> If a blinder soul there be,
> Let me guide him nearer Thee.
>
> J. G. WHITTIER

ASK Him to increase your powers of sympathy : to give you more quickness and depth of sympathy, in little things as well as great. Opportunities of doing a kindness are often lost from mere want of thought. Half a dozen lines of kindness may bring sunshine into the whole day of some sick person. Think of the pleasure you might give to some one who is much shut up, and who has fewer pleasures than you have, by sharing with her some little comfort or enjoyment that *you* have learnt to look upon as a necessary of life,—the pleasant drive, the new book, flowers from the country, etc. Try to put yourself in another's place. Ask ' What should I like myself, if I were hard-worked, or sick, or lonely ? ' Cultivate the *habit* of sympathy.

G. H. WILKINSON

I beseech you therefore, brethren, by the mercies of God, that ye present your bodies a living sacrifice, holy, acceptable unto God, which is your reasonable service.—ROM. xii. 1.

THOU hast my flesh, Thy hallowed shrine
  Devoted solely to Thy will ;
Here let Thy light forever shine,
  This house still let Thy presence fill ;
O Source of Life, live, dwell, and move
In me, till all my life be love !

JOACHIM LANGE

MAY it not be a comfort to those of us who feel we have not the mental or spiritual power that others have, to notice that the living sacrifice mentioned in Rom. xii. 1 is our 'bodies'? Of course, that includes the mental power, but does it not also include the loving, sympathizing glance, the kind, encouraging word, *the ready errand for another*, the work of our hands, opportunities for all of which come oftener in the day than for the mental power we are often empted to envy? May we be enabled to offer willingly that which we have.

ANON.

Seekest thou great things for thyself? seek them not.—JER. xlv. 5.

> I WOULD not have the restless will
>   That hurries to and fro,
> Seeking for some great thing to do,
>   Or secret thing to know ;
> I would be treated as a child,
>   And guided where I go.
>
> A. L. WARING

OH ! be little, be little ; and then thou wilt be content with little ; and if thou feel, now and then, a check or a secret smiting,— in *that* is the Father's love ; be not over-wise, nor over-eager, in thy own willing, running, and desiring, and thou mayest feel it so ; and by degrees come to the knowledge of thy Guide, who will lead thee, step by step, in the path of life, and teach thee to follow. Be still, and wait for light and strength.

I. PENINGTON

SINK into the sweet and blessed littleness, where thou livest by grace alone. Contemplate with delight the holiness and goodness in God, which thou dost not find in thyself. How lovely it is to be nothing when God is all !

G. TERSTEEGEN

*And that which fell among thorns are they,
which, when they have heard, go forth, and are
choked with cares, and riches and pleasures of this
life, and bring no fruit to perfection.*—LUKE viii. 14.

PRESERVE me from my calling's snare,
And hide my simple heart above,
Above the thorns of choking care,
The gilded baits of worldly love.

C. WESLEY

ANYTHING allowed in the heart which is
contrary to the will of God, let it seem
ever so insignificant, or be ever so deeply
hidden, will cause us to fall before our enemies.
Any root of bitterness cherished towards
another, any self-seeking, any harsh judgments
indulged in, any slackness in obeying the voice
of the Lord, any doubtful habits or surround-
ings, any one of these things will effectually
cripple and paralyse our spiritual life. I
believe our blessed Guide, the indwelling Holy
Spirit, is always secretly discovering these
things to us by continual little twinges and
pangs of conscience, so that we are left without
excuse.

H. W. S.

See that ye refuse not Him that speaketh.—HEB.
xii. 52.

> FROM the world of sin and noise
>   And hurry I withdraw ;
> For the small and inward voice
>   I wait with humble awe ;
> Silent am I now and still,
>   Dare not in Thy presence move ;
> To my waiting soul reveal
>   The secret of Thy love.
>
> C. WESLEY

WHEN therefore the smallest instinct or desire of thy heart calleth thee towards God, and a newness of life, give it time and leave to speak ; and take care thou refuse not Him that speaketh. . . . Be retired, silent, passive, and humbly attentive to this new risen light within thee.

WM. LAW

IT is hardly to be wondered at that he should lose the finer consciousness of higher powers and deeper feelings, not from any behaviour in itself wrong, but from the hurry, noise, and tumult in the streets of life, that, penetrating too deep into the house of life, dazed and stupefied the silent and lonely watcher in the chamber of conscience, far apart. He had no time to think or feel.

G. MACDONALD

Be silent, O all flesh, before the Lord.—ZECH. ii. 13.

> BE earth, with all her scenes, withdrawn ;
> Let noise and vanity be gone :
> In secret silence of the mind,
> My heaven, and there my God, I find.
>
> I. WATTS

IT is only with the pious affection of the will that we can be spiritually attentive to God. As long as the noisy restlessness of the thoughts goes on, the gentle and holy desires of the new nature are overpowered and inactive.

J. P. GREAVES

THERE is hardly ever a complete silence in our soul. God is whispering to us wellnigh incessantly. Whenever the sounds of the world die out in the soul, or sink low, then we hear these whisperings of God. He is always whispering to us, only we do not always hear, because of the noise, hurry, and distraction which life causes as it rushes on.

F. W. FABER

THE prayer of faith is a sincere, sweet, and quiet view of divine, eternal truth. The soul rests quiet, perceiving and loving God ; sweetly rejecting all the imaginations that present themselves, calming the mind in the Divine presence, and fixing it only on God.

MOLINOS

Being confident of this very thing, that He which hath begun a good work in you will perform it.—PHIL. i. 6.

He that endureth to the end shall be saved.—MATT. x. 22.

> FILL with inviolable peace ;
>   Stablish and keep my settled heart ;
> In Thee may all my wanderings cease,
>   From Thee no more may I depart :
> Thy utmost goodness called to prove,
> Loved with an everlasting love !
>
> C. WESLEY

IF any sincere Christian cast himself with his whole will upon the Divine Presence which dwells within him, he shall be kept safe unto the end. What is it that makes us unable to persevere ? Is it want of strength ? By no means. We have with us the strength of the Holy Spirit. When did we ever set ourselves sincerely to any work according to the will of God, and fail for want of strength ? It was not that strength failed the will, but that the will failed first. If we could but embrace the Divine will with the whole love of ours ; cleaving to it, and holding fast by it, we should be borne along as upon ' the river of the water of life '. We open only certain chambers of our will to the influence of the Divine will. We are afraid of being wholly absorbed into it. And yet, if we would have peace, we must be altogether united to Him.

H. E. MANNING

They that know Thy name will put their trust in Thee : for Thou, Lord, hast not forsaken them that seek Thee.—PS. ix. 10.

Yea, the Lord shall give that which is good.— PS. lxxxv. 12.

IN Thee I place my trust,
  On Thee I calmly rest ;
I know Thee good, I know Thee just,
  And count Thy choice the best.
                H. F. LYTE

THE souls that would really be richer in duty in some new position, are precisely those who borrow no excuses from the old one · who even esteem it full of privileges, plenteous in occasions of good, frequent in divine appeals, which they chide their graceless and unloving temper for not heeding more. Wretched and barren is the discontent that quarrels with its tools instead of with its skill ; and, by criticizing Providence, manages to keep up complacency with self. How gentle should we be, if we were not provoked ; how pious, if we were not busy ; the sick would be patient, only he is not in health ; the obscure would do great things, only he is not conspicuous !

                J. MARTINEAU

Am I my brother's keeper ?—GEN. iv. 9.

BECAUSE I held upon my selfish road,
And left my brother wounded by the way,
And called ambition duty, and pressed on—
    O Lord, I do repent.
                        SARAH WILLIAMS

HOW many are the sufferers who have fallen
amongst misfortunes along the wayside of
life ! ' By *chance*', we come that way ; chance,
accident, Providence, has thrown them in our
way ; we see them from a distance, like the
Priest, or we come upon them suddenly, like the
Levite ; our business, our pleasure, is inter-
rupted by the sight, is troubled by the delay ;
what are our feelings, what our actions towards
them ? . . . ' Who is thy neighbour ? ' It is
the sufferer, wherever, whoever, whatsoever
he be. Wherever thou hearest the cry of
distress, wherever thou seest any one brought
across thy path by the chances and changes of
life (that is, by the Providence of God), whom
it is in thy power to help,—he, stranger or
enemy though he be,—*he* is thy neighbour.
                        A. P. STANLEY

Walk worthy of the vocation wherewith ye are called, with all lowliness and meekness, with long-suffering, forbearing one another in love.—EPH. iv. 1, 2.

HELP us, O Lord, with patient love to bear
  Each other's faults, to suffer with true meekness ;
Help us each other's joys and griefs to share,
  But let us turn to Thee alone in weakness.

ANON.

YOU should make a special point of asking God every morning to give you, before all else, that true spirit of meekness which He would have His children possess. You must also make a firm resolution to practise yourself in this virtue, especially in your intercourse with those persons to whom you chiefly owe it. You must make it your main object to conquer yourself in this matter ; call it to mind a hundred times during the day, commending your efforts to God. It seems to me that no more than this is needed in order to subject your soul entirely to His will, and then you will become more gentle day by day, trusting wholly in His goodness. You will be very happy, my dearest child, if you can do this, for God will dwell in your heart ; and where He reigns all is peace. But if you should fail, and commit some of your old faults, do not be disheartened, but rise up and go on again, as though you had not fallen.

FRANCIS DE SALES

Now therefore keep thy sorrow to thyself, and bear with a good courage that which hath befallen thee —2 ESDRAS X. 15.

GO, bury thy sorrow,
  The world hath its share :
Go, bury it deeply,
  Go, hide it with care
Go, bury thy sorrow,
  Let others be blest ;
Go, give them the sunshine,
  And tell God the rest.

ANON:

OUR veiled and terrible guest [Trouble] brings for us, if we will accept it, the boon of fortitude, patience, self-control, wisdom, sympathy, faith. If we reject that, then we find in our hands the other gift,—cowardice, weakness, isolation, despair. If your trouble seems to have in it no other possibility of good, at least set yourself to bear it like a man. Let none of its weight come on other shoulders. Try to carry it so that no one shall even see it. Though your heart be sad within, let cheer go out from you to others. Meet them with a kindly presence, considerate words, helpful acts.

G. S. MERRIAM

Let them that suffer according to the will of God commit the keeping of their souls to Him in well-doing, as unto a faithful Creator.—1 PETER iv. 19.

The Lord is very pitiful, and of tender mercy.— JAMES V. 11.

ON Thy compassion I repose
In weakness and distress :
I will not ask for greater ease,
Lest I should love Thee less.
Oh, 'tis a blessed thing for me
To need Thy tenderness.

A. L. WARING

OH, look not at thy pain or sorrow, how great soever ; but look from them, look off them, look beyond them, to the Deliverer ! whose power is over them, and whose loving, wise, and tender spirit is able to do thee good by them. The Lord lead thee, day by day, in the right way, and keep thy mind stayed upon Him, in whatever befalls thee ; that the belief of His love and hope in His mercy, when thou art at the lowest ebb, may keep up thy head above the billows.

ISAAC PENINGTON

Blessed are the peacemakers : for they shall be called the children of God.—MATT. v. 9.

GRANT us Thy peace, down from Thy presence
    falling,
  As on the thirsty earth cool night-dews sweet ;
Grant us Thy peace, to Thy pure paths recalling,
  From devious ways, our worn and wandering feet.
                                        E. SCUDDER

O GOD, who art Peace everlasting, whose
  chosen reward is the gift of peace, and
who hast taught us that the peacemakers are
Thy children, pour Thy sweet peace into our
souls, that everything discordant may utterly
vanish, and all that makes for peace be sweet
to us forever.   Amen.

                          GELASIAN, A.D. 492

HAVE you ever thought seriously of the mean-
ing of that blessing given to the peacemakers ?
People are always expecting to get peace in
heaven ; but you know whatever peace they get
there will be ready-made.   Whatever making of
peace *they* can be blest for, must be on the earth
here : not the taking of arms against, but the
building of nests amidst, its ' sea of troubles '
[like the halcyons].   Difficult enough, you
think ?   Perhaps so, but I do not see that any of
us try.   We complain of the want of many
things—we want votes, we want liberty, we
want amusement, we want money.   Which of
us feels or knows that he wants peace ?

                                       J. RUSKIN

The eyes of all wait upon Thee ; and Thou givest them their meat in due season.—PS. cxlv. 15.

What time I am afraid, I will trust in Thee.—PS. lvi. 3.

LATE on me, weeping, did this whisper fall :
' Dear child, there is no need to weep at all !
Why go about to grieve and to despair ?
Why weep now through thy Future's eyes, and bear
In vain to-day to-morrow's load of care ? '

H. S. SUTTON

THE crosses of the present moment always bring their own special grace and consequent comfort with them ; we see the hand of God in them when it is laid upon us. But the crosses of anxious foreboding are seen out of the dispensation of God ; we see them without grace to bear them ; we see them indeed through a faithless spirit which banishes grace. So, everything in them is bitter and unendurable ; all seems dark and helpless. Let us throw self aside ; no more self-interest, and then God's will, unfolding every moment in everything, will console us also every moment for all that He shall do around us, or within us, for our discipline.

FÉNELON

His delight is in the law of the Lord. And he shall be like a tree planted by the rivers of water, that bringeth forth his fruit in his season ; his leaf also shall not wither ; and whatsoever he doeth shall prosper.—PS. i, 2, 3.

THE wind that blows can never kill
  The tree God plants ;
It bloweth east ; it bloweth west ;
The tender leaves have little rest,
But any wind that blows is best.
  The tree God plants
Strikes deeper root, grows higher still,
Spreads wider boughs, for God's good-will
  Meets all its wants.

LILLIE E. BARR

IT is a fatal mistake to suppose that we cannot be holy except on the condition of a situation and circumstances in life such as shall suit ourselves. It is one of the first principles of holiness to leave our times and our places, our going out and our coming in, our wasted and our goodly heritage entirely with the Lord. Here, O Lord, hast Thou placed us, and we will glorify Thee here !

T. C. UPHAM

IT is not by change of circumstances, but by fitting our spirits to the circumstances in which God has placed us, that we can be reconciled to life and duty.

F. W. ROBERTSON

O Lord, I am oppressed ; undertake for me.—
ISA. xxxviii. 14.

BEING perplexed, I say,
  Lord, make it right !
Night is as day to Thee,
  Darkness is light.
I am afraid to touch
Things that involve so much ;—
    My trembling hand may shake,
    My skill-less hand may break :
    Thine can make no mistake.

                  ANNA WARNER

THE many troubles in your household will tend to your edification, if you strive to bear them all in gentleness, patience, and kindness. Keep this ever before you, and remember constantly that God's loving eyes are upon you amid all these little worries and vexations, watching whether you take them as He would desire. Offer up all such occasions to Him, and if sometimes you are put out, and give way to impatience, do not be discouraged, but make haste to regain your lost composure.

                  FRANCIS DE SALES

If any man will come after me, let him deny himself, and take up his cross daily, and follow me.
—LUKE ix. 23.

> THERE lies thy cross ; beneath it meekly bow ;
>   It fits thy stature now ;
> Who scornful pass it with averted eye,
>   'Twill crush them by and by.
>
> J. KEBLE

TO take up the cross of Christ is no great action done once for all ; it consists in the continual practice of small duties which are distasteful to us.

J. H. NEWMAN

ON one occasion an intimate friend of his was fretting somewhat at not being able to put a cross on the grave of a relation, because the rest of the family disliked it. ' Don't you see,' he said to her, ' that by giving up your own way, you will be virtually putting a cross on the grave ? You'll have it in its effect. The one is but a stone cross, the other is a true spiritual cross.'

LIFE OF JAMES HINTON

I WOULD have you, one by one, ask yourselves, Wherein do I take up the cross daily ?

E. B. PUSEY

EVERY morning, receive thine own special cross from the hands of thy heavenly Father.

L. SCUPOLI

Pure religion and undefiled before God and the Father is this, To visit the fatherless and widows in their affliction, and to keep himself unspotted from the world.—JAMES i. 27.

NOT to ease and aimless quiet
  Doth that inward answer tend,
But to works of love and duty
  As our being's end.

J. G. WHITTIER

IT is surprising how practical duty enriches the fancy and the heart, and action clears and deepens the affections. Indeed, no one can have a true idea of right, until he does it ; any genuine reverence for it, till he has done it often and with cost ; any peace ineffable in it, till he does it always and with alacrity. Does any one complain, that the best affections are transient visitors with him, and the heavenly spirit a stranger to his heart ? Oh, let him not go forth, on any strained wing of thought, in distant quest of them ; but rather stay at home, and set his house in the true order of conscience ; and of their own accord the divinest guests will enter.

J. MARTINEAU

Continue in prayer, and watch in the same with thanksgiving.—COL. iv. 2.

Watch ye, stand fast in the faith, quit you like men, be strong.—1 COR. xvi. 13.

WE kneel how weak, we rise how full of power.
Why therefore should we do ourselves this wrong,
Or others—that we are not always strong,
That we are ever overborne with care,
That we should ever weak or heartless be,
Anxious or troubled, when with us is prayer,
And joy and strength and courage are with Thee ?
       R. C. TRENCH

IT is impossible for us to make the duties of our lot minister to our sanctification without a habit of devout fellowship with God. This is the spring of all our life, and the strength of it. It is prayer, meditation, and converse with God, that refreshes, restores, and renews the temper of our minds, at all times, under all trials, after all conflicts with the world. By this contact with the world unseen we receive continual accesses of strength. As our day, so is our strength. Without this healing and refreshing of spirit, duties grow to be burdens, the events of life chafe our temper, employments lower the tone of our minds, and we become fretful, irritable, and impatient.

       H. E. MANNING

This is a faithful saying, and these things I will that thou affirm constantly, that they which have believed in God might be careful to maintain good works.—TITUS iii. 8.

FAITH's meanest deed more favour bears
  Where hearts and wills are weighed,
Than brightest transports, choicest prayers,
  Which bloom their hour and fade.

J. H. NEWMAN

ONE secret act of self-denial, one sacrifice of inclination to duty, is worth all the mere good thoughts, warm feelings, passionate prayers, in which idle people indulge themselves.

J. H. NEWMAN

IT is impossible for us to live in fellowship with God without holiness in all the duties of life. These things act and react on each other. Without a diligent and faithful obedience to the calls and claims of others upon us, our religious profession is simply dead. To disobey conscience when it points to relative duties irritates the whole temper, and quenches the first beginnings of devotion. We cannot go from strife, breaches, and angry words, to God. Selfishness, an imperious will, want of sympathy with the sufferings and sorrows of other men, neglect of charitable offices, suspicions, hard censures of those with whom our lot is cast, will miserably darken our own hearts, and hide the face of God from us.

H. E. MANNING

Lord, not my feet only, but also my hands and my head.—JOHN xiii. 9.

TAKE my hands, and let them move
At the impulse of Thy love.

Take my feet, and let them be
Swift and ' beautiful ' for Thee.

Take my intellect, and use
Every power as Thou shalt choose.

F. R. HAVERGAL

IF a man may attain thereunto, to be unto God as his hand is to a man, let him be therewith content, and not seek further. That is to say, let him strive and wrestle with all his might to obey God and His commandments so thoroughly at all times, and in all things, that in him there be nothing, spiritual or natural, which opposeth God ; and that his whole soul and body, with all their members, may stand ready and willing for that to which God hath created them ; as ready and willing as his hand is to a man, which is so wholly in his power, that in the twinkling of an eye, he moveth and turneth it whither he will. And when we find it otherwise with us, we must give our whole diligence to amend our state.

THEOLOGIA GERMANICA

WHEN the mind thinks nothing, when the soul covets nothing, and the body acteth nothing that is contrary to the will of God, this is perfect sanctification.

ANONYMOUS, in an old Bible, 1599

Thy kingdom come.—MATT. vi. 10.

> THE kingdom of established peace,
>   Which can no more remove ;
> The perfect powers of godliness,
>   The omnipotence of love.
>
> C. WESLEY

MY child, thou mayest not measure out thine offering unto me by what others have done or left undone ; but be it thine to seek out, even to the last moment of thine earthly life, what is the utmost height of pure devotion to which I have called *thine own self*. Remember that, if thou fall short of this, each time thou utterest in prayer the words, ' Hallowed by Thy name, Thy kingdom come ', thou dost most fearfully condemn thyself, for is it not a mockery to ask for that thou wilt not seek to promote even unto the uttermost, within the narrow compass of thine own heart and spirit ?

THE DIVINE MASTER

IF you do not wish for His kingdom, don't pray for it. But if you do, you must do more than pray for it ; you must work for it.

J. RUSKIN

She obeyed not the voice ; she received not correction ; she trusted not in the Lord ; she drew not near to her God.—ZEPH. iii. 2.

OH ! let us not this thought allow ;
The heat, the dust upon our brow,
Signs of the contest, we may wear ;
Yet thus we shall appear more fair
    In our Almighty Master's eye,
Than if in fear to lose the bloom,
Or ruffle the soul's lightest plume,
    We from the strife should fly.

R. C. TRENCH

IF God requires anything of us, we have no right to draw back under the pretext that we are liable to commit some fault in obeying. It is better to obey imperfectly than not at all. Perhaps you ought to rebuke some one dependent on you, but you are silent for fear of giving way to vehemence ;—or you avoid the society of certain persons, because they make you cross and impatient. How are you to attain self-control, if you shun all occasions of practising it ? Is not such self-choosing a greater fault than those into which you fear to fall ? Aim at a steady mind to do right, go wherever duty calls you, and believe firmly that God will forgive the faults that take our weakness by surprise in spite of our sincere desire to please Him.

JEAN NICOLAS GROU

It is good that a man should both hope and quietly wait for the salvation of the Lord.—LAM. iii. 26.

Truly my soul waiteth upon God : from Him cometh my salvation.—PS. lxii. 1.

NOT so in haste, my heart ;
Have faith in God, and wait
Although He linger long,
He never comes too late.

ANON.

THE true use to be made of all the imperfections of which you are conscious is neither to justify, nor to condemn them, but to present them before God, conforming your will to His, and remaining in peace ; for peace is the divine order, in whatever state we may be.

FÉNELON

YOU will find it less easy to uproot faults, than to choke them by gaining virtues. Do not think of your faults ; still less of others' faults ; in every person who comes near you look for what is good and strong : honour that ; rejoice in it ; and, as you can, try to imitate it ; and your faults will drop off like dead leaves, when their time comes.

J. RUSKIN

Call unto me, and I will answer thee, and show thee great and mighty things which thou knowest not.—JER. xxxiii. 3.

And I have also given thee that which thou hast not asked.—1 KINGS iii. 13.

> NO voice of prayer to Thee can rise,
> But swift as light Thy love replies ;
> Not always what we ask, indeed,
> But, O most Kind ! what most we need.
>
> H. M. KIMBALL

IF you have any trial which seems intolerable, pray,—pray that it be relieved or changed. There is no harm in that. We may pray for anything, not wrong in itself, with perfect freedom, if we do not pray selfishly. One disabled from duty by sickness may pray for health, that he may do his work ; or one hemmed in by internal impediments may pray for utterance, that he may serve better the truth and the right. Or, if we have a besetting sin, we may pray to be delivered from it, in order to serve God and man, and not be ourselves Satans to mislead and destroy. But the answer to the prayer may be, as it was to Paul, not the removal of the thorn, but, instead, a growing insight into its meaning and value. The voice of God in our soul may show us, as we look up to Him, that His strength is enough to enable us to bear it.

J. F. CLARKE

Can ye drink of the cup that I drink of? and be baptized with the baptism that I am baptized with?
—MARK X. 38.

> WHATE'ER my God ordains is right;
>   Though I the cup must drink
> That bitter seems to my faint heart,
>   I will not fear nor shrink.
>
> S. RODIGAST

THE worst part of martyrdom is not the last agonizing moment; it is the wearing, daily steadfastness. Men who can make up their minds to hold out against the torture of an hour have sunk under the weariness and the harass of small prolonged vexations. And there are many Christians who have the weight of some deep, incommunicable grief pressing, cold as ice, upon their hearts. To bear that cheerfully and manfully is to be a martyr. There is many a Christian bereaved and stricken in the best hopes of life. For such a one to say quietly, 'Father, not as I will, but as Thou wilt', is to be a martyr. There is many a Christian who feels the irksomeness of the duties of life, and feels his spirit revolting from them. To get up every morning with the firm resolve to find pleasure in those duties, and do them well, and finish the work which God has given us to do, that is to drink Christ's cup. The humblest occupation has in it materials of discipline for the highest heaven.

F. W. ROBERTSON

For the whole world before thee is as a little grain of the balance, yea, as a drop of the morning dew that falleth down upon the earth. But Thou has! mercy upon all. For Thou lovest all the things that are.—WISDOM OF SOLOMON xi. 22–4.

OH ! Source divine, and Life of all,
  The Fount of Being's fearful sea,
Thy depth would every heart appal,
  That saw not love supreme in Thee.

J. STERLING

HE showed a little thing, the quantity of a hazel-nut, lying in the palm of my hand, as meseemed, and it was as round as a ball. I looked thereon with the eye of my understanding, and thought, ' *What may this be ?* ' and it was answered generally thus, ' *It is all that is made.*' I marvelled how it might last ; for methought it might suddenly have fallen to naught for littleness. And I was answered in my understanding, ' *It lasteth, and ever shall : For God loveth it. And so hath all thing being by the Love of God.*' In this little thing I saw three properties. The first is, that God made it. The second is, that God loveth it. The third is, that God keepeth it. For this is the cause which we be not all in ease of heart and soul : for we seek here rest in this thing which is so little, where no rest is in : and we know not our God that is all Mighty, all Wise, and all Good, for he is very rest. God wills to be known, and it pleaseth Him that we rest us in Him. For all that is beneath Him, sufficeth not us. MOTHER JULIANA, 1373

Whosoever will be great among you, shall be your minister ; and whosoever of you will be the chiefest, shall be servant of all. For even the Son of man came not to be ministered unto, but to minister.—MARK X. 43–5.

A CHILD'S kiss
Set on thy sighing lips, shall make thee glad ;
A poor man served by thee, shall make thee rich ;
A sick man helped by thee, shall make thee strong,
Thou shalt be served thyself by every sense
Of service which thou renderest.

E. B. BROWNING

LET every man lovingly cast all his thoughts and cares, and his sins too, as it were, on the Will of God. Morevoer, if a man, while busy in this lofty inward work, were called by some duty in the Providence of God to cease therefrom, and cook a broth for some sick person, or any other such service, he should do so willingly and with great joy. If I had to forsake such work, and go out to preach or aught else, I should go cheerfully, believing not only that God would be with me, but that he would vouchsafe me it may be even greater grace and blessing in that external work undertaken out of true love in the service of my neighbour, than I should perhaps receive in my season of loftiest contemplation.

JOHN TAULER

All the paths of the Lord are mercy and truth unto such as keep His covenant and His testimonies.
—PS. XXV. 10

SPEAK, Lord, for Thy servant heareth,
  Speak peace to my anxious soul,
And help me to feel that all my ways
  Are under Thy wise control ;

That He who cares for the lily,
  And heeds the sparrows' fall,
Shall tenderly lead His loving child ;
  For He made and loveth all.

ANON

IT is not by seeking more fertile regions where toil is lighter—happier circumstances free from difficult complications and troublesome people—but by bringing the high courage of a devout soul, clear in principle and aim, to bear upon what is given to us, that we brighten our inward light, lead something of a true life, and introduce the kingdom of heaven into the midst of our earthly day. If we cannot work out the will of God where God has placed us, then why has He placed us there ?

J. H. THOM

Pray for us unto the Lord thy God . . . that the Lord thy God may show us the way wherein we may walk, and the thing that we may do.—JER. xlii. 2, 3.

That which I see not, teach Thou me.—JOB xxxiv. 32.

O FATHER, hear!
The way is dark, and I would fain discern
What steps to take, into which path to turn;
   Oh! make it clear.

CHRISTIAN INTELLIGENCER

'WE can't choose happiness either for ourselves or for another; we can't tell where that will lie. We can only choose whether we will indulge ourselves in the present moment, or whether we will renounce that, for the sake of obeying the Divine voice within us,—for the sake of being true to all the motives that sanctify our lives. I know this belief is hard; it has slipped away from me again and again; but I have felt that if I let it go forever, I should have no light through the darkness of this life.'

GEORGE ELIOT

THERE was a care on my mind so to pass my time, that nothing might hinder me from the most steady attention to the voice of the true Shepherd.

JOHN WOOLMAN

Thou shalt hide them in the secret of Thy presence from the pride of man ; Thou shalt keep them secretly in a pavilion from the strife of tongues.
—PS. xxxi. 20.

THE praying spirit breathe,
　The watching power impart,
From all entanglements beneath
　Call off my anxious heart.
My feeble mind sustain,
　By worldly thoughts oppressed ;
Appear, and bid me turn again
　To my eternal rest.

C. WESLEY

AS soon as we are with God in faith and in love, we are in prayer.

FÉNELON

IF you could once make up your mind in the fear of God never to undertake more work of any sort than you can carry on calmly, quietly, without hurry or flurry, and the instant you feel yourself growing nervous and like one out of breath, would stop and take breath, you would find this simple common-sense rule doing for you what no prayers or tears could ever accomplish.

ELIZABETH PRENTISS

*How excellent is Thy loving-kindness, O God !
therefore the children of men put their trust under
the shadow of Thy wings.*—PS. xxxvi. 7.

*The eternal God is thy refuge, and underneath
are the everlasting arms.*—DEUT. xxxiii. 27.

> WITHIN Thy circling arms we lie,
>   O God ! in Thy infinity :
> Our souls in quiet shall abide,
>   Beset with love on every side.
>
> ANON.

'THE Everlasting Arms.' I think of that
whenever rest is sweet. How the whole
earth and the strength of it, that is almightiness,
is beneath every tired creature to give it rest ;
holding us, always ! No thought of God is
closer than that. No human tenderness of
patience is greater than that which gathers in
its arms a little child, and holds it, heedless of
weariness. And He fills the great earth, and
all upon it, with this unseen force of His love,
that never forgets or exhausts itself, so that
everywhere we may lie down in His bosom, and
be comforted.

A. D. T. WHITNEY

The word is very nigh unto thee, in thy mouth, and in thy heart, that thou mayest do it.—DEUT. XXX. 14.

BUT, above all, the victory is most sure
For him, who, seeking faith by virtue, strives
To yield entire obedience to the Law
Of Conscience ; Conscience reverenced and obeyed,
As God's most intimate presence in the soul,
And His most perfect image in the world.

W. WORDSWORTH

WHAT we call Conscience is the voice of Divine love in the deep of our being, desiring union with our will ; and which, by attracting the affections inward, invites them to enter into the harmonious contentment, and ' fulness of joy ' which attends the being joined by ' one spirit to the Lord '.

J. P. GREAVES

I REJOICE, that God has bestowed upon you a relish and inclination for the inner life. To be called to this precious and lofty life is a great and undeserved grace of God, to which we ought to respond with great faithfulness. God invites us to His fellowship of love, and wishes to prepare our spirit to be His own abode and temple.

GERHARD TERSTEEGEN

Show me Thy ways, O Lord ; teach me Thy paths.—PS. XXV. 4.

> WHEN we cannot see our way,
> Let us trust and still obey :
> He who bids us forward go,
> Cannot fail the way to show.
> Though the sea be deep and wide,
> Though a passage seem denied ;
> Fearless let us still proceed,
> Since the Lord vouchsafes to lead.
>
> ANON.

THAT which is often asked of God, is not so much His will and way, as His approval of our way.

S. F. SMILEY

THERE is nothing like the first glance we get at duty, before there has been any special pleading of our affections or inclinations. Duty is never uncertain at first. It is only after we have got involved in the mazes and sophistries of wishing that things were otherwise than they are, that it seems indistinct. Considering a duty is often only explaining it away. Deliberation is often only dishonesty. God's guidance is plain, when we are true.

F. W. ROBERTSON

When I awake, I am still with Thee.—PS. cxxxix. 18.

> LET the glow of love destroy
> Cold obedience faintly given ;
> Wake our hearts to strength and joy
> With the flushing eastern heaven.
> Let us truly rise, ere yet
> Life be set.
>
> ROSENROTH

WITH his first waking consciousness, he can set himself to take a serious, manly view of the day before him. He ought to know pretty well on what lines his difficulty is likely to come, whether in being irritable, or domineering, or sharp in his bargains, or self-absorbed, or whatever it be ; and now, in this quiet hour, he can take a good, full look at his enemy, and make up his mind to beat him. It is a good time, too, for giving his thoughts a range quite beyond himself,—beyond even his own moral struggles,—a good time, there in the stillness, for going into the realm of other lives. His wife,—what needs has she for help, for sympathy, that he can meet ? His children,—how can he make the day sweeter to them ? This acquaintance, who is having a hard time ; this friend, who dropped a word to you yesterday that you hardly noticed in your hurry, but that comes up to you now, revealing in him some finer trait, some deeper hunger, than you had guessed before,—now you can think these things over. So you get your day somewhat into right perspective and proportion before you begin it.

G. S. MERRIAM

Ye shall rejoice in all that ye put your hand unto, ye and your households, wherein the Lord thy God hath blessed thee.—DEUT. xii. 7.

SWEET is the smile of home ; the mutual look
　When hearts are of each other sure ;
Sweet all the joys that crowd the household nook,
　The haunts of all affections pure.

J. KEBLE

IS there any tie which absence has loosened, or which the wear and tear of every-day intercourse, little uncongenialities, unconfessed misunderstandings, have fretted into the heart, until it bears something of the nature of a fetter ? Any cup at our home-table whose sweetness we have not fully tasted, although it might yet make of our daily bread a continual feast ? Let us reckon up these treasures while they are still ours, in thankfulness to God.

ELIZABETH CHARLES

WE ought daily or weekly to dedicate a little time to the reckoning up of the virtues of our belongings,—wife, children, friends,—and contemplating them then in a beautiful collection. And we should do so now, that we may not pardon and love in vain and too late, after the beloved one has been taken away from us to a better world.

JEAN PAUL RICHTER

Yea, though I walk through the valley of the shadow of death, I will fear no evil ; for Thou art with me ; Thy rod and Thy staff, they comfort me.—PS. xxiii. 4.

O WILL, that willest good alone,
  Lead Thou the way, Thou guidest best ;
A silent child, I follow on,
  And trusting lean upon Thy breast.
And if in gloom I see Thee not,
  I lean upon Thy love unknown ;
In me Thy blessed will is wrought,
  If I will nothing of my own.

GERHARD TERSTEEGEN

THE devout soul is always safe in every state, if it makes everything an occasion either of rising up, or falling down into the hands of God, and exercising faith, and trust, and resignation to Him. The pious soul, that eyes only God, that means nothing but being His alone, can have no stop put to its progress ; light and darkness equally assist him : in the light he looks up to God, in the darkness he lays hold on God, and so they both do him the same good.

WM. LAW

When I sit in darkness, the Lord shall be a light unto me.—MICAH vii. 8.

There be many that say, Who will show us any good? Lord, lift Thou up the light of Thy countenance upon us.—PS. iv. 6.

HOW oft a gleam of glory sent
  Straight through the deepest, darkest night,
  Has filled the soul with heavenly light,
With holy peace and sweet content.

ANON.

SUPPOSE you are bewildered and know not what is right nor what is true. Can you not cease to regard whether you do or not, whether you be bewildered, whether you be happy? Cannot you utterly and perfectly love, and rejoice to be in the dark, and gloom-beset, because that very thing is the fact of God's Infinite Being as it is to you? Cannot you take this trial also into your own heart, and be ignorant, not because you are obliged, but because that being God's will, it is yours also? Do you not see that a person who truly *loves* is one with the Infinite Being—cannot be uncomfortable or unhappy? It is that which IS that he wills and desires and holds best of all to be. To know God is utterly to sacrifice self.

JAMES HINTON

My little children, let us not love in word, neither in tongue ; but in deed, and in truth.—I JOHN iii. 18.

But be ye doers of the word, and not hearers only. deceiving your own selves.—JAMES i. 22.

THRICE blest whose lives are faithful prayers,
  Whose loves in higher love endure ;
  What souls possess themselves so pure,
Or is there blessedness like theirs ?

                 A. TENNYSON

LET every creature have your love. Love, with its fruits of meekness, patience, and humility, is all that we can wish for to ourselves, and our fellow-creatures ; for this is to live in God, united to Him, both for time and eternity. To desire to communicate good to every creature, in the degree we can, and it is capable of receiving from us, is a divine temper ; for thus God stands unchangeably disposed towards the whole creation.

                 WM. LAW

WHAT shall be our reward for loving our neighbour *as* ourselves in this life ? That, when we become angels, we shall be enabled to love him *better* than ourselves.

               E. SWEDENBORG

Blessed are the pure in heart ; for they shall see God.—MATT. v. 8.

Follow peace with all men, and holiness, without which no man shall see the Lord.—HEB. xii. 14.

SINCE Thou Thyself dost still display
  Unto the pure in heart,
Oh, make us children of the day
  To know Thee as Thou art.
For Thou art light and life and love ;
  And Thy redeemed below
May see Thee as Thy saints above,
  And know Thee as they know.

J. MONTGOMERY

DOUBT, gloom, impatience, have been expelled ; joy has taken their place, the hope of heaven and the harmony of a pure heart, the triumph of self-mastery, sober thoughts, and a contented mind. How can charity towards all men fail to follow, being the mere affectionateness of innocence and peace ? Thus the Spirit of God creates in us the simplicity and warmth of heart which children have, nay, rather the perfections of His heavenly hosts, high and low being joined together in His mysterious work ; for what are implicit trust, ardent love, abiding purity, but the mind both of little children and of the adoring Seraphim !

J. H. NEWMAN

Lord, who shall abide in Thy tabernacle? Who shall dwell in Thy holy hill? He that walketh uprightly, and worketh righteousness, and speaketh the truth in his heart.—PS. XV. 1, 2.

HOW happy is he born or taught,
   That serveth not another's will,
Whose armour is his honest thought,
   And simple truth his utmost skill.

                 H. WOTTON

IF thou workest at that which is before thee, following right reason, seriously, vigorously, calmly, without allowing anything else to distract thee, but keeping thy divine part pure as if thou shouldest be bound to give it back immediately,—if thou holdest to this, expecting nothing, fearing nothing, but satisfied with thy present activity according to nature, and with heroic truth in every word and sound which thou utterest, thou wilt live happy. And there is no man who is able to prevent this.

                 MARCUS ANTONINUS

Be strong, all ye people of the land, saith the Lord, and work ; for I am with you, saith the Lord of hosts.—HAGGAI ii. 4.

YET the world is Thy field, Thy garden ;
  On earth art Thou still at home.
When Thou bendest hither Thy hallowing eye,
My narrow work-room seems vast and high,
Its dingy ceiling a rainbow-dome,
Stand ever thus at my wide-swung door,
  And toil will be toil no more.

L. LARCOM

THE situation that has not its duty, its ideal, was never yet occupied by man. Yes, here, in this poor, miserable, hampered, despicable Actual, wherein thou even now standest, here or nowhere is thy Ideal : work it out therefrom ; and working, believe, live, be free. Fool ! the Ideal is in thyself, the impediment too is in thyself : thy condition is but the stuff thou art to shape that same Ideal out of : what matters whether such stuff be of this sort or that, so the form thou givest it be heroic, be poetic. O thou that pinest in the imprisonment of the Actual, and criest bitterly to the gods for a kingdom wherein to rule and create, know this of a truth : the thing thou seekest is already with thee, ' here or nowhere ', couldst thou only see !

T. CARLYLE

I am purposed that my mouth shall not transgress.—PS. xvii. 3.

In the multitude of words there wanteth not sin : but he that refraineth his lips is wise.—PROV. X. 19.

PRUNE thou thy words ; the thoughts control
    That o'er thee swell and throng ;
They will condense within thy soul,
    And change to purpose strong.

J. H. NEWMAN

FEW men suspect how much mere talk fritters away spiritual energy,—that which should be spent in action, spends itself in words. Hence he who restrains that love of talk, lays up a fund of spiritual strength.

F. W. ROBERTSON

DO not flatter yourself that your thoughts are under due control, your desires properly regulated, or your dispositions subject as they should be to Christian pinciple, if your intercourse with others consists mainly of frivolous gossip, impertinent anecdotes, speculations on the character and affairs of your neighbours, the repetition of former conversations, or a discussion of the current petty scandal of society ; much less, if you allow yourself in careless exaggeration on all these points, and that grievous inattention to exact truth, which is apt to attend the statements of those whose conversation is made up of these materials.

H. WARE, JR.

Judge not, that ye be not judged.—MATT. vii. 1.

Why beholdest thou the mote that is in thy brother's eye ; but perceivest not the beam that is in thine own eye ?—LUKE vi. 41.

JUDGE not ; the workings of his brain
  And of his heart thou canst not see ;
What looks to thy dim eyes a stain,
  In God's pure light may only be
A scar, brought from some well-won field,
Where thou wouldst only faint and yield.

ADELAIDE A. PROCTER

WHEN you behold an aspect for whose constant gloom and frown you cannot account, whose unvarying cloud exasperates you by its apparent causelessness, be sure that there is a canker somewhere, and a canker not the less deeply corroding because concealed.

CHARLOTTE BRONTË

WHILE we are coldly discussing a man's career, sneering at his mistakes, blaming his rashness, and labelling his opinions—' Evangelical and narrow ', or ' Latitudinarian and Pantheistic ', or ' Anglican and supercilious '—that man, in his solitude, is perhaps shedding hot tears because his sacrifice is a hard one, because strength and patience are failing him to speak the difficult word, and do the difficult deed.

GEORGE ELIOT

Be strong, and of a good courage ; be not afraid, neither be thou dismayed : for the Lord thy God is with thee whithersoever thou goest.—JOSH. i. 9.

BY Thine unerring Spirit led,
  We shall not in the desert stray ;
We shall not full direction need,
  Nor miss our providential way ;
As far from danger as from fear,
While love, almighty love, is near.

CHARLES WESLEY

WATCH your way then, as a cautious traveller ; and don't be gazing at that mountain or river in the distance, and saying, ' How shall I ever get over them ? ' but keep to the present *little inch* that is before you, and accomplish *that* in the little moment that belongs to it. The mountain and the river can only be passed in the same way ; and, when you come to them, you will come to the light and strength that belong to them.

M. A. KELTY

LET not future things disturb thee, for thou wilt come to them, if it shall be necessary, having with thee the same reason which thou now usest for present things.

MARCUS ANTONINUS

Say to them that are of a fearful heart, Be strong, fear not.—ISA. XXXV. 4.

WHY shouldst thou fill to-day with sorrow
    About to-morrow,
       My heart ?
One watches all with care most true,
Doubt not that He will give thee too
       Thy part.

PAUL FLEMMING

THE crosses which we make for ourselves by a restless anxiety as to the future, are not crosses which come from God. We show want of faith in Him by our false wisdom, wishing to forestall His arrangements, and struggling to supplement His Providence by our own providence. The future is not yet ours ; perhaps it never will be. If it comes, it may come wholly different from what we have foreseen. Let us shut our eyes, then, to that which God hides from us, and keeps in reserve in the treasures of His deep counsels. Let us worship without seeing ; let us be silent ; let us abide in peace.

FÉNELON

I had fainted, unless I had believed to see the goodness of the Lord in the land of the living.—PS. xxvii. 13.

I will surely do thee good.—GEN. xxxii. 12.

THOU know'st not what is good for thee,
 But God doth know,—
Let Him thy strong reliance be,
 And rest thee so.

C. F. GELLERT

LET us be very careful of thinking, on the one hand, that we have no work assigned us to do, or, on the other hand, that what we have assigned to us is not the right thing for us. If ever we can say in our hearts to God, in reference to any daily duty, ' This is not my place ; I would choose something dearer ; I am capable of something higher ' ; we are guilty not only of rebellion, but of blasphemy. It is equivalent to saying, not only, ' My heart revolts against Thy commands ', but ' Thy commands are unwise ; Thine Almighty guidance is unskilful ; Thine omniscient eye has mistaken the capacities of Thy creature ; Thine infinite love is indifferent to the welfare of Thy child.'

ELIZABETH CHARLES

*And because ye are sons, God hath sent the spirit
of His Son into your hearts, crying, Abba, Father.*
—GAL. iv. 6.

O LORD, forgive my sin,
And deign to put within
A calm, obedient heart, a patient mind ;
That I may murmur not,
Though bitter seem my lot ;
For hearts unthankful can no blessing find.

RUTILIUS, 1604

RESIGNATION to the Divine Will signi-
fies a cheerful approbation and thankful
acceptance of everything that comes from God.
It is not enough patiently to submit, but we
must thankfully receive and fully approve of
everything that, by the order of God's provi-
dence, happens to us. For there is no reason
why we should be patient, but what is as good
and as strong a reason why we should be
thankful. Whenever, therefore, you find your-
self disposed to uneasiness or murmuring at
any thing that is the effect of God's providence
over you, you must look upon yourself as
denying either the wisdom or goodness of God.

WM. LAW

Ye shall not go out with haste, for the Lord will go before you ; and the God of Israel will be your rereward.—ISA. lii. 12.

He that believeth shall not make haste.—ISA. xxviii. 16.

> HOLY Spirit, Peace divine !
> Still this restless heart of mine ;
> Speak to calm this tossing sea,
> Stayed in Thy tranquillity.
>
> S. LONGFELLOW

IN whatever you are called upon to do, endeavour to maintain a calm, collected, and prayerful state of mind. Self-recollection is of great importance. ' It is good for a man to quietly wait for the salvation of the Lord.' He who is in what may be called a spiritual hurry, or rather who runs without having evidence of being spiritually sent, makes haste to no purpose.   T. C. UPHAM

THERE is great fret and worry in always running after work ; it is not good intellectually or spiritually.   ANNIE KEARY

WHENEVER we are outwardly excited we should cease to act ; but whenever we have a message from the spirit within, we should execute it with calmness. A fine day may excite one to act, but it is much better that we act from the calm spirit in any day, be the outward what it may.   J. P. GREAVES

As for me and my house, we will serve the Lord.
JOSH. xxiv. 15.

O HAPPY house ! and happy servitude !
  Where all alike one Master own ;
Where daily duty, in Thy strength pursued,
  Is never hard or toilsome known ;
Where each one serves Thee, meek and lowly,
  Whatever Thine appointment be,
Till common tasks seem great and holy,
  When they are done as unto Thee,

C. J. P. SPITTA

AT Dudson there was no rushing after any-
thing, either worldly or intellectual. It was
a home of constant activity, issuing from, and
retiring to, a centre of deep repose. There was
an earnest application of excellent sense to the
daily duties of life, to the minutest courtesy and
kindness, as well as to the real interests of
others. Everything great and everything little
seemed done in the same spirit, and with the
same degree of fidelity, because it was the will
of God ; and that which could not be traced to
His will was not undertaken at all. . . . Noth-
ing at Dudson was esteemed too little to be
cared for, and nothing too great to be under-
taken at the command of God ; and for this
they daily exercised their mental and bodily
powers on the things around them ; knowing
that our Lord thoroughly furnishes each of
His soldiers for his work, and places before
each the task he has to do.

M. A SCHIMMELPENNINCK

Now the Lord of peace Himself give you peace always, by all means.—2 THESS. iii. 16.

The Lord will give strength unto His people ; the Lord will bless His people with peace.—PS. xxix. 11.

IN the heart's depths a peace serene and holy
   Abides, and when pain seems to have its will,
Or we despair,—oh, may that peace rise slowly,
   Stronger than agony, and we be still.

S. JOHNSON

BUT if a man ought and is willing to lie still under God's hand, he must and ought also to lie still under all things, whether they come from God, himself, or the creatures, nothing excepted. And he who would be obedient, resigned, and submissive to God, must and ought to be also resigned, obedient, and submissive to all things, in a spirit of yielding, and not of resistance ; and take them in silence, resting on the hidden foundations of his soul, and having a secret inward patience, that enableth him to take all chances or crosses willingly ; and, whatever befalleth, neither to call for nor desire any redress, or deliverance, or resistance, or revenge, but always in a loving, sincere humility to cry, ' Father, forgive them, for they know not what they do ! '

THEOLOGIA GERMANICA

And when the people complained, it displeased the Lord.—NUM. xi. 1.

> WHEN thou hast thanked thy God
> For every blessing sent,
> What time will then remain
> For murmurs or lament ?
>
> R. C. TRENCH

LET him, with a cheerful and thankful spirit, yield himself up to suffer whatever God shall appoint unto him, and to fulfil, according to his power, by the grace of God, all His holy will to the utmost that he can discern it, and never complain of his distresses but to God alone with entire and humble resignation, praying that he may be strong to endure all his sufferings according to the will of God.

JOHN TAULER

HE who complains, or thinks he has a right to complain, because he is called in God's Providence to suffer, has something within him which needs to be taken away. A soul whose will is lost in God's will, can never do this. Sorrow may exist ; but complaint never.

CATHERINE ADORNA

Singing and making melody in your heart to the Lord.—EPH. V. 19.

Sanctify the Lord God in your hearts.—I PETER iii. 15.

THERE are in this loud stunning tide
 Of human care and crime,
With whom the melodies abide
 Of th' everlasting chime ;
Who carry music in their heart
Through dusky lane and wrangling mart,
Plying their daily task with busier feet,
Because their secret souls a holy strain repeat.

J. KEBLE

STRIVE to carry thyself with a total resignation to the Divine Will, that God may do with thee and all thine according to His heavenly pleasure, relying on Him as on a kind and loving Father. Never recall that intention, and though thou beest taken up about the affairs of the condition wherein God hath placed thee, yet thou wilt still be in prayer, in the presence of God, and in perpetual acts of resignation. 'A just man leaves not off to pray unless he leaves off to be just.' He always prays who always does well. The good desire is prayer, and if the desire be continued so also is the prayer.

M. MOLINOS

We desire that every one of you do show the same diligence to the full assurance of hope unto the end.—HEB. vi. 11.

The Lord is faithful, who shall stablish you, and keep you from evil.—2 THESS. iii. 3.

> LONG though my task may be,
>   Cometh the end.
> God 'tis that helpeth me,
> His is the work, and He
>   New strength will lend.

ANON.

SET yourself steadfastly to those duties which have the least attractive exterior; it matters not whether God's holy will be fulfilled in great or small matters. Be patient with yourself and your own failings; never be in a hurry, and do not yield to longings after that which is impossible to you. My dear sister, go on steadily and quietly; if our dear Lord means you to run, He will ' strengthen your heart '.

FRANCIS DE SALES

ALWAYS begin by doing that which costs me most, unless the easier duty is a pressing one. Examine, classify, and determine at night the work of the morrow; arrange things in the order of their importance, and act accordingly. Dread, above all things, bitterness and irritation. Never say, or indirectly recall anything to my advantage.

MADAME SWETCHINE

He that sinneth against Me wrongeth his own soul : all they that hate Me love death.—PROV. viii. 36.

But now being made free from sin, and become servants to God, ye have your fruit unto holiness, and the end everlasting life. For the wages of sin is death ; but the gift of God is eternal life through Jesus Christ our Lord.—ROM. vi. 22, 23.

> O SOVEREIGN Love, to Thee I cry !
> Give me Thyself, or else I die !
> Save me from death ; from hell set free !
> Death, hell, are but the want of Thee.
> Quickened by Thy imparted flame,
> Saved when possessed of Thee, I am :
> My life, my only heaven Thou art ;
> O might I feel Thee in my heart !
>
> C. WESLEY

SIN itself is hell, and death, and misery to the soul, as being a departure from goodness and holiness itself ; I mean from God, in conjunction with whom the happiness, and blessedness, and heaven of a soul doth consist. Avoid it, therefore, as you would avoid being miserable.

SAMUEL SHAW

' I COULDN'T live in peace if I put the shadow of a wilful sin between myself and God.'

GEORGE ELIOT

UNHOLY tempers are always unhappy tempers.

JOHN WESLEY

Mine iniquities have taken hold upon me, so that I am not able to look up ; therefore my heart faileth me. Be pleased, O Lord, to deliver me ; O Lord, make haste to help me.—PS. xl. 12, 13.

Sin shall not have dominion over you.—ROM. vi. 14.

O THOU, to whose all-searching sight
The darkness shincth as the light !
Search, prove my heart ; it pants for Thee :
Oh, burst these bonds, and set it free !

G. TERSTEEGEN

YES, this sin which has sent me weary-hearted to bed and desperate in heart to morning work, that has made my plans miscarry until I am a coward, that cuts me off from prayer, that robs the sky of blueness and the earth of spring-time, and the air of freshness, and human faces of friendliness,—this blasting sin which perhaps has made my bed in hell for me so long,—*this can be conquered.* I do not say annihilated, but, better than that, *conquered,* captured and transfigured into a *friend :* so that I at last shall say, ' My temptation has become my strength ! for to the very fight with it I owe my force.'

W. C. GANNETT

I am not worthy of the least of all the mercies, and of all the truth, which Thou hast showed unto Thy servant.—GEN. xxxii. 10.

SOME murmur if their sky is clear,
　And wholly bright to view,
If one small speck of dark appear
　In their great heaven of blue :
And some with thankful love are filled,
　If but one streak of light,
One ray of God's good mercy, gild
　The darkness of their night.

R. C. TRENCH

HABITUAL sufferers are precisely those who least frequently doubt the Divine benevolence, and whose faith and love rise to the serenest cheerfulness. Possessed by no idea of a prescriptive right to be happy, their blessings are not benumbed by anticipation, but come to them fresh and brilliant as the first day's morning and evening light to the dwellers in Paradise. With the happy it is their constant peace that seems to come by nature, and to be blunted by its commonness,—and their griefs to come from God, sharpened by their sacred origin ; with the sufferer, it is his pain that appears to be a thing of course, and to require no explanation, while his relief is reverently welcomed as a divine interposition, and, as a breath of Heaven, caresses the heart into melodies of praise.

J. MARTINEAU

Hath the Lord as great delight in burnt-offerings and sacrifices, as in obeying the voice of the Lord? Behold, to obey is better than sacrifice.—1 SAM. XV. 22.

Fear ye not, stand still, and see the salvation of the Lord, which He will show to you to-day.—EXOD. XIV. 13.

> THE folded hands seem idle :
> If folded at His word,
> 'Tis a holy service, trust me,
> In obedience to the Lord.

> ANNA SHIPTON

IT is not the multitude of hard duties, it is not constraint and contention that advance us in our Christian course. On the contrary, it is the yielding of our wills without restriction and without choice, to tread cheerfully every day in the path in which Providence leads us, to seek nothing, to be discouraged by nothing, to see our duty in the present moment, to trust all else without reserve to the will and power of God.

FÉNELON

GODLINESS is the devotion of the soul to God, as to a living person whose will is to be its law, whose love is to be its life. It is the habit of living before the face of God, and not the simply doing certain things.

J. B. BROWN

*Except your righteousness shall exceed the right-
eousness of the scribes and Pharisees, ye shall in
no case enter into the kingdom of heaven.*—MATT.
V. 20.

> THE freedom from all wilful sin,
> The Christian's daily task,—
> Oh these are graces far below
> What longing love would ask !
> Dole not thy duties out to God.
>
> F. W. FABER

YOU perhaps will say that all people fall
short of the perfection of the Gospel, and
therefore you are content with your failings.
But this is saying nothing to the purpose : for
the question is not whether Gospel perfection
can be fully attained, but whether you come
as near it as a sincere intention and careful
diligence can carry you. Whether you are not
in a much lower state than you might be if you
sincerely intended and carefully laboured to
advance yourself in all Christian virtues.

WM. LAW

WE know not exactly how low the least degree
of obedience is, which will bring a man to
heaven ; but this we are quite sure of, that he
who aims no higher will be sure to fall short
even of that, and that he who goes farthest
beyond it will be most blessed.

JOHN KEBLE

Thus saith the Lord, thy Redeemer, the Holy One of Israel ; I am the Lord thy God which teacheth thee to profit, which leadeth thee by the way thou shouldest go.—ISA. xlviii. 17.

I SEEK Thy aid, I ask direction,
  Teach me to do what pleaseth Thee ;
I can bear toil, endure affliction,
  Only Thy leadings let me see.

ANON.

OF all paths a man could strike into, there *is*, at any given moment, a *best path* for every man ; a thing which, here and now, it were of all things *wisest* for him to do ; which could he but be led or driven to do, he were then doing ' like a man ', as we phrase it. His success, in such case, were complete, his felicity a maximum. This path, to find this path, and walk in it, is the one thing needful for him.

T. CARLYLE

EVERY man has his own vocation. There is one direction in which all space is open to him. He has faculties silently inviting him thither to endless exertion. He is like a ship in a river ; he runs against obstructions on every side but one ; on that side all obstruction is taken away, and he sweeps serenely over a deepening channel into an infinite sea.

R. W. EMERSON

Be not overcome of evil, but overcome evil with good.—ROM. xii. 21.

> COME, in this accepted hour ;
>   Bring Thy heavenly kingdom in ;
> Fill us with Thy glorious power,
>   Rooting out the seeds of sin.
>
> C. WESLEY

IF we wish to overcome evil, we must overcome it by good. There are doubtless many ways of overcoming the evil in our own hearts, but the simplest, easiest, most universal, is to overcome it by active occupation in some good word or work. The best antidote against evil of all kinds, against the evil thoughts which haunt the soul, against the needless perplexities which distract the conscience, is to keep hold of the good we have. Impure thoughts will not stand against pure words, and prayers, and deeds. Little doubts will not avail against great certainties. Fix your affections on things above, and then you will be less and less troubled by the cares, the temptations, the troubles of things on earth.

A. P. STANLEY

I am the Almighty God ; walk before me, and be thou perfect.—GEN. xvii. 1.

Consecrate yourselves to-day to the Lord.—EXOD. xxxii. 29.

TAKE my life, and let it be
Consecrated, Lord, to Thee.

Take my moments and my days ;
Let them flow in ceaseless praise.

F. R. HAVERGAL

I HAVE noticed that wherever there has been a faithful following of the Lord in a consecrated soul, several things have inevitably followed, sooner or later. Meekness and quietness of spirit become in time the characteristics of the daily life. A submissive acceptance of the will of God as it comes in the hourly events of each day ; pliability in the hands of God to do or to suffer all the good pleasure of his will ; sweetness under provocation ; calmness in the midst of turmoil and bustle ; yieldingness to the wishes of others, and an insensibility to slights and affronts ; absence of worry or anxiety ; deliverance from care and fear ;—all these, and many similar graces, are invariably found to be the natural outward development of that inward life which is hid with Christ in God.

H. W. S.

Father, if Thou be willing, remove this cup from me ; nevertheless, not my will, but Thine, be done.—LUKE xxii. 42.

JUST as Thou wilt is just what I would will ;
Give me but this, the heart to be content,
And, if my wish is thwarted, to lie still,
Waiting till puzzle and till pain are spent,
And the sweet thing made plain which the Lord
    meant.

                        SUSAN COOLIDGE

LET your will be one with His will, and be glad to be disposed of by Him. He will order all things for you. What can cross your will, when it is one with His will, on which all creation hangs, round which all things revolve ? Keep your hearts clear of evil thoughts ; for as evil choices estrange the will from His will, so evil thoughts cloud the soul, and hide Him from us. Whatever sets us in opposition to Him makes our will an intolerable torment. So long as we will one thing and He another, we go on piercing ourselves through and through with a perpetual wound ; and His will advances moving on in sanctity and majesty, crushing ours into the dust.

                        H. E. MANNING

Teach me to do Thy will ; for Thou art my God : Thy spirit is good ; lead me into the land of uprightness.—PS. cxliii. 10.

THE battle of our life is won,
And heaven begun,
When we can say, 'Thy will be done!'
But, Lord, until
These restless hearts in Thy deep love are still,
We pray Thee, 'Teach us how to do Thy will'!
LUCY LARCOM

'YOU are seeking your own will, my daughter. You are seeking some good other than the law you are bound to obey. But how will you find good ? It is not a thing of choice ; it is a river that flows from the foot of the Invisible Throne, and flows by the path of obedience. I say again, man cannot choose his duties. You may choose to forsake your duties, and choose not to have the sorrow they bring. But you will go forth, and what will you find, my daughter ? Sorrow without duty —bitter herbs, and no bread with them.'

GEORGE ELIOT

HOWEVER dark and profitless, however painful and weary, existence may have become ; however any man, like Elijah, may be tempted to cast himself down beneath the juniper-tree, and say, 'It is enough, O Lord!'—life is not done, and our Christian character is not won, so long as God has anything left for us to suffer, or anything left for us to do.

F. W. ROBERTSON

The Lord is my strength, and my shield ; my heart trusted in Him, and I am helped : therefore my heart greatly rejoiceth ; and with my song will I praise Him.—PS. xxviii. 7.

WELL may Thy happy children cease
From restless wishes, prone to sin,
And, in Thy own exceeding peace,
Yield to Thy daily discipline.

A. L. WARING

TALK of hair-cloth shirts, and scourgings, and sleeping on ashes, as means of saint-ship ! there is no need of them in our country. Let a woman once look at her domestic trials as her hair-cloth, her ashes, her scourges,—accept them,—rejoice in them,—smile and be quiet, silent, patient, and loving under them,—and the convent can teach her no more ; she is a victorious saint.

H. B. STOWE

PERHAPS it is a greater energy of Divine Provi-dence, which keeps the Christian from day to day, from year to year—praying, hoping, run-ning, believing—against all hindrances—which maintains him as a *living* martyr, than that which bears him up for an hour in sacrificing himself at the stake.

R. CECIL

For I am persuaded that neither death, nor life, nor angels, nor principalities, 'nor powers, nor things present, nor things to come, nor height, nor depth, nor any other creature, shall be able to separate us from the love of God, which is in Christ Jesus our Lord.—ROM. viii. 38, 39.

I KNOW not what the future hath
   Of marvel or surprise,
Assured alone that life and death
   His mercy underlies.

J. G. WHITTIER

BE of good faith, my dear Friends, look not out at any thing ; fear none of those things ye may be exposed to suffer, either outwardly or inwardly ; but trust the Lord over all, and your life will spring, and grow, and refresh you, and ye will learn obedience and faithfulness daily more and more, even by your exercises and sufferings ; yea, the Lord will teach you the very mystery of faith and obedience ; the wisdom, power, love, and goodness of the Lord ordering *every* thing for you, and ordering *your* hearts in every thing.

I. PENINGTON

Turn ye to the stronghold, ye prisoners of hope.—
ZECH. ix. 12.

Their strength is to sit still.—ISA. xxx. 7.

O POWER to do ; O baffled will !
  O prayer and action ! ye are one.
Who may not strive, may yet fulfil
The harder task of standing still,
  And good but wished with God is done.
                  J. G. WHITTIER

THAT God has circumscribed our life may
add a peculiar element of trial, but often
it defines our way and cuts off many tempting
possibilities that perplex the free and the
strong ; whilst it leaves intact the whole body
of spiritual reality, with the Beatitude thereon,
' that if we know these things, happy are we if
we do them '. We know that God orders the
lot ; and to meet it with the energies it requires
and permits, neither more nor less,—to fill it
at every available point with the light and
action of an earnest and spiritually inventive
mind, though its scene be no wider than a sick
chamber, and its action narrowed to patient
suffering, and gentle, cheerful words, and
all the light it can emit the thankful quiet of a
trustful eye,—without chafing as though God
had misjudged our sphere, and placed us wrong,
and did not know where we could best serve
Him,—this is what, in that condition, we *have
to do.*

                  J. H. THOM

Therefore I take pleasure in infirmities, in reproaches, in necessities, in persecutions, in distresses for Christ's sake : for when I am weak, then am I strong.—2 COR. xii. 10.

WHATE'ER God does is well !
In patience let us wait ;
He doth Himself our burdens bear,
    He doth for us take care,
And He, our God, knows all our weary days.
    Come, give Him praise.

B. SCHMOLCKE

NOTHING else but this seeing God in everything will make us loving and patient with those who annoy and trouble us. They will be to us then only the instruments for accomplishing His tender and wise purposes towards us, and we shall even find ourselves at last inwardly thanking them for the blessings they bring us. Nothing else will completely put an end to all murmuring or rebelling thoughts.

H. W. S.

THE subjection of the will is accomplished by calmly resigning thyself up in everything that internally or externally vexes thee ; for it is thus only that the soul is prepared for the reception of divine influences. Prepare the heart like clean paper, and the Divine Wisdom will imprint on it characters to His own liking.

M. MOLINOS

I know the thoughts that I think toward you, saith the Lord, thoughts of peace, and not of evil, to give you an expected end.—JER. xxix. 11.

THY thoughts are good, and Thou art kind,
   E'en when we think it not ;
How many an anxious, faithless mind
   Sits grieving o'er its lot,
And frets, and pines by day and night,
As God had lost it out of sight,
   And all its wants forgot.

P. GERHARDT

YOU are never to complain of your birth, your training, your employments, your hardships ; never to fancy that you could be something if only you had a different lot and sphere assigned you. God understands His own plan, and He knows what you want a great deal better than you do. The very things that you most deprecate, as fatal limitations or obstructions, are probably what you most want. What you call hindrances, obstacles, discouragements, are probably God's opportunities. Bring down your soul, or, rather, bring it up to receive God's will and do His work, in your lot, in your sphere, under your cloud of obscurity, against your temptations, and then you shall find that your condition is never opposed to your good, but really consistent with it.

H. BUSHNELL

*Behold, I have refined thee, but not with silver ;
I have chosen thee in the furnace of affliction.*—ISA.
xlviii. 10.

BE patient, suffering soul ! I hear thy cry.
The trial fires may glow, but I am nigh.
   I see the silver, and I will refine
   Until My image shall upon it shine.
Fear not, for I am near, thy help to be ;
Greater than all thy pain, My love for Thee.

H. W. C.

GOD takes a thousand times more pains
with us than the artist with his picture, by
many touches of sorrow, and by many colours
of circumstance, to bring man into the form
which is the highest and noblest in His sight,
if only we received His gifts and myrrh in the
right spirit. . . . But when the cup is put
away, and these feelings are stifled or un-
heeded, a greater injury is done to the soul than
can ever be amended. For no heart can con-
ceive in what surpassing love God giveth us
this myrrh ; yet this which we ought to receive
to our soul's good, we suffer to pass by us in
our sleepy indifference, and nothing comes of it.
Then we come and complain : ' Alas, Lord !
I am so dry, and it is so dark within me ! ' I
tell thee, dear child, open thy heart to the pain,
and it will do thee more good than if thou
wert full of feeling and devoutness.

J. TAULER

That good thing which was committed unto thee,
keep by the Holy Ghost which dwelleth in us.—
2 TIM. i. 14.

> OH that the Comforter would come !
> Nor visit as a transient guest,
> But fix in me His constant home,
> And keep possession of my breast ;
> And make my soul His loved abode,
> The temple of indwelling God !
>
> C. WESLEY

THY spirit should become, while yet on earth, the peaceful throne of the Divine Being ; think, then, how quiet, how gentle and pure, how reverent, thou shouldest be.

GERHARD TERSTEEGEN

I CANNOT tell you how much I love you. But that which of all things I have most at heart, with regard to you, is the real progress of your soul in the divine life. Heaven seems to be awakened in you. It is a tender plant. It requires stillness, meekness, and the unity of the heart, totally given up to the unknown workings of the Spirit of God, which will do all its work in the calm soul, that has no hunger or desire but to escape out of the mire of its earthly life into its lost union and life in God. I mention this, out of a fear of your giving in to an eagerness about many things, which, though seemingly innocent, yet divide and weaken the workings of the divine life within you.

WM. LAW

*And Enoch walked with God; and he was not;
for God took him.*—GEN. v. 24.

> OH for a closer walk with God,
>   A calm and heavenly frame;
> A light to shine upon the road
>   That leads me to the Lamb!
>
> W. COWPER

IS it possible for any of us in these modern
days to so live that we may walk with God?
Can we walk with God in the shop, in the office,
in the household, and on the street? When
men exasperate us, and work wearies us, and
the children fret, and the servants annoy, and
our best-laid plans fall to pieces, and our castles
in the air are dissipated like bubbles that break
at a breath, then can we walk with God? That
religion which fails us in the every-day trials
and experiences of life has somewhere in it a
flaw. It should be more than a plank to sustain
us in the rushing tide, and land us exhausted
and dripping on the other side. It ought, if it
come from above, to be always, day by day, to
our souls as the wings of a bird, bearing us away
from and beyond the impediments which seek
to hold us down. If the Divine Love be a con-
scious presence, an indwelling force with us, it
will do this.

CHRISTIAN UNION

Of whom the whole family in heaven and earth is named.—EPH. iii. 15.

> ONE family, we dwell in Him ;
>   One church above, beneath ;
> Though now divided by the stream,—
>   The narrow stream of death.
>
> One army of the living God,
>   To His command we bow :
> Part of His host has crossed the flood,
>   And part is crossing now.
>
> C. WESLEY

LET us, then, learn that we can never be lonely or forsaken in this life. Shall they forget us because they are 'made perfect'? Shall they love us the less because they now have power to love us more? If we forget them not, shall they not remember us with God? No trial, then, can isolate us, no sorrow can cut us off from the Communion of Saints. Kneel down, and you are with them ; lift up your eyes, and the heavenly world, high above all perturbation, hangs serenely overhead ; only a thin veil, it may be, floats between. All whom we loved, and all who loved us, whom we still love no less, while they love us yet more, are ever near, because ever in His presence in whom we live and dwell.

H. E. MANNING

Wherefore seeing we also are compassed about with so great a cloud of witnesses, let us lay aside every weight, and the sin which doth so easily beset us, and let us run with patience the race that is set before us.—HEB. xii. 1.

WHEN the powers of hell prevail
  O'er our weakness and unfitness,
Could we lift the fleshly veil,
  Could we for a moment witness
Those unnumbered hosts that stand
Calm and bright on either hand ;

Oh, what joyful hope would cheer,
  Oh, what faith serene would guide us !
Great may be the danger near.
  Greater are the friends beside us.

ANON.

WE are compassed about by a cloud of witnesses, whose hearts throb in sympathy with every effort and struggle, and who thrill with joy at every success. How should this thought check and rebuke every worldly feeling and unworthy purpose, and enshrine us, in the midst of a forgetful and unspiritual world, with an atmosphere of heavenly peace ! They have overcome—have risen—are crowned, glorified ; but still they remain to us, our assistants, our comforters, and in every hour of darkness their voice speaks to us : ' So we grieved, so we struggled, so we fainted, so we doubted ; but we have overcome, we have obtained, we have seen, we have found,—and in our victory behold the certainty of thy own.'

B.H. STOWE

Wherefore putting away lying, speak every man truth with his neighbour : for we are members one of another.—EPH. iv. 25.

IN conversation be sincere ;
Keep conscience as the noontide clear ;
Think how All-seeing God thy ways
And all thy secret thoughts surveys.

THOMAS KEN

THE essence of lying is in deception, not in words ; a lie may be told by silence, by equivocation, by the accent on a syllable, by a glance of the eye attaching a peculiar significance to a sentence ; and all these kinds of lies are worse and baser by many degrees than a lie plainly worded ; so that no form of blinded conscience is so far sunk as that which comforts itself for having deceived because the deception was by gesture or silence, instead of utterance.

J. RUSKIN

HE that is habituated to deceptions and artificialities in trifles, will try in vain to be true in matters of importance ; for truth is a thing of habit rather than of will. You cannot in any given case by any sudden and single effort will to be true, if the habit of your life has been insincerity.

F. W. ROBERTSON

A soft answer turneth away wrath : but grievous words stir up anger.—PROV. XV. I.

Doest thou well to be angry ?—JONAH iv. 4.

RENEW Thine image, Lord, in me,
Lowly and gentle may I be ;
 No charms but these to Thee are dear ;
No anger mayst Thou ever find,
No pride in my unruffled mind,
 But faith, and heaven-born peace be there.
                              P. GERHARDT

NEITHER say nor do aught displeasing to thy neighbour ; and if thou hast been wanting in charity, seek his forgiveness, or speak to him with gentleness. Speak always with mildness and in a low tone of voice.

                              L. SCUPOLI

INJURIES hurt not more in the receiving than in the remembrance. A small injury shall go as it comes ; a great injury may dine or sup with me ; but none at all shall lodge with me. Why should I vex myself because another hath vexed me ? Grief for things past that cannot be remedied, and care for things to come that cannot be prevented, may easily hurt, can never benefit me. I will therefore commit myself to God in both, and enjoy the present.

                              JOSEPH HALL

The temple of God is holy, which temple ye are.—
1 COR. iii. 17.

NOW shed Thy mighty influence abroad
On souls that would their Father's image bear ;
Make us as holy temples of our God,
Where dwells forever calm, adoring prayer.

C. J. P. SPITTA

THIS pearl of eternity is the church or temple of God within thee, the consecrated place of divine worship, where alone thou canst worship God in spirit and in truth. When once thou art well grounded in this inward worship, thou wilt have learned to live unto God above time and place. For every day will be Sunday to thee, and, wherever thou goest, thou wilt have a priest, a church, and an altar along with thee. For when God has all that he should have of thy heart, when thou art wholly given up to the obedience of the light and spirit of God within thee, to will only in His will, to love only in His love, to be wise only in His wisdom, then it is that everything thou dost is as a song of praise, and the common business of thy life is a conforming to God's will on earth as angels do in heaven.

WM. LAW

*He will fulfil the desire of them that fear Him :
He also will hear their cry, and will save them.—*
PS. cxlv. 19.

*Delight thyself also in the Lord ; and He shall
give thee the desires of thine heart.—*PS. xxxvii. 4.

THOUGH to-day may not fulfil
All thy hopes, have patience still ;
For perchance to-morrow's sun
Sees thy happier days begun.

P. GERHARDT

HIS great desire and delight is God ; and
by desiring and delighting, he hath Him.
*Delight thou in the Lord, and He shall give thee
thy heart's desire,—*HIMSELF ; and then surely
thou shalt have all. Any other thing *commit it
to Him*, and he shall bring it to pass.

R. LEIGHTON

ALL who call on God in true faith, earnestly
from the heart, will certainly be heard, and will
receive what they have asked and desired,
although not in the hour or in the measure, or
the very thing which they ask ; yet they will
obtain something greater and more glorious
than they had dared to ask.

MARTIN LUTHER

I was not disobedient unto the heavenly vision.—
ACTS xxvi. 19.

*The Lord our God will we serve, and His voice
will we obey.*—JOSH. xxiv. 24.

> I WILL shun no toil or woe,
> Where Thou leadest I will go,
>   Be my pathway plain or rough ;
> If but every hour may be
> Spent in work that pleases Thee,
>   Ah, dear Lord, it is enough !
>
>   G. TERSTEEGEN

ALL these longings and doubts, and this in-
ward distress, are the voice of the Good
Shepherd in your heart, seeking to call you out
of all that is contrary to His will. Oh, let me
entreat of you not to turn away from His
gentle pleadings.

               H. W. S.

THE fear of man brings a snare. By halting in
our duty and giving back in the time of trial, our
hands grow weaker, our ears grow dull as to
hearing the language of the true Shepherd ; so
that when we look at the way of the righteous, it
seems as though it was not for us to follow
them.

               J. WOOLMAN

Lo, I come to do Thy will, O God.—HEB. x. 9.

Teach me to do Thy will, for Thou art my God.
—PS. cxliii. 10.

> LO ! I come with joy to do
>   The Father's blessed will ;
> Him in outward works pursue,
>   And serve His pleasure still.
> Faithful to my Lord's commands,
>   I still would choose the better part ;
> Serve with careful Martha's hands,
>   And loving Mary's heart.
>
> C. WESLEY

A SOUL cannot be regarded as truly sub-
dued and consecrated in its will, and as
having passed into union with the Divine will,
until it has a disposition to do promptly and
faithfully all that God requires, as well as to
endure patiently and thankfully all that He
imposes.

T. C. UPHAM

WHEN we have learned to offer up every duty
connected with our situation in life as a sacrifice
to God, a settled employment becomes just a
settled habit of prayer.

THOMAS ERSKINE

' *DO the duty which lies nearest thee*,' which
thou knowest to be a duty. Thy second duty
will already have become clearer.

T. CARLYLE

*Say not thou, I will hide myself from the Lord :
shall any remember. me from above ? I shall not
be remembered among so many people : for what
is my soul among such an infinite number of
creatures ?*—ECCLESIASTICUS, xvi. 17.

AMONG so many, can He care ?
Can special love be everywhere ?
A myriad homes,—a myriad ways,—
And God's eye over every place ?

I asked : my soul bethought of this ;—
In just that very place of His
Where He hath put and keepeth you,
God hath no other thing to do !

A. D. T. WHITNEY

GIVE free and bold play to those instincts of
the heart which believe that the Creator
must care for the creatures He has made, and
that the only real effective care for them must
be that which takes each of them into His love,
and knowing it separately surrounds it with His
separate sympathy. There is not one life which
the Life-giver ever loses out of His sight ; not
one which sins so that He casts it away ; not one
which is not so near to Him that whatever
touches it touches Him with sorrow or with
joy.

PHILLIPS BROOKS

In Him we live, and move, and have our being.---
ACTS xvii. 28.

*Whither shall I go from Thy spirit ? or whither
shall I flee from Thy presence ?*—PS. cxxxix. 7.

YEA ! In Thy life our little lives are ended,
  Into Thy depths our trembling spirits fall ;
In Thee enfolded, gathered, comprehended,
  As holds the sea her waves—Thou hold'st us all.
                                    E. SCUDDER

WHERE then is *our* God ? You say, He
is *everywhere* : then show me *anywhere*
that you have met Him. You declare Him
everlasting : then tell me *any moment* that He
has been with you. You believe Him ready to
succour them that are tempted, and to lift those
that are bowed down : then in what passionate
hour did you subside into His calm grace ? in
what sorrow lose yourself in His ' more exceed-
ing ' joy ? These are the testing questions by
which we may learn whether we too have raised
our altar to an ' unknown God ' and pay the
worship of the blind ; or whether we commune
with Him ' in whom we live, and move, and
have our being '.

                                    J. MARTINEAU

Walk worthy of the Lord unto all pleasing, being fruitful in every good work, and increasing in the knowledge of God ; strengthened with all might, according to His glorious power, unto all patience and long-suffering with joyfulness.—COL. i. 10, 11.

TO be the thing we seem,
To do the thing we deem
   Enjoined by duty ;
To walk in faith, nor dream
Of questioning God's scheme
   Of truth and beauty.

ANON.

TO shape the whole Future is not our problem ; but only to shape faithfully a small part of it, according to rules already known. It is perhaps possible for each of us, who will with due earnestness inquire, to ascertain clearly what he, for his own part, ought to do ; this let him, with true heart, do, and continue doing. The general issue will, as it has always done, rest well with a Higher Intelligence than ours. . . . This day thou knowest ten commanded duties, seest in thy mind ten things which should be done for one that thou doest ! *Do* one of them ; this of itself will show thee ten others which can and shall be done.

T. CARLYLE

I must work the works of Him that sent me, while it is day ; the night cometh, when no man can work.—JOHN ix. 4.

Wherefore have ye not fulfilled your task?— EXOD. v. 14.

> He who intermits
> The appointed task and duties of the day
> Untunes full oft the pleasures of the day ;
> Checking the finer spirits that refuse
> To flow, when purposes are lightly changed.
> W. WORDSWORTH

BY putting off things beyond their proper times, one duty treads upon the heels of another, and all duties are felt as irksome obligations,—a yoke beneath which we fret and lose our peace. In most cases the consequence of this is, that we have no time to do the work as it ought to be done. It is therefore done precipitately, with eagerness, with a greater desire simply to get it done, than to do it well, and with very little thought of God throughout.

F. W. FABER

SUFFICIENT for each day is the *good* thereof, equally as the evil. We must do at once, and with our might, the merciful deed that our hand findeth to do,—else it will never be done, for the hand will find other tasks, and the arrears fall through. And every unconsummated good feeling, every unfulfilled purpose that His spirit has prompted, shall one day charge us as faithless and recreant before God.

J. H. THOM

Blessed is the man whom Thou chastenest, O Lord, and teachest him out of Thy law.—PS. xciv. 12.

Truly this is a grief, and I must bear it.—JER. x. 19.

> HOLD in thy murmurs, heaven arraigning !
> The patient see God's loving face ;
> Who bear their burdens uncomplaining,
> 'Tis they that win the Father's grace.
>
> ANON.

DO not run to this and that for comfort when you are in trouble, but bear it. Be uncomfortably quiet—be uneasily silent—be patiently unhappy.

J. P. GREAVES

HARD words *will* vex ; unkindness *will* pierce ; neglect *will* wound ; threatened evils *will* make the soul quiver ; sharp pain or weariness *will* rack the body, or make it restless. But what says the Psalmist ? ' When my heart is vexed, I will complain.' To whom ? Not *of* God, but *to* God.

E. B. PUSEY

SURELY, I have thought, I do not want to have a grief which would not be a grief. I feel that I shall be able to take up my cross in a religious spirit soon, and then it will be all right.

JAMES HINTON

Thou art my servant ; I have formed thee ; thou art my servant ; O Israel, thou shalt not be forgotten of me.—ISA. xliv. 21.

OH, give Thy servant patience to be still,
    And bear Thy will ;
Courage to venture wholly on the arm
    That will not harm ;
The wisdom that will never let me stray
    Out of my way ;
The love, that, now afflicting, knoweth best
    When I should rest.

J. M. NEALE

ACCEPT His will entirely, and never suppose that you could serve Him better in any other way. You can never serve Him well, save in the way He chooses. Supposing that you were never to be set free from such trials, what would you do ? You would say to God, ' I am Thine—if my trials are acceptable to Thee, give me more and more.' I have full confidence that this is what you would say, and then you would not think more of it—at any rate, you would not be anxious. Well, do the same now. Make friends with your trials, as though you were always to live together ; and you will see that when you cease to take thought for your own deliverance, God will take thought for you ; and when you cease to help yourself eagerly, He will help you.

FRANCIS DE SALES

AH, if you knew what peace there is in an accepted sorrow !

MADAME GUYON

Fear thou not ; for I am with thee : be not dismayed ; for I am thy God : I will strengthen thee ; yea, I will help thee ; yea, I will uphold thee with the right hand of my righteousness.—ISA. xli. 10.

LORD, be Thou near and cheer my lonely way ;
  With Thy sweet peace my aching bosom fill ;
Scatter my cares and fears ; my griefs allay,
    And be it mine each day
    To love and please, Thee still.

P. CORNEILLE

WHAT if the wicked nature, which is as a sea casting out mire and dirt, rage against thee ? There is a river, a sweet, still, flowing river, the streams whereof will make glad thy heart. And, learn but in quietness and stillness to retire to the Lord, and wait upon Him ; in whom thou shalt feel peace and joy, in the midst of thy trouble from the cruel and vexatious spirit of this world. So, wait to know thy work and service to the Lord every day, in thy place and station ; and the Lord make thee faithful therein, and thou wilt want neither help, support, nor comfort.

I. PENINGTON

*Thou wilt keep him in perfect peace, whose mind
is stayed on Thee ; because he trusteth in Thee.—*
ISA. xxvi 3.

WHAT comforts, Lord, to those are given,
Who seek in Thee their home and rest !
They find on earth an opening heaven,
And in Thy peace are amply blest.

W. C. DESSLER

GOD is a tranquil Being, and abides in a
tranquil eternity. So must thy spirit
become a tranquil and clear little pool, wherein
the serene light of God can be mirrored.
Therefore shun all that is disquieting and dis-
tracting, both within and without. Nothing in
the whole world is worth the loss of thy peace ;
even the faults which thou hast committed
should only humble, but not disquiet thee.
God is full of joy, peace, and happiness. En-
deavour then to obtain a continually joyful
and peaceful spirit. Avoid all anxious care,
vexation, murmuring, and melancholy, which
darken thy soul, and render thee unfit for the
friendship of God. If thou dost perceive
such feelings arising, turn gently away from
them.

G. TERSTEEGEN

Every day will I bless Thee, and I will praise Thy name for ever and ever.—PS. cxlv. 2.

Commit thy works unto the Lord, and thy thoughts shall be established.—PROV. xvi. 3.

LORD, I my vows to Thee renew ;
Disperse my sins as morning dew ;
Guard my first springs of thought and will,
And with Thyself my spirit fill.

THOMAS KEN

MORNING by morning think, for a few moments, of the chief employments of the day, any one thing of greater moment than others, thine own especial trial, any occasions of it which are likely to come that day, and by one short strong act commend thyself beforehand in all to God ; offer all thy thoughts, words, and deeds to Him—to be governed, guided, accepted by Him. . . . Choose some great occasions of the day, such as bring with them most trial to thee, on which, above others, to commend thyself to God.

E. B. PUSEY

WILL you not, before venturing away from your early quiet hour, ' commit thy works ' to Him definitely, the special things you have to do to-day, and the unforeseen work which He may add in the course of it ?

F. R. HAVERGAL

Hereby know we that we dwell in Him, and He in us, because He hath given us of His Spirit.—
1 JOHN iv. 13.

WITHIN ! within, oh turn
  Thy spirit's eyes, and learn
Thy wandering senses gently to control ;
Thy dearest Friend dwells deep within thy soul,
  And asks thyself of thee,
That heart, and mind, and sense, He may make whole
  In perfect harmony.

G. TERSTEEGEN

WAIT patiently, trust humbly, depend only upon, seek solely to a God of Light and Love, of Mercy and Goodness, of Glory and Majesty, ever dwelling in the inmost depth and spirit of your soul. There you have all the secret, hidden, invisible Upholder of all the creation, whose blessed operation will always be found by a humble, faithful, loving, calm, patient introversion of your heart to Him, who has His hidden heaven within you, and which will open itself to you, as soon as your heart is left wholly to His eternal, ever-speaking word, and ever-sanctifying spirit within you. Beware of all eagerness and activity of your own natural spirit and temper. Run not in any hasty ways of your own. Be patient under the sense of your own vanity and weakness ; and patiently wait for God to do His own work, and in His own way.

WM. LAW

If any man among you seem to be religious, and bridleth not his tongue, but deceiveth his own heart, this man's religion is vain.—JAMES i. 26.

I said, I will take heed to my ways, that I sin not with my tongue.—PS. xxxix. 1.

NO sinful word, nor deed of wrong,
Nor thoughts that idly rove ;
But simple truth be on our tongue,
And in our hearts be love.

ST. AMBROSE

LET us all resolve,—First, to attain the grace of SILENCE ; Second, to deem all FAULT-FINDING that does no good a SIN, and to resolve, when we are happy ourselves, not to poison the atmosphere for our neighbours by calling on them to remark every painful and disagreeable feature of their daily life ; Third, to practise the grace and virtue of PRAISE.

HARRIET B. STOWE

SURROUNDED by those who constantly exhibit defects of character and conduct, if we yield to a complaining and impatient spirit, we shall mar our own peace without having the satisfaction of benefiting others.

T. C. UPHAM

Ye have need of patience, that, after ye have done the will of God, ye might receive the promise. —HEB. X. 36.

SWEET Patience, come :
Not from a low and earthly source,—
Waiting, till things shall have their course,—
Not as accepting present pain
In hope of some hereafter gain,—
Not in a dull and sullen calm,—
But as a breath of heavenly balm,
Bidding my weary heart submit
To bear whatever God sees fit ;
Sweet Patience, come !

HYMNS OF THE CHURCH MILITANT

PATIENCE endues her scholars with content of mind, and evenness of temper, preventing all repining grumbling, and impatient desires, and inordinate affections ; disappointments here are no crosses, and all anxious thoughts are disarmed of their sting ; in her habitations dwell quietness, submission, and long-suffering, all fierce turbulent inclinations are hereby allayed. The eyes of the patient fixedly wait the inward power of God's providence, and they are thereby mightily enabled towards their salvation and preservation.

THOMAS TRYON

Man shall not live by bread alone, but by every word that proceedeth out of the mouth of God.—MATT. iv. 4.

A man's life consisteth not in the abundance of the things which he possesseth.—LUKE xii. 15.

WHATE'ER God does is well,
Whether He gives or takes !
And what we from His hand receive
    Suffices us to live.
He takes and gives, while yet He loves us still.
    Then love His will.

B. SCHMOLCK

IS that beast better, that hath two or three mountains to graze on, than a little bee, that feeds on dew or manna, and lives upon what falls every morning from the storehouse of heaven, clouds, and providence ?

JEREMY TAYLOR

FOR myself I am certain that the good of human life cannot lie in the possession of things which for one man to possess is for the rest to lose, but rather in things which all can possess alike, and where one man's wealth promotes his neighbour's.

B. SPINOZA

EVERY lot is happy to a person who bears it with tranquillity.

BOËTHIUS

Your Father knoweth what things ye have need of.—MATT. vi. 8.

Seek ye first the kingdom of God, and His right-eousness, and all these things shall be added unto you.—MATT. vi. 33.

THY kingdom come, with power and grace,
 To every heart of man ;
Thy peace, and joy, and righteousness
 In all our bosoms reign.

C. WESLEY

GOD bids us, then, by past mercies, by present grace, by fears of coming ill, by hopes in His goodness, earnestly, with our whole hearts, seek Him and His righteousness, and all these things, all ye need for soul and body, peace, comfort, joy, the overflowing of His consolations, shall be added over and above to you.

E. B. PUSEY

GRANT us, O Lord, we beseech Thee, always to seek Thy kingdom and righteousness, and of whatsoever Thou seest us to stand in need, mercifully grant us an abundant portion. Amen.

BE content to be a child, and let the Father proportion out daily to thee what light, what power, what exercises, what straits, what fears, what troubles He sees fit for thee.

I. PENINGTON

I have taught thee in the way of wisdom ; I have led thee in right paths.—PROV. iv. 11.

WE know not what the path may be
As yet by us untrod ;
But we can trust our all to Thee,
Our Father and our God.

WM. J. IRONS

WE have very little command over the circumstances in which we may be called by God to bear our part—unlimited command over the temper of our souls, but next to no command over the outward forms of trial. The most energetic will cannot order the events by which our spirits are to be perilled and tested. Powers quite beyond our reach—death, accident, fortune, another's sin—may change in a moment all the conditions of our life. With to-morrow's sun existence may have new and awful aspects for any of us.

J. H. THOM

OH, my friend, look not *out* at what stands in the way ; what if it look dreadfully as a lion, is not the Lord stronger than the mountains of prey ? but look *in*, where the law of life is written, and the will of the Lord revealed, that thou mayest know what is the Lord's will concerning thee.

I. PENINGTON

Be of good courage, and He shall strengthen your heart, all ye that hope in the Lord.—PS. xxxi. 24.

Let not your heart be troubled, neither let it be afraid.—JOHN xiv. 27.

IN heavenly love abiding,
  No change my heart shall fear ;
And safe is such confiding,
  For nothing changes here.

A. L. WARING

A TRUE Christian, that hath power over his own will, may live nobly and happily, and enjoy a clear heaven within the serenity of his own mind perpetually. When the sea of this world is most rough and tempestuous about him, then can he ride safely at anchor within the haven, by a sweet compliance of his will with God's will. He can look about him, and with an even and indifferent mind behold the world either to smile or frown upon him ; neither will he abate of the least of his contentment for all the ill and unkind usage he meets withal in this life. He that hath got the mastery over his own will feels no violence from without, finds no contests within ; and when God calls for him out of this state of mortality, he finds in himself a power to lay down his own life ; neither is it so much taken from him, as quietly and freely surrendered up by him.

DR. JOHN SMITH

And the Lord, He it is that doth go before thee ;
He will be with thee, He will not fail thee, neither
forsake thee : fear not, neither be dismayed.—
DEUT. xxxi. 8.

> KNOW well, my soul, God's hand controls
>   Whate'er thou fearest ;
> Round Him in calmest music rolls
>   Whate'er thou hearest.

J. G. WHITTIER

THE lessons of the moral sentiment are, once for all, an emancipation from that anxiety which takes the joy out of all life. It teaches a great peace. It comes itself from the highest place. It is that, which being in all sound natures, and strongest in the best and most gifted men, we know to be implanted by the Creator of men. It is a commandment at every moment, and in every condition of life, to do the duty of that moment, and to abstain from doing the wrong.

R. W. EMERSON

GO face the fire at sea, or the cholera in your friend's house, or the burglar in your own, or what danger lies in the way of duty, knowing you are guarded by the cherubim of Destiny.

R. W. EMERSON

Behold, I am with thee, and will keep thee in all places whither thou goest.—GEN. xxviii. 15.

BE quiet, soul :
Why shouldst thou care and sadness borrow,
Why sit in nameless fear and sorrow,
The livelong day ?
God will mark out thy path to-morrow
In His best way.

ANON.

I HAD hoped, Madame, to find you here, and was rejoicing in that hope ; but God has sent you elsewhere. The best place is wherever He puts us, and any other would be undesirable, all the worse because it would please our fancy, and would be of our own choice. Do not think about distant events. This uneasiness about the future is unwholesome for you. We must leave to God all that depends on Him, and think only of being faithful in all that depends upon ourselves. When God takes away that which He has given you, He knows well how to replace it, either through other means or by Himself.

FÉNELON

The Lord hath been mindful of us : He will bless us.—PS. CXV. 12.

MY Father ! what am I, that all
Thy mercies sweet like sunlight fall
 So constant o'er my way ?
That Thy great love should shelter me,
And guide my steps so tenderly
 Through every changing day ?

ANON.

WHAT a strength and spring of life, what hope and trust, what glad, unresting energy, is in this one thought,—to serve Him who is ' my Lord ', ever near me, ever looking on ; seeing my intentions before He beholds my failures ; knowing my desires before He sees my faults ; cheering me to endeavour greater things, and yet accepting the least ; inviting my poor service, and yet, above all, content with my poorer love. Let us try to realize this, whatsoever, wheresoever we be. The humblest and the simplest, the weakest and the most encumbered, may love Him not less than the busiest and strongest, the most gifted and laborious. If our heart be clear before Him ; if He be to us our chief and sovereign choice, dear above all, and beyond all desired ; then all else matters little. That which concerneth us He will perfect in stillness and in power.

H. E. MANNING

*Yea, I have loved thee with an everlasting love ;
therefore with loving-kindness have I drawn thee.—*
JER. xxxi. 3.

ON the great love of God I lean,
Love of the Infinite, Unseen,
With nought of heaven or earth between.
    This God is mine, and I am His ;
    His love is all I need of bliss.

                        H. BONAR

IF ever human love was tender, and self-sacrificing, and devoted ; if ever it could bear and forbear ; if ever it could suffer gladly for its loved ones ; if ever it was willing to pour itself out in a lavish abandonment for the comfort or pleasure of its objects ; then infinitely more is Divine love tender, and self-sacrificing, and devoted, and glad to bear and forbear, and to suffer, and to lavish its best of gifts and blessings upon the objects of its love. Put together all the tenderest love you know of, the deepest you have ever felt, and the strongest that has ever been poured out upon you, and heap upon it all the love of all the loving human hearts in the world, and then multiply it by infinity, and you will begin, perhaps, to have some faint glimpse of what the love of God is.

                        H. W. S.

*My sons, be not now negligent : for the Lord
hath chosen you to stand before Him, to serve Him.*
—2 CHRON. xxix. 11.

> BRIGHT be my prospect as I pass along ;—
>   An ardent service at the cost of all,—
> Love by untiring ministry made strong,
>   And ready for the first, the softest call.
>   A. L. WARING

THERE are many things that appear trifles,
which greatly tend to enervate the soul,
and hinder its progress in the path to virtue and
glory. The habit of indulging in things which
our judgment cannot thoroughly approve, grows
stronger and stronger by every act of self-
gratification, and we are led on by degrees to an
excess of luxury which must greatly weaken our
hands in the spiritual warfare. If we do not
endeavour to do that which is right in every
particular circumstance, though trifling, we
shall be in great danger of letting the same
negligence take place in matters more essential.
                               MARGARET WOODS

THE will can only be made submissive by
frequent self-denials, which must keep in sub-
jection its sallies and inclinations. Great weak-
ness is often produced by indulgences which
seem of no importance.
                               M. MOLINOS

Why art thou cast down, O my soul ? and why art thou disquieted in me ? hope thou in God ; for I shall yet praise Him for the help of His countenance.—PS. xlii. 5.

We are troubled on every side, yet not distressed.
—2 COR. iv. 8.

> OH, my soul, why are thou vexed ?
>   Let things go e'en as they will ;
> Though to thee they seem perplexed,
>   Yet His order they fulfil.
>
> A. H. FRANCKE

THE vexation, restlessness, and impatience which small trials cause, arise wholly from our ignorance and want of self-control. We may be thwarted and troubled, it is true, but these things put us into a condition for exercising patience and meek submission, and the self-abnegation wherein alone the fullness of God is to be found.

DE RENTY

EVERY day deny yourself some satisfaction ;—bearing all the inconveniences of life (for the love of God), cold, hunger, restless nights, ill health, unwelcome news, the faults of servants, contempt, ingratitude of friends, malice of enemies, calumnies, our own failings, lowness of spirits, the struggle in overcoming our corruptions ;—bearing all these with patience and resignation to the will of God. Do all this as unto God, with the greatest privacy.

BISHOP WILSON

Charity envieth not . . . thinketh no evil.—
I COR. xiii. 4, 5.

*Why dost thou judge thy brother? or why dost
thou set at nought thy brother?*—ROM. xiv. 10.

He that despiseth his neighbour, sinneth.—PROV.
xiv. 21.

LOOK thou with pity on a brother's fall,
But dwell not with stern anger on his fault;
The grace of God alone holds thee, holds all;
Were that withdrawn, thou too wouldst swerve and
    halt.

J. EDMESTON

IF, on hearing of the fall of a brother, however
differing or severed from us, we feel the least
inclination to linger over it, instead of hiding it
in grief and shame, or veiling it in the love
which covereth a multitude of sins; if, in
seeing a joy or a grace or an effective service
given to others, we do not rejoice, but feel
depressed, let us be very watchful; the most
diabolical of passions may mask itself as
humility, or zeal for the glory of God.

ELIZABETH CHARLES

LOVE taketh up no malign elements; its spirit
prompteth it to cover in mercy all things that
ought not to be exposed, to believe all of good
that can be believed, to hope all things that a
good God makes possible, and to endure all
things that the hope may be made good.

J. H. THOM

Therefore thou art inexcusable, O man, whosoever thou art that judgest : for wherein thou judgest another, thou condemnest thyself ; for thou that judgest doest the same things.—ROM. ii. 1.

SEARCH thine own heart. What paineth thee
  In others, in thyself may be ;
All dust is frail, all flesh is weak ;
  Be thou the true man thou dost seek.

                J. G. WHITTIER

A SAINT'S life in one man may be less than common honesty in another. From *us*, whose consciences He has reached and enlightened, God may look for a martyr's truth, a Christian's unworldly simplicity, before He will place us on a level even with the average of the exposed classes. We perhaps think our lives at least harmless. We do not consider what He may think of them, when compared with the invitations of His that we have slighted, with the aims of His Providence we are leaving without our help, with the glory for ourselves we are refusing and casting away, with the vast sum of blessed work that daily faithfulness in time can rear without overwork on any single day.

                J. H. THOM

Now the God of hope fill you with all joy and peace in believing, that ye may abound in hope, through the power of the Holy Ghost.—ROM. XV. 13.

> TO heaven I lift my waiting eyes;
>   There all my hopes are laid;
> The Lord that built the earth and skies
>   Is my perpetual aid.
>
> I. WATTS

GROVEL not in things below, among earthly cares, pleasures, anxieties, toils, if thou wouldst have a good strong hope on high. Lift up thy cares with thy heart to God, if thou wouldst hope in Him. Then see what in thee is most displeasing to God. This it is which holdeth thy hope down. Strike firmly, repeatedly, in the might of God, until it give way. Thy hope will soar at once with thy thanks to God who delivereth thee.

E. B. PUSEY

THE snares of the enemy will be so known to thee and discerned, the way of help so manifest and easy, that their strength will be broken, and the poor entangled bird will fly away singing, from the nets and entanglements of the fowler; and praises will spring up, and great love in thy heart to the Forgiver and Redeemer.

I. PENINGTON

Fight the good fight of faitn, lay hold on eternal life, whereunto thou art also called.—1 TIM. vi. 12.

OH, dream no more of quiet life ;
Care finds the careless out ; more wise to vow
  Thy heart entire to faith's pure strife ;
So peace will come, thou knowest not when or
    how.

LYRA APOSTOLICA

WHO art thou that complainest of thy life of toil ? Complain not. Look up, my wearied brother ; see thy fellow-workmen there, in God's Eternity ; surviving there, they alone surviving ; sacred band of the Immortals, celestial body-guard of the empire of mankind. To thee Heaven, though severe, is *not* unkind ; Heaven is kind,—as a noble mother ; as that Spartan mother, saying while she gave her son his shield, ' With it, my son, or upon it.' Thou too shalt return *home* in honour ; to thy far-distant Home, in honour ; doubt it not,—if in the battle thou keep thy shield ! Thou, in the Eternities and deepest death-kingdoms art not an alien ; thou everywhere art a denizen. Complain not.

T. CARLYLE

The God of all grace, who hath called us unto His eternal glory by Christ Jesus, after that ye have suffered a while, make you perfect, stablish, strengthen, settle you.—I PETER V. 10.

Take heed, and be quiet ; fear not, neither be faint-hearted.—ISA. vii. 4.

> HOW shalt thou bear the cross that now
>   So dread a weight appears ?
> Keep quietly to God, and think
>   Upon the Eternal Years.
>
> F. W. FABER

GOD forgive them that raise an ill report upon the sweet cross of Christ ; it is but our weak and dim eyes, that look but to the black side, that makes us mistake ; those that can take that crabbed tree handsomely upon their backs, and fasten it on cannily, shall find it such a burden as wings unto a bird, or sails to a ship.

S. RUTHERFORD

BLESSED is any weight, however overwhelming, which God has been so good as to fasten with His own hand upon our shoulders.

F. W. FABER

WE cannot say this or that trouble shall not befall, yet we may, by help of the Spirit, say, nothing that doth befall shall make me do that which is unworthy of a Christian.

R. SIBBES

This God is our God for ever and ever : He will be our guide even unto death.—PS. xlviii. 14.

For the Lord shall be thy confidence.—PROV. iii. 26.

BE still, my soul ! Thy God doth undertake
To guide the future, as He has the past :
Thy hope, thy confidence, let nothing shake,
All now mysterious shall be bright at last.

J. BORTHWICK.

HE has kept and folded us from ten thousand ills when we did not know it : in the midst of our security we should have perished every hour, but that He sheltered us ' from the terror by night and from the arrow that flieth by day '—from the powers of evil that walk in darkness, from snares of our own evil will. He has kept us even against ourselves, and saved us even from our own undoing. Let us read the traces of His hand in all our ways, in all the events, the chances, the changes of this troubled state. It is He that folds and feeds us, that makes us to go in and out,—to be faint, or to find pasture,—to lie down by the still waters, or to walk by the way that is parched and desert.

H. E. MANNING

WE are never without help. We have no right to say of any good work, it is too hard for me to do, or of any sorrow, it is too hard for me to bear ; or of any sinful habit, it is too hard for me to overcome.

ELIZABETH CHARLES

Acquaint now thyself with Him, and be at peace.
—JOB xxii. 21.

*All thy children shall be taught of the Lord,
and great shall be the peace of thy children.*—ISA.
liv. 13.

> UNITE, my roving thoughts, unite
> In silence soft and sweet ;
> And thou, my soul, sit gently down
> At thy great Sovereign's feet.
>
> P. DODDRIDGE

YES ! blessed are those holy hours in which
the soul retires from the world to be alone
with God. God's voice, as Himself, is every-
where. Within and without, He speaks to our
souls, if we would hear. Only the din of the
world, or the tumult of our own hearts, deafens
our inward ear to it. Learn to commune with
Him in stillness, and He, whom thou hast
sought in stillness, will be with thee when thou
goest abroad.

E. B. PUSEY.

THE great step and direct path to the fear and
awful reverence of God, is to meditate, and
with a sedate and silent hush to turn the eyes
of the mind inwards ; there to seek, and with a
submissive spirit wait at the gates of Wisdom's
temple ; and then the Divine Voice and Distin-
guishing Power will arise in the light and centre
of a man's self.

THOMAS TRYON

Blessed be the God and Father of our Lord Jesus Christ, who hath blessed us with all spiritual blessings.—EPH. i. 3.

As sorrowful, yet alway rejoicing.—2 COR. vi. 10.

IT is not happiness I seek,
Its name I hardly dare to speak ;
It is not made for man or earth,
And Heaven alone can give it birth.

There is a something sweet and pure,
Through life, through death it may endure ;
With steady foot I onward press,
And long to win that Blessedness.

LOUISA J. HALL

THE elements of *happiness* in this present life no man can command, even if he could command himself, for they depend on the action of many wills, on the purity of many hearts, and by the highest law of God the holiest must ever bear the sins and sorrows of the rest ; but over the *blessedness* of his own spirit circumstance need have no control ; God has therein given an unlimited power to the means of preservation, of grace and growth, at every man's command.

J. H. THOM

THERE is in man a higher than love of happiness : he can do without happiness, and instead thereof find blessedness.

T. CARLYLE

For this shall every one that is godly pray unto Thee in a time when Thou mayest be found : surely in the floods of great waters they shall not come nigh unto him.—PS. xxxii. 6.

BE not o'ermastered by thy pain,
  But cling to God, thou shalt not fall.
The floods sweep over thee in vain,
  Thou yet shalt rise above them all ;
For when thy trial seems too hard to bear,
Lo ! God, thy King, hath granted all thy prayer.
           Be thou content.

P. GERHARDT

IT is the Lord's mercy, to give thee breathings after life, and cries unto Him against that which oppresseth thee ; and happy wilt thou be, when He shall fill thy soul with that which He hath given thee to breathe after. Be not troubled ; for if troubles abound, and there be tossing, and storms, and tempests, and no peace, nor anything visible left to support ; yet, lie still, and sink beneath, till a secret hope stir, which will stay the heart in the midst of all these ; until the Lord administer comfort, who knows how and what relief to give to the weary traveller, that knows not where it is, nor which way to look, nor where to expect a path.

I. PENINGTON

Behold, we count them happy which endure.—
JAMES V. 11.

*If ye endure chastening, God dealeth with you
as with sons.*—HEB. xii. 7.

> TRIALS must and will befall ;
> But with humble faith to see
> Love inscribed upon them all,
> This is happiness to me.
>
> W. COWPER

BE not afraid of these trials which God may
see fit to send upon thee. It is with the
wind and storm of tribulation that God separ-
ates the true wheat from the chaff. Always
remember, therefore, that God comes to thee
in thy sorrows, as really as in thy joys. He lays
low, and He builds up. Thou wilt find thyself
far from perfection, if thou dost not find God in
everything.

M. MOLINOS

GOD hath provided a sweet and quiet life for
His children, could they improve and use it ;
a calm and firm conviction in all the storms and
troubles that are about them, however things go,
to find content, and be careful for nothing.

R. LEIGHTON

Oh that Thou wouldest bless me indeed, and that Thine hand might be with me, and that Thou wouldest keep me from evil, that it may not grieve me !—1 CHRON. iv. 10.

Ye shall serve the Lord your God, and He shall bless thy bread and thy water.—EXOD. xxiii. 25.

WHAT I possess, or what I crave,
   Brings no content, great God, to me,
If what I would, or what I have,
   Be not possest, and blest, in Thee ;
What I enjoy, O make it mine,
   In making me that have it, Thine.

                       J. QUARLES

OFFER up to God all pure affections, desires, regrets, and all the bonds which link us to home, kindred, and friends, together with all our works, purposes, and labours. These things, which are not only lawful, but sacred, become then the matter of thanksgiving and oblation. Memories, plans for the future, wishes, intentions ; works just begun, half done, all but completed ; emotions, sympathies, affections,—all these things throng tumultuously and dangerously in the heart and will. The only way to master them is to offer them up to Him, as once ours, under Him, always His by right.

                       H. E. MANNING

*I delight to do Thy will, O my God : yea, Thy
law is within my heart.*—PS. xl. 8.

A PATIENT, a victorious mind,
That life and all things casts behind,
  Springs forth obedient to Thy call ;
A heart that no desire can move,
But still to adore, believe, and love,
  Give me, my Lord, my Life, my All.

P. GERHARDT

THAT piety which sanctifies us, and which
is a true devotion to God, consists in doing
all His will precisely at the time, in the situa-
tion, and under the circumstances, in which He
has placed us. Perfect devotedness requires,
not only that we do the will of God, but that
we do it with love. God would have us serve
Him with delight ; it is our hearts that He
asks of us.

FÉNELON

DEVOTION is really neither more nor less than
a general inclination and readiness to do that
which we know to be acceptable to God. It is
that ' free spirit ', of which David spoke when
he said, ' I will run the way of Thy command-
ments, when Thou hast set my heart at liberty.'
People of ordinary goodness walk in God's way,
but the devout run in it, and at length they
almost fly therein. . . . To be truly devout, we
must not only do God's will, but we must do it
cheerfully.

FRANCIS DE SALES

So teach us to number our days, that we may apply our hearts unto wisdom.—PS. XC. 12.

Seek ye not what ye shall eat, or what ye shall drink, neither be ye of doubtful mind.—LUKE xii. 29.

OUR days are numbered : let us spare
Our anxious hearts a needless care :
'Tis Thine to number out our days ;
'Tis ours to give them to Thy praise.

MADAME GUYON

EVERY day let us renew the consecration to God's service ; every day let us, in His strength, pledge ourselves afresh to do His will, even in the veriest trifle, and to turn aside from anything that may displease Him. . . . He does not bid us bear the burdens of to-morrow, next week, or next year. Every day we are to come to Him in simple obedience and faith, asking help to keep us, and aid us through that day's work ; and to-morrow, and to-morrow, and to-morrow, through years of long to-morrows, it will be but the same thing to do ; leaving the future always in God's hands, sure that He can care for it better than we. Blessed trust ! that can thus confidingly say, " This hour is mine with its present duty ; the next is God's, and when it comes, His presence will come with it."

ANON.

And as many as walk according to this rule, peace be on them, and mercy, and upon the Israel of God.—GAL. vi. 16.

LORD, I have given my life to Thee,
    And every day and hour is Thine,—
What Thou appointest let them be ;
    Thy will is better, Lord, than mine.

A. WARNER

BEGIN at once ; before you venture away from this quiet moment, ask your King to take you wholly into His service, and place all the hours of this day quite simply at His disposal, and ask Him to make and keep you *ready* to do just exactly what He appoints. Never mind about to-morrow ; one day at a time is enough. Try it to-day, and see if it is not a day of strange, almost curious peace, so sweet that you will be only too thankful, when to-morrow comes, to ask Him to take it also,—till it will become a blessed habit to hold yourself simply and 'wholly at Thy commandment for *any* manner of service'. The 'whatsoever' is not necessarily active work. It may be waiting (whether half an hour or half a lifetime), learning, suffering, sitting still. But shall we be less ready for these, if any of them are His appointments for to-day ? Let us ask Him to prepare us for all that He is preparing for us.

F. R. HAVERGAL

Return unto thy rest, O my soul ; for the Lord hath dealt bountifully with thee.—PS. cxvi. 7.

We which have believed do enter into rest.—HEB. iv. 3.

REST is not quitting
    The busy career ;
Rest is the fitting
    Of self to its sphere.

'Tis loving and serving
    The highest and best !
'Tis onwards, unswerving,—
    And that is true rest.

J. S. DWIGHT

AS a result of this strong faith, the inner life of Catherine of Genoa was characterized, in a remarkable degree, by what may be termed rest, or quietude ; which is only another form of expression for true interior peace. It was not, however, the quietude of a lazy inaction, but the quietude of an inward acquiescence ; not a quietude which feels nothing and does nothing, but that higher and divine quietude which exists by feeling and acting in the time and degree of God's appointment and God's will. It was a principle in her conduct, to give herself to God in the discharge of duty ; and to leave all results without solicitude in His hands.

T. C. UPHAM

Thou understandest my thought afar off.—PS. CXXXIX. 2.

Who can understand his errors? cleanse Thou me from secret faults.—PS. XIX. 12.

MY newest griefs to Thee are old;
  My last transgression of Thy law,
Though wrapped in thought's most secret fold,
  Thine eyes with pitying sadness saw.
                    H. M. KIMBALL

LORD our God, great, eternal, wonderful in glory, who keepest covenant and promises for those that love Thee with their whole heart, who art the Life of all, the Help of those that flee unto Thee, the Hope of those who cry unto Thee, cleanse us from our sins, secret and open; and from every thought displeasing to Thy goodness,—cleanse our bodies and souls, our hearts and consciences, that with a pure heart, and a clear soul, with perfect love and calm hope, we may venture confidently and fearlessly to pray unto Thee. Amen.

                    COPTIC LITURGY OF ST. BASIL

THE dominion of any sinful habit will fearfully estrange us from His presence. A single consenting act of inward disobedience in thought or will is enough to let fall a cloud between Him and us, and to leave our hearts cheerless and dark.

                    H. E. MANNING

The fruit of the Spirit is love, joy, peace, long-suffering, gentleness, goodness, faith, meekness, temperance.—GAL. V. 22, 23.

Herein is my Father glorified, that ye bear much fruit ; so shall ye be my disciples.—JOHN xv. 8.

O BREATH from out the Eternal Silence ! blow
  Softly upon our spirits' barren ground ;
The precious fullness of our God bestow,
  That fruits of faith, love, reverence may abound.
G. TERSTEEGEN

IS it possible we should be ignorant whether we feel tempers contrary to love or no ?—whether we rejoice always, or are burdened and bowed down with sorrow ?—whether we have a praying, or a dead, lifeless spirit ?—whether we can praise God, and be resigned in all trials, or feel murmurings, fretfulness, and impatience under them ?—is it not easy to know if we feel anger at provocations, or whether we feel our tempers mild, gentle, peaceable, and easy to be entreated, or feel stubbornness, self-will, and pride ? whether we have slavish fears, or are possessed of that perfect love which casteth out all fear that hath torment ?

HESTER ANN ROGERS

We trust in the living God.—1 TIM. iv. 10.

THY secret judgment's depths profound
   Still sings the silent night ;
The day, upon his golden round,
   Thy pity infinite.
I. WILLIAMS.   *Tr. from Latin*

NOW that I have no longer any sense for the transitory and perishable, the universe appears before my eyes under a transformed aspect. The dead, heavy mass which did but stop up space has vanished, and in its place there flows onward, with the rushing music of mighty waves, an eternal stream of life, and power, and action, which issues from the original source of all life,—from Thy life, O Infinite One ! for all life is Thy life, and only the religious eye penetrates to the realm of true Beauty.
J. G. FICHTE

WHAT is Nature ? Art thou not the ' Living Garment ' of God ? O Heavens, is it, in very deed, He then that ever speaks through thee ; that lives and loves in thee, that lives and loves in me ? Sweeter than dayspring to the ship-wrecked in Nova Zembla ; ah ! like the mother's voice to her little child that strays bewildered, weeping, in unknown tumults ; like soft streamings of celestial music to my too exasperated heart, came that Evangel. The Universe is not dead and demoniacal, a charnel-house with spectres ; but godlike, and my Father's.
T. CARLYLE

O Lord, be gracious unto us ; we have waited for Thee.—ISA. xxxiii. 2.

And now, Lord, what wait I for ? my hope is in Thee.—PS. xxxix. 7.

> HE never comes too late ;
>   He knoweth what is best ;
> Vex not thyself in vain ;
>   Until He cometh, rest.
>
> B. T.

WE make mistakes, or what we call such. The nature that could fall into such mistake exactly needs, and in the goodness of the dear God is given, the living of it out. And beyond this, I believe more. That in the pure and patient living of it out we come to find that we have fallen, not into hopeless confusion of our own wild, ignorant making ; but that the finger of God has been at work among our lines, and that the emerging is into His blessed order ; that He is forever making up for us our own undoings ; that He makes them up beforehand ; that He evermore restoreth our souls.

A. D. T. WHITNEY

THE Lord knows how to make stepping-stones for us of our defects, even ; it is what He lets them be for. He remembereth—He remembered in the making—that we are but dust ; the dust of earth, that He *chose* to make something little lower than the angels out of.

A. D. T. WHITNEY

*Take no thought how or what ye shall speak :
for it shall be given you in that same hour what ye
shall speak.*—MATT. X. 19.

> JUST to follow hour by hour
>   As He leadeth ;
> Just to draw the moment's power
>   As it needeth.
>
> F. R. HAVERGAL

YOU have a disagreeable duty to do at twelve
o'clock. Do not blacken nine, and ten,
and eleven, and all between, with the colour of
twelve. Do the work of each, and reap your
reward in peace. So when the dreaded moment
in the future becomes the present, you shall
meet it walking in the light, and that light will
overcome its darkness. The best preparation
is the present well seen to, the last duty done.
For this will keep the eye so clear and the body
so full of light that the right action will be
perceived at once, the right words will rush
from the heart to the lips, and the man, full of
the Spirit of God because he cares for nothing
but the will of God, will trample on the evil
thing in love, and be sent, it may be, in a chariot
of fire to the presence of his Father, or stand
unmoved amid the cruel mockings of the men
he loves.

G. MACDONALD

*Hast thou not known? hast thou not heard,
that the everlasting God, the Lord, the Creator of
the ends of the earth, fainteth not, neither is weary?
He giveth power to the faint ; and to them that
have no might be increaseth strength.*—ISA. xl. 28,
29.

> WORKMAN of God ! oh, lose not heart,
>   But learn what God is like ;
> And in the darkest battle-field
>   Thou shalt know where to strike.
>
> F. W. FABER

FOR the rest, let that vain struggle to read
the mystery of the Infinite cease to harass
us. It is a mystery which, through all ages,
we shall only read here a line of, there another
line of. Do we not already know that the name
of the Infinite is GOOD, is GOD ? Here on earth
we are as soldiers, fighting in a foreign land,
that understand not the plan of the campaign,
and have no need to understand it ; seeing well
what is at our hand to be done. Let us do it like
soldiers, with submission, with courage, with a
heroic joy. Behind us, behind each one of us,
lie six thousand years of human effort, human
conquest : before us is the boundless Time,
with its as yet uncreated and unconquered
continents and Eldorados, which we, even we,
have to conquer, to create ; and from the
bosom of Eternity there shine for us celestial
guiding stars.   T. CARLYLE

I will wait upon the Lord, that hideth His face from the house of Jacob, and I will look for Him.—
ISA. viii. 17.

WHAT heart can comprehend Thy name,
   Or, searching, find Thee out ?
Who art within, a quickening flame,
   A presence round about.

Yet though I know Thee but in part,
   I ask not, Lord, for more :
Enough for me to know Thou art,
   To love Thee and adore.

F. L. HOSMER

STAND up, O heart ! and yield not one inch of thy rightful territory to the usurping intellect. Hold fast to God in spite of logic, and yet not quite blindly. Be not torn from thy grasp upon the skirts of His garments by any wrench of atheistic hypothesis that seeks only to hurl thee into utter darkness ; but refuse not to let thy hands be gently unclasped by that loving and pious philosophy that seeks to draw thee from the feet of God only to place thee in His bosom. Trustfully, though tremblingly, let go the robe, and thou shalt rest upon the heart and clasp the very living soul of God.

JAMES HINTON

Thou, therefore, endure hardness, as a good soldier of Jesus Christ.—2 TIM. ii. 3.

WHERE our Captain bids us go,
'Tis not ours to murmur, ' No '.
   He that gives the sword and shield,
   Chooses too the battle-field
On which we are to fight the foe.

ANON.

OF nothing may we be more sure than this ; that, if we cannot sanctify our present lot, we could sanctify no other. Our heaven and our Almighty Father are there or nowhere. The obstructions of that lot are given for us to heave away by the concurrent touch of a holy spirit, and labour of strenuous will ; its gloom, for us to tint with some celestial light ; its mysteries are for our worship ; its sorrows for our trust ; its perils for our courage ; its temptations for our faith. Soldiers of the cross, it is not for us, but for our Leader and our Lord, to choose the field ; it is ours, taking the station which He assigns, to make it the field of truth and honour, though it be the field of death.

J. MARTINEAU

Giving thanks unto the Father, which hath made us meet to be partakers of the inheritance of the saints in light.—COL. i. 12.

THE souls most precious to us here
  May from this home have fled ;
But still we make one household dear ;
  One Lord is still our head.
Midst cherubim and seraphim
  They mind their Lord's affairs ;
Oh ! if we bring our work to Him
  Our work is one with theirs.

T. H. GILL

WE are apt to feel as if nothing we could do on earth bears a relation to what the good are doing in a higher world ; but it is not so. Heaven and earth are not so far apart. Every disinterested act, every sacrifice to duty, every exertion for the good of ' one of the least of Christ's brethren ', every new insight into God's works, every new impulse given to the love of truth and goodness, associates us with the departed, brings us nearer to them, and is as truly heavenly as if we were acting, not on earth, but in heaven. The spiritual tie between us and the departed is not felt as it should be. Our union with them daily grows stronger, if we daily make progress in what they are growing in.

WM. E. CHANNING

That ye, being rooted and grounded in love, may be able to comprehend with all saints what is the breadth, and length, and depth, and height ; and to know the love of Christ, which passeth knowledge, that ye might be filled with all the fulness of God.— EPH. iii. 17–19.

O LOVE that passeth knowledge, thee I need ;
  Pour in the heavenly sunshine ; fill my heart ;
Scatter the cloud, the doubting, and the dread,—
  The joy unspeakable to me impart.

                                        H. BONAR

TO examine its evidence is not to try Christianity ; to admire its martyrs is not to try Christianity ; to compare and estimate its teachers is not to try Christianity ; to attend its rites and services with more than Mahometan punctuality is not to try or know Christianity. But for one week, for one day, to have lived in the pure atmosphere of faith and love to God, of tenderness to man ; to have beheld earth annihilated, and heaven opened to the prophetic gaze of hope ; to have seen evermore revealed behind the complicated troubles of this strange, mysterious life, the unchanged smile of an eternal Friend, and everything that is difficult to reason solved by that reposing trust which is higher and better than reason,— to have known and felt this, I will not say for a *life*, but for a single blessed hour, *that*, indeed, is to have made experiment of Christianity.

                              WM. ARCHER BUTLER

The peace of God, which passeth all understanding, shall keep your hearts and minds through Christ Jesus.—PHIL. iv. 7.

Let the peace of God rule in your hearts.—COL. iii. 15.

DROP Thy still dews of quietness,
  Till all our strivings cease ;
Take from our souls the strain and stress,
And let our ordered lives confess
  The beauty of Thy peace.

J. G. WHITTIER

' THESE things write we unto you, that your
joy may be full.' What is fullness of
joy but *peace* ? Joy is tumultuous only when it
is not full ; but peace is the privilege of those
who are ' filled with the knowledge of the glory
of the Lord, as the waters cover the sea '.
' Thou wilt keep him in perfect peace, whose
mind is stayed on Thee, because he trusteth in
Thee.' It is peace, springing from trust and
innocence, and then overflowing in love towards
all around him. He who is anxious, thinks of
himself, is suspicious of danger, speaks
hurriedly, and has no time for the interests of
others ; he who lives in peace is at leisure,
wherever his lot is cast.

J. H. NEWMAN

THROUGH the spirit of Divine Love let the
violent, obstinate powers of thy nature be
quieted, the hardness of thy affections softened,
and thine intractable self-will subdued ; and
as often as anything contrary stirs within thee,
immediately sink into the blessed Ocean of
meekness and love.

G. TERSTEEGEN

Wherefore thou art no more a servant, but a son ; and if a son, then an heir of God through Christ.—
GAL. iv. 7.

NOT by the terrors of a slave
  God's sons perform His will,
But with the noblest powers they have
  His sweet commands fulfil.

ISAAC WATTS

OUR thoughts, good or bad, are not in our command, but every one of us has at all hours duties to *do*, and these he can do negligently, like a slave, or faithfully, like a true servant. ' *Do* the duty that is nearest thee '— that first, and that well ; all the rest will disclose themselves with increasing clearness, and make their successive demand. Were your duties never so small, I advise you, set yourself with double and treble energy and punctuality, to do them, hour after hour, day after day.

T. CARLYLE

WHATEVER we are, high or lowly, learned or unlearned, married or single, in a full house or alone, charged with many affairs or dwelling in quietness, we have our daily round of work, our duties of affection, obedience, love, mercy, industry, and the like ; and that which makes one man to differ from another is not so much what things he does, as his manner of doing them.

H. E. MANNING

Now the God of peace make you perfect in every good work, to do His will, working in you that which is well-pleasing in His sight.—HEB. xiii. 20, 21.

Be ready to every good work.—TITUS iii. 1.

so, firm in steadfast hope, in thought secure,
  In full accord to all Thy world of joy,
May I be nerved to labours high and pure,
  And thou Thy child to do Thy work employ.
                                    J. STERLING

BE with God in thy outward works, refer them to Him, offer them to Him, seek to do them in Him and for Him, and He will be with thee in them, and they shall not hinder, but rather invite His presence in thy soul. Seek to see Him in all things, and in all things He will come nigh to thee.

                                    E. B. PUSEY

NOTHING less than the majesty of God, and the powers of the world to come, can maintain the peace and sanctity of our homes, the order and serenity of our minds, the spirit of patience and tender mercy in our hearts. Then will even the merest drudgery of duty cease to humble us, when we transfigure it by the glory of our own spirit.

                                    J. MARTINEAU

Finally, brethren, whatsoever things are true, whatsoever things are honest, whatsoever things are just, whatsoever things are pure, whatsoever things are lovely, whatsoever things are of good report,— think on these things.—PHIL. iv. 8.

As he thinketh in his heart, so is he.—PROV. xxiii. 7.

STILL may Thy sweet mercy spread
A shady arm above my head,
About my paths ; so shall I find
The fair centre of my mind
Thy temple, and those lovely walls
Bright ever with a beam that falls
Fresh from the pure glance of Thine eye,
Lighting to eternity.

R. CRASHAW

MAKE yourselves nests of pleasant thoughts. None of us yet know, for none of us have been taught in early youth, what fairy palaces we may build of beautiful thought—proof against all adversity. Bright fancies, satisfied memories, noble histories, faithful sayings, treasure-houses of precious and restful thoughts, which care cannot disturb, nor pain make gloomy, nor poverty take away from us,—houses built without hands, for our souls to live in.

J. RUSKIN

FOR nowhere either with more quiet or more freedom from trouble does a man retire than into his own soul ; particularly when he has within him such thoughts, that by looking into them he is immediately in perfect tranquillity. And I affirm that tranquillity is nothing else than the good ordering of the mind.

MARCUS ANTONINUS

O Lord, I know that the way of man is not in himself : it is not in man that walketh to direct his steps.—JER. x. 23.

I will direct all his ways.—ISA. xlv. 13.

> COME, Light serene and still !
> Our darkened spirits fill
> With thy clear day :
> Guide of the feeble sight,
> Star of grief's darkest night,
> Reveal the path of right,
> Show us Thy way.
>
> ROBERT II. OF FRANCE

THERE had been solemn appointed seasons in Anna's life, when she was accustomed to enter upon a full and deliberate survey of her business in this world. The claims of each relationship, and the results of each occupation, were then examined in the light of eternity. It was then, too, her fervent prayer to be enabled to discern the will of God far more perfectly, not only in the indications given of it for her guidance through each day's occupations, but as it might concern duties not yet brought home to her conscience, and therefore unprovided for in her life.

ANNA, OR PASSAGES FROM HOME LIFE

Forgetting those things which are behind, and reaching forth unto those things which are before, I press toward the mark.—PHIL. iii. 13, 14.

YET I argue not
Against Heaven's hand or will, nor bate a jot
Of heart or hope ; but still bear up and steer
Right onward.

J. MILTON

IT is not by regretting what is irreparable that true work is to be done, but by making the best of what we are. It is not by complaining that we have not the right tools, but by using well the tools we have. What we are, and where we are, is God's providential arrangement,— God's doing, though it may be man's misdoing ; and the manly and the wise way is to look your disadvantages in the face, and see what can be made out of them. Life, like war, is a series of mistakes, and he is not the best Christian nor the best general who makes the fewest false steps. He is the best who wins the most splendid victories by the retrieval of mistakes. Forget mistakes ; organize victory out of mistakes.

F. W. ROBERTSON

INDEX OF AUTHORS
OF THE PROSE SELECTIONS

INDEX OF AUTHORS

OF THE POETICAL SELECTIONS